EXCHANGE   LIBRARY
(St. Peter's Square)

This book must be returned on or before the date last stamped
or a fine will be charged.

1 OCT 64			

713D

Josiah Gilbert Holland

JOSIAH GILBERT HOLLAND

JOSIAH GILBERT HOLLAND

in Relation to His Times

By

HARRY HOUSTON PECKHAM

Philadelphia

UNIVERSITY OF PENNSYLVANIA PRESS

LONDON: HUMPHREY MILFORD: OXFORD UNIVERSITY PRESS

1940

Copyright 1940

University of Pennsylvania Press

Manufactured in the United States of America

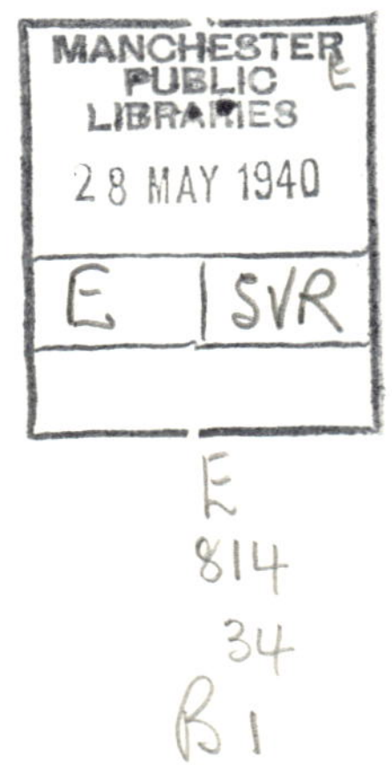

Preface

AMERICAN-BORN readers who are near or past the fifty-year
mark will hardly need to be told who J. G. Holland was, or
why a study of his life and work is an undertaking distinctly
worth while. To the vast majority of younger readers it will
probably be a revelation to learn of the phenomenal popularity and prestige of this erstwhile famous American poet,
novelist, essayist, lecturer, and editor. It will certainly be a
revelation to them to learn that on the day after Holland's
death the New York *Times* referred to him as "one of the
most celebrated writers . . . this country has produced," [1]
and that on the same day a very prominent Middle Western
newspaper declared that "by the death of J. G. Holland . . .
the literary world lost one of its brightest lights." [2] The story
of Holland's meteoric rise, his huge and loyal following, and
his ultimate eclipse is a significant and engrossing narrative
—as significant and engrossing as that of the changes that
took place in American life, American taste, and American
thought during the middle and later years of the last century.

Except for very short sketches prepared for works of reference,[2] only two biographical studies of Josiah Gilbert Holland have ever been published. One of these two, a seven-page
memorial magazine article by Edward Eggleston, is necessarily inadequate because of its extreme brevity. The other,
an interesting and appreciative book by Mrs. H. M. Plunkett,
is much fuller in scope and is—I am assured by living members of the Holland family—factually accurate as far as it
goes. Mrs. Plunkett, a western Massachusetts journalist, gathered most of her materials from the direct testimony of Mrs.

[1] See below, p. 206.

[2] By far the best of these is the sketch written by the late William B. Cairns
for the *Dictionary of American Biography* (IX, 146–148).

J. G. Holland and painstakingly recorded her data in a manner that met with the full approval of Mrs. Holland.[3] The Plunkett book, however, has a number of serious weaknesses. In the first place, it is totally lacking in documentation. In the second place, it is amazingly uninformative as regards specific dates and places and the identification of persons. In the third place, it is (as Professor Cairns truly remarks) "uncritical."[4] It goes on the naïve assumption that Holland's writings are of permanent intrinsic value, and it makes neither a detailed nor a systematic effort to analyze and appraise Holland's work. It is, in short, lamentably deficient in objectivity, except in matters of indisputable biographical fact.

The present volume attempts to be both biographical and critical. In it I have made the greatest possible use of all of Mrs. Plunkett's data that seemed valuable; but I have also endeavored to fill in many biographical gaps. Through the use of letters, newspaper files, county and regional histories, historical-social studies, and the personal recollections of a few of Holland's near relatives and intimate contemporaries, I am presenting a great deal of material that I consider both fresh and important. Over and above biographical considerations, I am, I believe, analyzing Holland's writings in far more detail than they have ever been analyzed before. In evaluating Holland and his work, I have attempted to consider him, both as a phenomenon and as an influence, in relation to his times and his social and intellectual background.

For a large part of my material, I am deeply indebted to various persons. Especially do I wish to express my thanks to Mrs. John K. Howe, of Springfield, Massachusetts, the eldest of Holland's three surviving children; to Mr. Hiller C. Wellman, City Library Association, Springfield, Massachusetts; to Mrs. Isabel R. Dickinson, Springfield, Massachusetts; to Miss Anne Clark Carlisle, Forbes Library, Northampton, Massa-

---

[3] For this information I am indebted to Holland's daughter, Mrs. John K. Howe.

[4] *Dictionary of American Biography,* IX, 148.

chusetts; to Dr. William E. Leonard, Hadley, Massachusetts; to the late Robert Underwood Johnson, distinguished New York author; to Mr. J. H. Poli, Production Department, Charles Scribner's Sons; to Mr. H. R. McIlwaine, Virginia State Library, Richmond; to Miss Mary C. Venn, Oberlin College Library; to Mrs. Marguerite H. Anderson, Indiana State Library, Indianapolis; to Mrs. Thomas A. Stuart, Lafayette, Indiana; to Mr. John I. Owen, Department of English, University of Illinois; to Mr. Paul M. Angle, Illinois State Historical Library, Springfield; to Mr. Joseph Miller, Jr., Secretary of the New York City Board of Education; to Miss Adair Black, Secretary of the Brick Church, New York City; to Mrs. George Inness, Jr., of Greenwich, Connecticut, daughter of Holland's business partner, Roswell Smith; to Mr. Ira H. Brainerd, of New York City; to Miss Mary A. Benjamin, of New York City, owner of three unpublished Holland letters; and to Miss Anne C. Keating, Librarian of the Edwin Watts Chubb Library, Ohio University. I wish also to state my appreciation of the excellent facilities afforded me by the newspaper-file departments of the Wisconsin State Historical Library and the Ohio State Historical and Archaeological Museum respectively. Finally, I desire to express my deep gratitude to Professor Harry Hayden Clark, nationally recognized authority on American literature, for invaluable advice with regard to the assembling and the presentation of my material.

The following publishers have generously consented to the use of excerpts from copyrighted works:

D. Appleton-Century Company: William H. Herndon and Jesse W. Weik's *Abraham Lincoln* and Arthur Hobson Quinn's *American Fiction*

Harvard University Press: Frank Luther Mott's *A History of American Magazines, 1741–1850*

D. C. Heath and Company: William Henry Hudson's *An Introduction to the Study of Literature*

Houghton Mifflin Company: Henry A. Beers's *Nathaniel Parker Willis,* Martha D. Bianchi's *Life and Letters of Emily*

Dickinson, William W. Ellsworth's *A Golden Age of Authors,* and E. P. Whipple's *American Literature and Other Papers*

Little, Brown and Company: Robert Underwood Johnson's *Remembered Yesterdays*

The Macmillan Company: Carl Russell Fish's *The Rise of the Common Man,* Allan Nevins' *The Emergence of Modern America,* Henry Kalloch Rowe's *The History of Religion in the United States,* and Carl Van Doren's *The American Novel*

A. C. McClurg & Co.: James Onderdonk's *History of American Verse*

Charles Scribner's Sons: Mrs. H. M. Plunkett's *Josiah Gilbert Holland* and all the works of J. G. Holland; also the portrait used as a frontispiece in this volume.

H. H. P.

Ohio University
Athens, Ohio
August 8, 1939

Contents

I

First Years

On Sunday, April 4, 1813,[1] Harrison and Anna Holland got religion. What they were converted *from*, no records indicate; but it is fairly safe to infer that this inoffensive young mechanic and his bride of less than three years were not plucked as brands from the burning. What they were converted *to* was, naturally, Congregationalism; for the scene of their conversion was the western Massachusetts village of Belchertown. The venerable Belchertown pastor, Justus Forward, who had wedded Harrison and Anna on November 5, 1810, had prayed and exhorted constantly for their conversion; but it had remained for Forward's successor, Experience Porter, to effect their ingathering.[1] Under ordinary circumstances the addition of two obscure names to the roster of a New England rural church is of slight consequence to American civilization. This particular addition, however, was probably momentous; for seven summers later, on July 24, 1819, the already six-times maternal [2] Anna Holland gave birth to a son, Josiah Gilbert. The birthplace was a squat, low-roofed cottage to the northwest of Belchertown village, near the present hamlet of Dwight.[3]

Conceived and suckled in Calvinistic piety, Josiah Gilbert Holland grew to be a paragon of all the copy-book virtues. More than that, he grew to be the best-selling American

---

[1] This information is contained in the J. G. Holland Memorial Address delivered by Rev. P. W. Lyman at Belchertown, Mass., Oct. 16, 1881. An unpublished copy of this address is on file in the Forbes Library, Northampton, Mass.

[2] The seven children of Harrison and Anna Holland were Charles (who died in infancy), Goodrich, James Harvey, Louisa, Lucretia, Clarissa, and Josiah Gilbert. For this information I am indebted to J. G. Holland's daughter, Mrs. John K. Howe.

[3] See *History of the Connecticut Valley*, 2 vols. Philadelphia, 1879, II, 836.

author of edifying books in his generation,[4] the major prophet of the unsophisticated, the supreme apostle to the naïve.

Before we look further into the life and the family connections of Josiah Holland, we shall do well to consider the background of his parents' conversion to religion. The late eighteenth century in general, and the Revolutionary War in particular, had dealt severely with the old New England Calvinism. Like every war, the Revolution had fostered unchristian rapacity and cruelty, and it had turned men's thoughts from God to politics, from individual soul-searching to national rights. It had created or enhanced the prestige of public men who were frankly heterodox, such as Benjamin Franklin, Thomas Jefferson, and Thomas Paine. Its Franco-American alliance of 1778 had brought many Americans into close and sympathetic contact with the ideas of Voltaire and other French skeptics. It had caused increasing numbers of persons to lend attentive ears to the Universalist preaching of John Murray, and to read with avidity such liberal theological works as the younger Charles Chauncy's *Salvation of All Men* (1782). Within a little more than a decade after the close of the war Paine's more radical *Age of Reason* (1794) had appeared and, as James Truslow Adams says, had "created an unprecedented sensation." [5] In another eleven years Harvard College was to make Unitarianism its official creed by "the election in 1805 of an avowed Unitarian, Henry Ware, to the Hollis Professorship of Theology." [6]

Inevitably, however, these assaults upon orthodoxy were met with vigorous counter-attacks. Universalism and Unitarianism, deism and agnosticism, might make a concerted drive against the old-time religion; but the latter held its ground the more stubbornly. Harvard and even Yale might become "hot-

[4] A recent researcher states: "At the time of his death in 1881 Dr. Holland was the most successful man of letters in the United States." Margaret Bloom: "Emily Dickinson and Dr. Holland." *University of California Chronicle,* Berkeley, Jan., 1933, XXXV, 96.

[5] James Truslow Adams: *New England in the Republic,* Boston, 1926, p. 219.

[6] William Warren Sweet: *The Story of Religions in America,* New York and London, 1930, p. 348.

beds of infidelity"; [7] Unitarianism might become "the religion of all the higher social circles of Massachusetts"; [8] but such developments made the plain people of New England all the more staunch in their opposition to all forms of theological liberalism. The founding of the orthodox Andover Theological Seminary in 1808 was clearly a protest against the new Unitarianism of Harvard; [9] and the opening of Park Street ("Brimstone Corner") Church in Boston in 1810 was as clearly a movement to defend the "faith of the fathers." [10] "By the end of the [eighteenth] century," says Professor Henry Kalloch Rowe, "a need of vigorous constructive preaching was apparent everywhere. The popular revival of religion that was noticeable after the turn of the century soon gave evidence of the importance of evangelism." [11] Despite all the inroads of heterodoxy, therefore, Congregationalism continued to be the faith of the masses in New England. More than that, it remained the established state religion of Massachusetts until 1833.[12] And even in the closing years of the nineteenth century it had almost twice as many adherents in the Bay State as its strongest Protestant rival.[13]

Here, then, we have the setting for the conversion of Harrison and Anna Holland. In this connection, it should be added that the Hollands embraced the faith during what J. G. Holland's biographer, Mrs. Plunkett, has called "a remarkable revival of religion," [14] and that they were but two of more than a hundred converts.[14] Undoubtedly the War of 1812 produced its reaction of irreligion, but when Harrison and Anna Holland accepted Christianity that war was only a few months old. Then, too, "Mr. Madison's War" was of rela-

---

[7] Adams, *op. cit.*, p. 219.

[8] *Ibid.*, p. 355.

[9] Sweet, *op. cit.*, p. 348.

[10] Henry Kalloch Rowe: *The History of Religion in the United States,* New York, 1924, p. 127.

[11] *Ibid.*, pp. 62–63.

[12] *Ibid.*, p. 50.

[13] According to the United States census of 1890, the Congregationalists led all Protestant denominations in Massachusetts with 101,830 members. The Baptists, with 59,890, were a rather poor second.

[14] Mrs. H. M. Plunkett: *Josiah Gilbert Holland,* New York, 1894, p. 2.

tively short duration, and it was always unpopular in New England.[15]

The geography of Belchertown, Massachusetts, is of more than passing religious interest; for only a dozen miles to the west lies Northampton, where Solomon Stoddard and his famous grandson Jonathan Edwards had established a strong evangelistic tradition in the eighteenth century—had, indeed, given impetus to the Great Awakening of about 1740.[16] The potency of the revivalistic preaching of Experience Porter may, then, be readily conjectured. Under the eloquent urgings of so zealous a follower of Stoddard and Edwards, the sinner who could remain unrepentant was indeed hardened. To quote Professor Rowe once more, "With the prevailing belief in the deadliness of sin and the horrors of hell, the exhorters had weapons as powerful with their hearers as the anathema and excommunication of the Roman Catholic church of the Middle Ages." [17] The foregoing quotation has particular reference to frontier camp meetings, but the evangelistic preaching in the rural meetinghouses of western Massachusetts in the early nineteenth century could hardly have been very different from that which Professor Rowe describes. All in all, it is no wonder that Harrison and Anna Holland were persuaded to become God-fearing, hell-fearing Christians.

The Hollands, it would appear, were always godly folk; for John and Judith Holland, the founders of the family in America, had been pillars in the congregation of the Reverend John White at Plymouth, England; and a decade or so after the landing of the *Mayflower* they were still singing psalms to the glory of Jehovah and the edification of the same John White—but, by this time, at Dorchester, Massachusetts.[18] When we next hear definitely of the Hollands, late in the eighteenth century, we learn of one Luther Holland, a veteran of General Gates's army and a fire-engine maker at

15 Adams, *op. cit.,* pp. 271–272.
16 Rowe, *op. cit.,* pp. 46, 60.
17 *Ibid.,* p. 66.
18 Plunkett, *op. cit.,* p. 1. See also *History of the Connecticut Valley,* II, 863.

Petersham, Worcester County. Luther's third son was Harrison Holland.[18]

Of the Gilberts, paternal ancestors of Anna Holland, we know less. There is, however, no reason to suppose that the Gilberts were a whit more reprobate than the Hollands. Certainly they were not buccaneers or even Unitarians. When we first meet these Gilberts, in the latter part of the eighteenth century, we find them domiciled at Hebron, Tolland County, Connecticut, a haven of refuge from the growing heterodoxy of eastern Massachusetts. Anna's father, John Gilbert, was a Revolutionary veteran and had attained to the fairly impressive rank of major. Anna was born at Hebron, but within a few years of her birth her family must have moved up the Willimantic Valley into Massachusetts, for her son's biographer informs us that she grew to womanhood in the Gilbert homestead at Belchertown.[19]

Josiah Gilbert Holland's childhood was hardly a happy one. If his father was "a modest, thoroughly earnest Christian," [19] he was neither worldly-wise nor provident. Perhaps he had no opportunity to be either the one or the other. Forty years later Josiah was to write of him:

> A practical old man, and yet a dreamer,
>   He thought that in some strange, unlooked-for way
> His mighty Friend in heaven, the great Redeemer,
>   Would honor him with wealth some golden day.[20]

One wonders at the word "practical,"—unless it be applied merely to the old man's mechanical ingenuity. That the older Holland was a dreamer, with a Micawber-like penchant for awaiting an illusory prosperity, there can be no doubt. The brutal truth was that Harrison Holland was a rolling stone, a migratory ne'er-do-well. Within less than a score of years he and his family dwelt in no fewer than five western Massachu-

---

[18] Plunkett, *op. cit.*, p. 1. See also *History of the Connecticut Valley*, II, 863.
[19] *Ibid.*, p. 2.
[20] From "Daniel Gray." *Atlantic Monthly*, Aug., 1859, IV, 195.

setts communities: Belchertown (twice), Heath, South Hadley, Granby, and Northampton, to be specific.[21]

The difficulty was that Harrison Holland was a product of the pre-machine age, unable to adjust himself to the industrial revolution. Once he had made a fairly good living as a wool-carder in his own little establishment; but in the eighteen-twenties, when textile mills began to dot the landscape of southern New England, he became a lost spirit. Other handi-craftsmen might stoically or sullenly accept low wages and grinding routine as factory operatives, but not Harrison Hol-land. After a brief venture as a wagon-wheel maker at Heath, he preferred to work sporadically as a farmers' "hired hand" and to let his half-grown daughters eke out the remainder of a bare livelihood by braiding palm-leaf hats.[22]

Meanwhile the mind of this Yankee mystic was often colored with pleasant, roseate dreams. While his older boys, Goodrich and Harvey, were working in a silk mill, he conceived an im-portant labor-saving and time-saving device in the form of a reel for holding silk as it was unwound from the cocoon. The invention was perfected, and it was a success. As late as the eighteen-nineties it continued in wide use. But Harrison Hol-land realized little profit from it. Too simple-minded or too impecunious to secure a patent for his invention, he lived to see others reap the reward of his ingenuity.[23] It must have been this circumstance that Josiah had in mind when, many years later, he created the character of Paul Benedict, defrauded inventor of the "Belcher" rifle, in the novel *Sevenoaks*. Bene-dict, however, found a guardian angel in the form of an able New York lawyer, and became a millionaire.[24] That is the distinction between romance and life.

But if the Hollands were desperately poor, they were eth-ically and doctrinally sound. To borrow a phrase more familiar to mundane Episcopalians than to flesh-mortifying Calvinists,

[21] *History of the Connecticut Valley,* II, 863.
[22] Plunkett, *op. cit.,* p. 5.
[23] *Ibid.,* pp. 3–5.
[24] *Sevenoaks,* p. 452.

they led "a godly, righteous, and sober life." [25] The Saturday evening ceremony of polishing copper-toed boots and laying out homespun Sabbath jackets and pantaloons must have been a commonplace to Josiah and his brothers—as much a commonplace as the long Sunday sermons on election and reprobation and the cold Sunday dinners of beef and mutton. Their trips to the midweek prayer meetings with their elders must have been frequent, if not regular. And if they still needed spiritual refreshment, they undoubtedly got an extra-abundance of it at the annual revivals. On the very Sunday afternoons when the British Puritan child, John Ruskin, was learning long chapters of the King James Bible by heart or renewing his acquaintance with *The Pilgrim's Progress*,[26] his little American contemporary, Josiah Holland, was doubtless doing the same thing with quite as much zeal if with a more meager intellectual background. And this was not all. During the family residence at Granby, when Josiah was about sixteen, the Holland spiritual adviser was the Reverend Eli Moody, an ardent devotee of theological polemics. Parson Moody, seeing in the youngest Holland a potential theologian, encouraged the boy to call often at the manse and borrow learned disquisitions on Puritan divinity. Thus it was that during adolescent years Josiah Gilbert Holland pored over such weighty tomes as Nathanael Emmons' sermons (in six volumes), Edward Dorr Griffin's *Kingdom of Christ*, Samuel Hopkins' *System of Doctrines*, and the younger Jonathan Edwards' *Discourses on the Atonement*.[27] The Harrison Hollands, of course, owned few books; in fact, they did not even take a county newspaper.[28] Apropos of Josiah Holland's theological reading, it must be borne in mind that in the New

[25] General Confession, Morning Prayer and Evening Prayer, *Book of Common Prayer*.

[26] John Ruskin: *Praeterita*, p. 1. *Selections and Essays*, edited by Frederick William Roe, New York, 1918.

[27] For identification of Parson Moody, see *History of the Connecticut Valley*, I, 171. For general reference to the theological works, see Plunkett, *op. cit.*, p. 11.

[28] Plunkett, *op. cit.*, p. 11.

England of a hundred years ago such reading was by no means unheard of, even among normal, healthy boys in their teens. Until the middle years of the nineteenth century nearly all articulate New Englanders were theologians.[29] Josiah Holland, then, read theological tracts for the simple reason that they were far more accessible than any other literary works.

Is it not a wonder that such a plethora of religiosity did not breed a generation of agnostics or libertines or both? Or is it? At any rate, one recalls few heretical or epicurean geniuses who were reared in such an environment as that of Josiah Holland. True, there were Lowell and Holmes, both of them sons of orthodox Congregational ministers. But Lowell and Holmes were not innocent rustics; they grew up among the urbanities of Cambridge and Boston. Then, too, it must be remembered that New England Congregationalism has always been more dignified and intelligent than the types of evangelical piety that flourished—and still flourish—in the villages of the South and the West. Its revivals have been less emotional, its clergy less illiterate.[30]

Of Josiah Gilbert Holland's school days there is not much to record. That he had the advantage (or disadvantage) of attending several schools is obvious from the peregrinations of the family. That he was an elegant penman, a champion "speller-down," and a facile writer of pretty verses is of more than passing interest. That he was neither too delicate nor too priggish to win more than his share of tussles on the playgrounds is gratifying to report.[31] And that during extra-scholastic hours he ran errands, split kindling, weeded gardens, and drove cows to and from pasture is to be taken for granted.

Josiah's secondary education, wherein the young lad undoubtedly acquired more Latin and other humanistic learning than many a present-day American collegian ever gets, was

---

[29] The Hartford Wits were perhaps the most conspicuous exception to this rule. Even they, however, were by no means devoid of religious interest, as may be seen from Timothy Dwight's revision of Isaac Watts's Psalms.

[30] See below, p. 14.

[31] Plunkett, *op. cit.*, pp. 9–12.

obtained at Northampton High School, at that time one of the few good public secondary institutions of learning in western Massachusetts.[32] Josiah being now at an age when it was considered necessary that he be gainfully employed, he became inmate and general chore-boy in the home of a leading Northampton citizen, Judge Charles Augustus Dewey.[32] In this connection it should be observed that a century ago a high-school education was by no means a commonplace thing, even in Massachusetts. It was, in fact, less of a commonplace, more of a social and cultural distinction, than a college education is today. As late as 1840 there were scarcely more than a dozen high schools in Massachusetts, "and a similar number in other States." [33] But Josiah Gilbert Holland, as his biographer assures us, was an ambitious lad; he had resolved "to be an educated gentleman." [32]

Young Holland's contact with Judge Dewey was peculiarly fortunate, for the latter's culture was as mellow as his character and his judicial attainments were high. A graduate of Williams College and an erstwhile law apprentice of the elder Theodore Sedgwick, Dewey served with notable distinction both as district attorney and as associate justice of the Massachusetts Supreme Court.[34] Extant portraits of Judge Dewey reveal a solemn-looking, almost a cross-looking old gentleman, whose austerity appears accentuated by an early-Victorian combination of shaven lip, shaven chin, and luxuriant side-whiskers. Beneath the stern countenance, however, there is a gracious touch of color: a fancy striped waistcoat bespeaking a human, almost a lovable tinge of vanity.[35] And in this instance the waistcoat must be more revelatory than the visage itself; for the testimony of contemporaries assures us that Charles Augustus Dewey enjoyed the affection as well as the esteem of

[32] Plunkett, *op. cit.*, p. 13.

[33] Ellwood P. Cubberley: Article on education in the United States. *Encyclopaedia Britannica*, Fourteenth Edition. 24 vols. London and New York, 1929, 1930, VII, 993.

[34] For data on Judge Dewey, see William T. Davis: *Bench and Bar of the Commonwealth of Massachusetts*, Boston, 1900, I, 291.

[35] See photographic reproduction of portrait, *The Meadow City's Quarter-Millennial Book*, Northampton, Mass., 1904, p. 483.

colleagues and neighbors alike. In later years Josiah Holland, though markedly reluctant to talk about the hardships and privations of his childhood and youth, often spoke feelingly of the Judge.[36] In the spacious, column-fronted Dewey mansion on Elm Street—known to recent generations of Smith College undergraduates as a commodious dormitory—the chore-boy was shown almost as many kindly considerations as if he had been a member of the family.[36] Here, in all probability, he first made acquaintance with secular classics: the Waverley Novels, the *Spectator,* the plays of Shakespeare, and the poetry of Milton, Pope, Gray, Cowper, and Burns. Here, too, under the stabilizing influence of Judge Dewey, he undoubtedly learned something that had been pathetically lacking in the example if not the precepts of his own home: the value of persistence in some one field of endeavor.

Those early years of Holland's stay in Northampton had, however, one untoward result. It was during his high-school days that his naturally rugged constitution underwent its first serious breakdown. The change from an outdoor to a sedentary existence was made too suddenly, and it was made at a fairly critical time of life. Growing too rapidly, exercising and eating too little, and studying too much—often under a very feeble tallow light—Josiah realized, for almost the first time, that he had physical limitations.[37] His intellectual and artistic limitations, unfortunately, he never quite realized. But this last is another story; it belongs in later chapters.

We must now revert to those pretty schoolboy verses, mentioned in an earlier paragraph. How numerous these verses were, or how varied in theme or style, we have no means of knowing; but one of them, an apostrophe to a comet, prompted Josiah's teachers to make rash predictions regarding his future as a man of letters.[38] And even during pre-school days he made

[36] For personal reminiscences not otherwise documented, I am indebted to Holland's daughter, Mrs. John K. Howe. For information about the Dewey mansion and its present use, I am indebted to Miss Anne Clark Carlisle, Forbes Library, Northampton, Mass.

[37] Plunkett, *op. cit.,* p. 14.

[38] *Ibid.,* p. 12.

a stanza about the edibility of pigeon meat—a stanza that his father considered worthy of preservation.[39] Josiah's earliest published verses, however, appeared in the *Youth's Companion* in August, 1837, when Josiah was in his nineteenth year. This piece, a touching little account of a tree planted by one of Judge Dewey's small sons a short time before the child's death, marks what we might call the beginning of Josiah Gilbert Holland's literary career. The importance always attached to this poem by its author is attested in the author's own words, written in 1881 in a letter to an admirer in Ohio:

I was then seventeen [40] years old, and that was forty-four years ago. I took the printed copy containing it from the Post-office, peeped within, and then walked home on air. I shall probably never be so absorbingly happy as I was then. Earth has nothing like it—earth never had anything like it—for me. I have seen my work in type since then, till I have tired of the sight of it, but I can never forget the great joy of that occasion.[41]

One other incident of Josiah's adolescent years shows him to have been at least a dreamer, if not a poet. For a brief time he worked at a textile mill at South Hadley, but he found the routine there decidedly irksome. One day at the loom, while more occupied in building air castles than in watching his threads, he drew a sharp rebuke from the overseer. Turning defiantly upon his monitor, he exclaimed in outraged tones, "I'll give you to understand, if I live many years, I was born for something other than to tend a spinning-jenny!" [42] If by "something other" he meant that he was ultimately to enjoy his brief day as America's best paid, best publicized writer,[43] his words were truly prophetic.

[39] *Ibid.*, p. 9.
[40] As a matter of fact, Josiah was just past eighteen at that time, for the poem bears the date August 18, 1837.
[41] Plunkett, *op. cit.*, p. 14.
[42] *Ibid.*, p. 10.
[43] See above, p. 2, footnote 1.

II

Finding a Career

When Josiah Holland expressed the resolve to become an educated gentleman, he must have pondered wistfully upon the fact that the college named for Lord Jeffrey Amherst lay within ten miles of his birthplace, and that Williams, Dartmouth, and Yale were not too remote from any of the towns in which he had spent his childhood and youth. The possibility of Harvard, of course, never entered his head; for Harvard, as we have already observed, had become too heretical for the orthodox son of orthodox parents. But college a hundred years ago was an exclusive affair, for the favored few.[1] Certainly it was not for the lad who was obliged to support not only himself but also, to a considerable extent, his family.

Holland's biographer is annoyingly vague about the period between his graduation from Northampton High School and his attaining his majority—approximately two years—but the records set forth a few interesting facts.

Josiah Holland, as we have already seen, was a versatile person. An expert maker of quill pens—the only kind known in those days—and an extraordinarily adept penman, he found remunerative employment as a teacher of longhand.[2] Among men and women eager to improve their chirography, young Holland's fame as a writing master spread over a wide radius

[1] According to the United States census of 1850, there were only 11,903 college students in the entire country. See J. D. B. DeBow (Superintendent of U.S. Census): *Statistical View of the United States, Being a Compendium of the Seventh Census*, p. 145, Washington, 1854. "A chief purpose of most colleges [between 1830 and 1850] was still the preservation of a learned clergy. . . . Most doctors and lawyers still continued to receive their instruction by apprenticeship." Carl Russell Fish: *The Rise of the Common Man*, New York, 1927, pp. 214–215.

[2] Plunkett, *op. cit.*, p. 16.

—even across the New Hampshire state line to the villages of Chesterfield and Hinsdale. In fact, there apparently came a time when the size and the number of his classes in penmanship were limited solely by the extent of territory that could be covered by a day on horseback. His largest writing class was conducted in the office of the *Hampshire Gazette,* in Northampton, and his advertisement announced, "All pupils are required to furnish their own lights." [3]

And this was by no means everything in his repertory of talents. Josiah Gilbert Holland could sing tenor and recite declamations as gracefully as he could indite copy-book maxims.[4] He could, moreover, make inexpensive portraits by the new mechanical process invented a few years earlier by a Frenchman named Louis Jacques Daguerre.[5] In his rooms in the old Canal Building in Northampton, he maintained a well-equipped studio for that purpose.[5] Did Berkshire villagers wish to learn the arts of singing and elocution? Did they wish to have their pictures taken? If so, they had in their midst a young man of more varied talents than the learned Dr. Johnson or the versatile Dr. Goldsmith.

If Josiah Gilbert Holland could have afforded a college course, he would undoubtedly have become a preacher. Much as he loved the writing of verses, much as he yearned for literary fame, he could hardly have considered belles-lettres as more than an avocation. In 1840, despite the well-established success of Irving and Cooper and the crescent popularity of Longfellow, no sensible young American had serious expectations of earning his livelihood by his pen alone.[6] Moreover, Josiah Holland had been reared in an atmosphere of such unremitting spiritual endeavor that the salvation of souls must have appeared far more important to him than any secular calling. Indeed, the fondest dream that Mrs. Harrison Hol-

3 Clifton Johnson: *Historic Hampshire in the Connecticut Valley,* Springfield, Mass., 1932, p. 75.

4 Plunkett, *op. cit.,* p. 17.

5 Edward Eggleston: "Josiah Gilbert Holland," *Century Magazine,* December, 1881, I, 162.

6 Fish, *op. cit.,* p. 106.

land cherished for her son Josiah was "that he might be a minister." [7] But why a long college course as a preparation for the ministry? Even to this day, are not the woods (and the mountains and the prairies) full of ardent gospelers who never saw the inside of an accredited college, whose fire and zeal far surpass either their theology or their grammar? Of course the reader who would ask these questions would be thinking, quite erroneously, in terms of what Mr. Mencken has called "the Bible belt." He would need to be reminded that New England Congregational ministers, however narrow and intolerant some of them may be, are not illiterate—that they are as inevitably college-bred as Episcopal or even Unitarian ministers. As a recent American church historian has pointed out, nearly all of the New England Congregational clergy at the time of the Revolutionary War were graduates of Harvard or Yale.[8] And with the subsequent development of such colleges as Dartmouth, Williams, Bowdoin, and Amherst, there is every reason to assume that the tradition of a college-bred New England Congregational ministry was fully maintained in the generations succeeding the Revolution.

Since Josiah Holland could not afford Yale or Dartmouth or Williams or Amherst, to say nothing of an intensive course at Andover Seminary, he must reluctantly choose a calling other than the ministry. For the routine and barter of business, we may well infer, the son of Harrison Holland had no bent; and anyhow, no capital with which to open even a small establishment. For the profession of law, we are told, he had no enthusiasm either.[9] Now a youth as declamatory as Josiah might well have hankered for a legal and political career; but manifestly he did not. Perhaps he had no fondness for debate; certainly no accessible record has listed debating among his numerous activities. And it is more than likely that most of the lawyers of his acquaintance were worldlings or shysters or both. Daniel Webster, most eminent New England lawyer and

[7] Plunkett, *op. cit.*, p. 9.
[8] Sweet, *op. cit.*, p. 256.
[9] Plunkett, *op. cit.*, p. 16.

statesman of the time, was already regarded by many pious New Englanders as both a reprobate and a renegade.[10] Following the stormy term of John Quincy Adams (1825–1829), the country was to elect only two more New England Presidents, Pierce and Coolidge, in a hundred years. The nation was turning to the South and the West for its political leaders. In 1840, few dreams of fame in Capitol or in White House could have stirred the breasts of New England youths.

As for country-school teaching, it was not really a profession for men at all. Rather, it was one of two less dignified things: an avocation for farmers, or a stop-gap for youths of varied ambitions whose lack of funds prevented their completing college courses in successive years.

The one calling that remained was medicine. And it is not difficult to understand why Josiah Holland, despite his apparent lack of interest in science, should finally have hit upon the medical profession. Surely ministering to the body would be, next to ministering to the spirit, the most altruistic work that a man could choose to do. Moreover, at this very time in Josiah's life—the year that he reached his majority—there came to him and his family a crushing sorrow that quickened his desire for conserving human life. In or near that year— within a space of fifteen months, to be exact—all three of Josiah's sisters, Louisa, Lucretia, and Clarissa, died: two from consumption, and one from measles.[11] What a devastating blow to a single family! What a cruel pity that three young lives should be sacrificed, perhaps needlessly, upon the altar of helpless ignorance! Here was an opportunity to prevent similar tragedies in other families—an opportunity to become a more sagacious, more advanced, more skilful doctor than any who had gone before.

But if a man had neither the time nor the money to qualify as a minister of the gospel, how could he hope to qualify as a doctor of medicine? The answer is easy. In 1840, New Englanders had the quaint notion that inasmuch as the body is

---

[10] Henry Cabot Lodge: *Daniel Webster*, Boston, 1883, p. 356.
[11] Plunkett, *op. cit.*, p. 7.

transitory and the soul immortal, the spiritual healer should be a far more learned man than the physical healer [12]—that upon the former there rested an infinitely graver responsibility than upon the latter. The same fantastic idea had, of course, prevailed through the centuries in old England, a far less pietistic land than the region lying between Quebec and Long Island. As late as the days of Napoleon and the corporeal Prince Regent—the days of Josiah Gilbert Holland's infancy—a hundred English country parishes might boast their learned doctors of divinity; yet from Southampton to the Tweed River there was not one first-rate college of medicine.[13] Witness John Keats, the liveryman's boy, apprenticed to a surgeon in much the way in which some Jim Brown or Tom Smith was apprenticed to a bootmaker or a tailor!

In Massachusetts, in 1840, the study of medicine required just half as much time as the study of divinity. And, whereas the matriculant at Yale or at any other reputable college of liberal arts must have had an adequate humanistic preparatory course, any sufficiently mature youth who was well grounded in the three "R's" could enter upon the formal study of medicine.[14] Two years' study was required for the obtaining of the M.D. degree; but of that two years, only six months had to be spent in an accredited medical school. For the remaining year and a half the candidate might—and commonly did—read and experiment in the office and under the tutelage of some experienced general practitioner.[15]

A lamentably scant preparation for the profession upon which human life itself depends! We are shocked; but that is because we are children of another century. For better or for worse, we think differently from our great-grandsires. Let our spiritual doctors be what they may—provided they are inoffensive—our physickers must be men of knowledge and skill.

[12] See above, p. 12, footnote 1.

[13] H. D. Traill, and J. S. Mann: *Social England*, 6 vols., New York, 1909, Vol. VI, Section I, p. 92.

[14] For the relatively low standing of the medical profession in this country in 1840, see Fish, *op. cit.*, p. 210.

[15] Plunkett, *op. cit.*, pp. 16, 17.

Since the soul is intangible and unproved, one mortal's guess about it is as good as another's. Since ethics appears more a matter of gregarious adjustment than of supernatural revelation, we put more trust in our scientists and quasi-scientists, our psychologists and our sociologists, than in our theologians or even our philosophers. The realms of anatomy and chemistry are, if still a long way from being completely explored, at least well charted. From test-tube and thermometer, from miscroscope and X-ray, we get workable evidence. From the meditations of the mystics, no matter how profound, we get what appear at best but little more than "hunches." Josiah Holland, however, was reared in an even earlier and more naïve time than what Mrs. Wharton has called the Age of Innocence; and he was a more thoroughgoing product of his age than May Welland or Newland Archer could ever have been of theirs. Perhaps, by the way, Josiah would have been innocent in any age.

Josiah's medical education was begun in 1841, in the office of two Northampton physicians, Benjamin Barrett and Daniel Thompson, at that time probably the two leading doctors of the community.[16] Dr. Barrett, who was about forty-five years old, was an outstanding citizen as well as an exceptionally competent physician. A graduate of Harvard College and of the Harvard Medical School, he was undoubtedly one of the most cultivated, best-versed members of his profession in Massachusetts. And his high medical attainments did not prevent him from taking an active part both in politics and in business. Indeed, he found time to honor his community as a state legislator and as treasurer of the Northampton Savings Bank. The Barrett Gymnasium at Amherst College, by the way, is a monument to Dr. Barrett's public spirit.[17] Dr. Thompson, who was four years his partner's junior, had received most of his medical training under the preceptorship of Dr. Barrett. Thompson, though always less prominent than Barrett, and perhaps less broadly cultivated, was considered fully as good a

---

[16] Plunkett, *op. cit.*, p. 17.

[17] For data on Dr. Barrett, see Solomon Clark: *Antiquities of Northampton, Massachusetts,* Northampton, 1882, p. 279.

doctor and a most estimable gentleman as well. Consequently, although Josiah Holland in later years seldom mentioned either of his Northampton medical mentors, we may assume that his contact with them was quite as salutary as his contact with Judge Dewey had been. Of the two doctors, Thompson unquestionably exerted the more intimate if not the more potent influence upon Holland. Between Thompson and Holland there existed the common bond of having sat at the feet of the wise Dr. Barrett.[18] Moreover, during these eighteen months of his career young Holland lodged at the Thompson residence on old South Street, opposite Rahar's Inn.[19]

Holland's medical education was completed in the Berkshire Medical College at Pittsfield. That institution, long since defunct, was once famed throughout lower New England and upstate New York; for its president, Dr. H. H. Childs, was an outstanding physician as well as an able executive.[20] All this, however, was before the days when the larger cities, with their superior clinical advantages, came almost to monopolize the medical colleges of this country.

The records of Josiah's career as a medical student at Pittsfield are scant. From them, however, we learn that "he applied himself with unremitting industry," [21] that he wrote a paper on "The Theory of Sensation," and that he received his diploma on November 3, 1843.[21] We learn also that during his two brief terms at Pittsfield he found time to address an open letter in verse to the pupils of a young ladies' seminary—a letter in which he sportively complained of the haughty maidens' propensity for snubbing the young men of the medical college.[21]

Springfield was the town in which Dr. Holland decided to hang up his shingle—a decision easily explainable to the student of western Massachusetts history. If the young profes-

<hr>

[18] For data on Dr. Thompson, see Richard L. Gay: *Gazetteer of Hampshire County, Massachusetts,* Springfield, n.d., p. 355.

[19] For this information I am indebted to Miss Anne Clark Carlisle, Forbes Library, Northampton, Mass.

[20] Plunkett, *op. cit.,* p. 18. See also Frank W. Blackmar: *Charles Robinson, the First Free-State Governor of Kansas,* Topeka, Kansas, 1900, p. 19.

[21] Plunkett, *op. cit.,* pp. 17–20.

sional was to "grow up with the town," Springfield was indeed the town to grow up with. The opening of the Boston-Springfield section of the Boston & Albany Railroad in 1839, and the completion of the road to Albany in 1841, made it apparent that Springfield, already a considerable trading center, was to become the metropolis of western Massachusetts. It was now only a question of time until this flourishing river village of ten thousand people [22] would be upon the main artery of traffic between Boston and the principal cities of the West, and it was only a question of a little longer time until it would be one of the chief railroad junction points between New York and eastern Canada. Meanwhile, its industrial expansion was keeping abreast of its growth in trade and traffic; for, along with its inevitable textile mills, it already possessed railroad shops and a large United States armory and arsenal.[23]

One of Josiah's Pittsfield classmates, Charles Bailey, from near Boston, shared Holland's faith in the future of Springfield; and so it was that in the spring of 1844 the two young doctors established a partnership in an office on Main Street.[24]

Dr. Holland's brief career as a practising physician was not conspicuously successful. True, he did help to quell an epidemic of erysipelas,[25] and he made a personally favorable impression upon many of the leading citizens of the community. But Springfield had its quota of well-established physicians, and it probably offered less opportunity to the novice than many a smaller, less thriving town. Moreover, Dr. Holland's zeal for his profession was by no means constant, a fact that is well attested by one incident related by his biographer. Two pupils in a young ladies' boarding-school having been stricken with scarlatina, the principal of the school summoned Dr. Holland to attend them. "But what did he do with the grand open-

[22] According to the United States census of 1840, the population of Springfield was 10,985.

[23] See George S. Merriam: *The Life and Times of Samuel Bowles,* New York, 1885, I, 13.

[24] Plunkett, *op. cit.,* p. 21.

[25] *Ibid.,* p. 22.

ing? The call came when he was at work on a poem . . . 'The Fays of the Fountain,' and he said, 'You go, Bailey; make some excuse; tell 'em I can't come.' " [26] No wonder Bailey and Holland agreed to disagree at the end of two and a half years!

Dr. Holland's second and last medical partnership was with Charles Robinson, another Pittsfield graduate, who was later to win political laurels as Governor of Kansas. The Holland-Robinson partnership seems to have been less fortuitous than the Holland-Bailey partnership had been; for in earlier years there had apparently been a closer intimacy between Holland and Robinson than between Holland and Bailey. Robinson had been Holland's roommate at Pittsfield; and in 1843, upon beginning the practice of medicine in Holland's native village of Belchertown, he had formed contacts with many of Holland's childhood friends.[27] It must, however, be admitted that Holland's second medical partnership proved quite as much of a fiasco as his first had been. Indeed, the chief fruit of this later enterprise was the establishment of a hospital exclusively for women, a project which soon proved to have been much more ambitious than feasible. Founded without important financial backing, and at a time when there was no popular demand for such an institution, the enterprise was bound to fail. Its demise occurred within six months.[28]

And so Dr. Holland had failed in the profession which he had so carefully, indeed, prayerfully, chosen. Like father, like son! Here, despite the stabilizing influence of Judge Dewey and Doctors Barrett and Thompson, we perceive the outcropping of the restive, indecisive spirit of poor old Harrison Holland. The net results of these three years in Springfield had been about as follows: first, a wealth of practical if somewhat bitter and financially profitless experience; second, a realization that medicine was not Josiah Holland's forte; third, some pleasant and highly advantageous social contacts.

To complicate the situation, the young doctor had com-

---

[26] Plunkett, *op. cit.*, p. 21.
[27] Blackmar, *op. cit.*, pp. 20, 21.
[28] See Plunkett, *op. cit.*, p. 26.

mitted matrimony on October 7, 1845,[29] a year and a half after
the formation of the Holland-Bailey partnership. For Josiah,
at least, the romance had begun in Northampton on a winter
evening of 1843–1844, at a party at the home of William A.
Hawley, then editor of the *Hampshire Gazette*. The Hawley
"sociable," presumably a church affair, must have been a rather
large gathering, for at it Holland saw a number of strangers
to whom he was not introduced. One such stranger was a
pretty, brown-haired girl of twenty or twenty-one, a visitor
from Springfield, whom Josiah was to admire from afar all
evening. He was never to forget her. A few months later, in
Springfield, he was to meet and know her as Miss Elizabeth
Chapin, for the activities of the two young people in the South
(Congregational) Church threw them into frequent contact
with each other.[30]

Miss Chapin was the scion of an old and substantial Springfield family that Dr. Holland has characterized as follows in
his novel *The Bay Path:*

Deacon Samuel Chapin lived a long and useful life. He was a
diligent, persevering, reliable man—a faithful public servant, and
an invaluable man in the Church. He was blessed with a large
family of children, and they were all boys; and they had large families of children who were all boys, who, in turn, had large families
of boys. The consequence was that Springfield became filled with
good people bearing that name, and the name was spread all over
New England, so that, at this day, there are many thousands who
bear the blood and the name of Deacon Samuel Chapin.[31]

Elizabeth Chapin was one of the five children of Whitfield
Chapin, who had died in 1833, when Elizabeth was ten years
old.[30] Whitfield Chapin had at one time prospered on a modest
scale in the lumber business,[32] but for some years previous to

[29] *Ibid.*, pp. 20, 24. For specific information not given by Mrs. Plunkett, I
am indebted to Holland's daughter, Mrs. John K. Howe, and to Mr. Hiller C.
Wellman, City Library Association, Springfield, Mass.
[30] See above, footnote 29.
[31] J. G. Holland: *The Bay-Path*, New York, 1857, 1909, pp. 400–401.
[32] See Charles Wells Chapin: *Sketches of the Old Inhabitants and Other Citizens of Springfield*, Springfield, Mass., 1893, p. 123.

his death he had been in straitened circumstances. Elizabeth, however, had been sent to live with a well-to-do uncle in Albany, who had seen to it that the girl was afforded the best social and cultural advantages of the aristocratic little New York capital, including a course in a young ladies' seminary—a course that was probably superior, in many respects, to what Josiah Holland had had at Northampton High School.[33]

Concerning the appearance of Miss Chapin and her bridegroom at the time of their marriage, we shall let the latter's biographer speak:

A miniature of Mrs. Holland, made at this time, shows her with a fair complexion, a rosy bloom, a pair of remarkably frank and fearless bluish-gray eyes, and a wealth of soft brown hair. She was of medium height, but looked fairly petite beside the tall and stalwart figure of her husband. His dark-olive complexion and black eyes and hair gave him a Spanish look, but when illuminated in talking or in lecturing, his face had a remarkable brilliancy of expression, and the two presented that happy contrast which some philosophers deem essential to perfect mutual admiration in husband and wife.[34]

With regard to the salient traits of Mrs. Holland's character, we may pertinently speak a little later.

At the beginning of 1847 Josiah Holland found himself face to face with a crucial situation. Twenty-seven years old, unprepared for any calling except the one in which he had already failed, and married to a woman bred to far greater refinements and comforts of existence than he, the young man was challenged by a most serious predicament.

It was at this juncture that Josiah made his first try at journalism. Prompted, perhaps, by the success of his friend William A. Hawley, of the *Hampshire Gazette,* and certainly inspired by his bent for scribbling, he founded the *Bay State Weekly* in January, 1847. In this venture he had the assistance of one Horace S. Taylor, who contracted to do the printing.

---

[33] For this information I am indebted to Mrs. John K. Howe.
[34] Plunkett, *op. cit.,* pp. 25–26.

This newspaper, like the Holland-Robinson hospital, gave up the ghost in six months, and its subscription list was sold to the *Springfield Republican*.[35]

There was now nothing left for young Holland to do but turn to the old stop-gap of schoolmastering. And so in the summer of 1847, when he was offered a position in a privately endowed school at Richmond, Virginia, he fairly jumped at the opportunity. Since the stipend offered was undoubtedly small, and since Mrs. Holland's widowed mother was in precarious health, it was decided that Josiah should go south alone.[36]

Records regarding the institution at Richmond are virtually nonexistent;[37] but inasmuch as one of Holland's contemporaries speaks of it as a "commercial college,"[38] we may reasonably suppose that it was Holland's skill as a penman which chiefly recommended him to the school authorities. Of course the word "college" gives us no intimation as to the academic standing of the institution, but we are perfectly safe in averring that it was no college in any proper sense of the term. In all the South, at that time, the number of genuine colleges could probably be counted upon the fingers of one's two hands;[39] and in Richmond there was only one college—a Baptist, non-commercial institution which dated from 1832. As a matter of fact, this "commercial college" might well have been a children's institution; for in the South, in those days, all grades of education were administered far more extensively under private auspices than through state support.[40] As a present-day historian expresses the matter, "The enthusiasm

[35] Plunkett, *op. cit.*, pp. 22–23.

[36] *Ibid.*, p. 26.

[37] Histories of Richmond, old Richmond directories, and archives of the Virginia Historical Library fail utterly to disclose the identity of the "college" in which Holland taught, and surviving members of the Holland family do not remember even the name of the institution.

[38] Plunkett, *op. cit.*, p. 107.

[39] According to the United States census of 1850 there were forty colleges in the South (as compared with 119 for the entire United States). See DeBow, *op. cit.*, p. 145. Of these forty Southern colleges, however, only a very few—such as William and Mary and the University of Virginia—could have compared at all favorably with the best colleges in the North.

[40] Fish, *op. cit.*, p. 226.

for popular education that swept over the North stopped short at the Potomac and the Ohio." [41]

One wishes that the letters written by Josiah Holland to his wife during the autumn of 1847 were extant. Surely they would recount a most revealing tale. Here was a provincial New Englander, thrown for the first time in his callow life into a realm almost as foreign as London or Edinburgh would have been. Here was an untraveled villager transported suddenly into the amenities of the most urbane state capital in Dixie, a town which, with its thirty thousand inhabitants,[42] was three times as large and ten times as metropolitan as the Springfield of that day. Famed for its Edgar Allan Poe and its *Southern Literary Messenger,* this proud Virginia city had become one of the four or five chief cultural centers of the nation. Moreover, as "the home of an aristocracy born in . . . great houses" [43] and "surrounded by servants and family portraits," [43] as a place with "brilliant . . . social activities" and "a taste for the arts," [43] and as a community in which Episcopalianism enjoyed far greater prestige than Calvinism, the Virginia capital and metropolis must easily have surpassed all but the very largest Northern cities of that day in politeness and sophistication. How those "nice people" of Richmond, those pleasure-loving Episcopalians, with their wine-drinking, whist-playing rectors, must have startled and shocked poor Josiah Holland! One fancies that his letters to Elizabeth must have been very different in tone from the letters that young William Tecumseh Sherman was writing from the South to Ellen Ewing in Ohio. Sherman, it will be recalled, was frankly enamored of the lovely Southern belles that he danced with.[44] Alas! what a figure Josiah Gilbert Holland would have cut at the polka or the german! What a figure indeed, when his wildest dissipation must have been an occasional Presbyterian "sociable"! One doubts that he even availed himself of the

<hr>

[41] S. E. Morison: *Oxford History of the United States,* 2 vols. London, 1927, II, 20.

[42] According to the census of 1850, the population of Richmond was 27,570.

[43] Hervey Allen: *Israfel,* New York, 1934, p. 78.

[44] Lloyd Lewis: *Sherman, Fighting Prophet,* New York, 1932, p. 69.

opportunity—probably the first of his life—to see the majestic Edwin Forrest do Brutus or Hamlet; for as much as a decade later his opinion of the theatre did not differ materially from that of every evangelist who ever "revived." His writings in the eighteen-fifties leave no room for doubt on that score.[45] Not until he removed to New York, a generation after his years in the South, did he speak with even the most reserved tolerance of play-acting and play-going.[46]

There are two kinds of provincial people who some day travel far from home. Those of the first group adapt themselves to their new environments; that is, when in Rome they go Roman. Those of the second group carry their original environments with them, so to speak; that is, they either hold aloof from their new milieu or else they try to reform it. Josiah Gilbert Holland unquestionably belonged to the second group; throughout his stay in Richmond he appears to have been serenely certain of his moral superiority to the best F.F.V. society—as serenely certain as the missionary lady from, let us say, Ottawa, Kansas, is of her moral superiority to the heathen Chinese. Josiah was occasionally worried about a few details of the Calvinistic creed and even the Scriptures; [47] but these worries concerned theology, not ethics. That the devout Congregationalists of Massachusetts had the highest moral standards in the world, he could hardly have doubted for a moment. At this point in his life Josiah Holland could not have differed much from the typical Puritan characterized so aptly by Henry K. Rowe.

He believed all men sinners before God, bound in the grip of Satanic power, and if a man would escape the evil he must be continually on the alert to break loose from temptation and sin. The sins that troubled him were not the social sins of greed and injustice and harsh attitudes of man to man, but the frivolity and superficiality of life, and the unresisted inclination to self-

<hr>

45 J. G. Holland: *Timothy Titcomb's Letters*, New York, 1858, p. 79. See also Merriam, *op. cit.*, I, 62.

46 See below, pp. 198–199.

47 Plunkett, *op. cit.*, p. 106.

indulgence. . . . He inclined to exalt his own virtues in contrast to the vices he saw around him.[48]

Josiah was destined to remain at the "commercial college" in Richmond for only one term. Then, at the beginning of 1848, he was called to a teaching position in a much more primitive Southern town, Vicksburg, Mississippi.[49]

Removal from Virginia to Mississippi marked, in its way, as great a transition as removal from Massachusetts to Virginia. True, Virginia and Mississippi were both "South," and as such they possessed in common many manners, customs, and traditions that were sharply at variance with those of New England. To go, however, from the Old Dominion to the Bayou State was to go from the settled East to the frontier West, from the most thickly populated commonwealth on the South Atlantic seaboard [50] to one of the most sparsely peopled states east of the Mississippi,[50] from a middle-Atlantic climate to a subtropical climate. In Virginia Josiah Holland had seen crops and vegetation not markedly different from those of his home state; a red clay soil and an abundance of tobacco had been the most striking new phenomena that he had observed. In Mississippi he was to see vast fields of the cotton which in those days was milled largely in his native Massachusetts.[51] In Virginia he had touched the fringe of the black belt—just enough of it to introduce him to the Southern attitude toward interracial relations; in Mississippi he was to find himself in a region where blacks were already more numerous than whites.[52] In Richmond he had been in a city which, though

[48] Rowe, *op. cit.*, pp. 19–20.

[49] Plunkett, *op. cit.*, p. 26.

[50] According to the United States census of 1850, Virginia was the fourth state in the Union in population; Mississippi, the fifteenth. Virginia (area, 42,627 square miles) had 1,421,661 inhabitants; Mississippi (area, 46,865 square miles), 606,526 inhabitants. See *World Almanac,* New York, 1937, pp. 242, 243, 948.

[51] Fish, *op. cit.,* p. 68. See also Morison, *op. cit.,* Vol. II, p. 13. See also Mabel B. Casner and Ralph Henry Gabriel: *Exploring American History,* New York, 1931, pp. 380–381.

[52] According to the United States census of 1850, 37% of the total population of Virginia was Negro; 51.2% of the total population of Mississippi was Negro. See DeBow, *op. cit.,* p. 85.

smaller than the Western towns of Cincinnati and St. Louis, was as metropolitan as any American community outside of New York, Philadelphia, and Boston; in Vicksburg he was to be in a much smaller, cruder, less promising village than Springfield.

The new position that Josiah Holland had accepted was that of superintendent of schools and principal of the Main Street School in Vicksburg.[53] Since there was also an opening for a woman teacher, who was to have charge of the primary department at the munificent stipend of ten dollars a week,[54] and since Mrs. Chapin's health appeared somewhat improved, it was agreed that Elizabeth should join her husband and serve as his assistant. This meant, of course, that Josiah must return to Massachusetts and get Elizabeth,[55] for in the eighteen-forties a trip from New England to the Gulf region was no journey for a woman to take alone.

The new work upon which the Hollands were now embarking was indeed a missionary enterprise—an enterprise from which their friends in Springfield had endeavored to dissuade them.[55] Vicksburg, a twenty-four-year-old village [56] which straggled clumsily along a high bluff overlooking the east bank of Old Man River, had only one railroad_ a line connecting it with Jackson, the state capital.[57] It was not to see its first northbound train for several years; and though the steam packets which docked at Vicksburg en route from St. Louis to New Orleans gave the town some access to the outside world and some promise of future growth, the raw village must have appeared the "jumping-off place," even to so relatively unsophisticated a couple as Josiah and Elizabeth Holland. The streets of Vicksburg were, according to the vagaries of the weather, either puddles of mud or beds of dust, in which wallowed pigs, buzzards, and goats. The dwellings, except for

<hr>

[53] Plunkett, *op. cit.*, pp. 26, 193.

[54] *Ibid.*, p. 27.

[55] Eggleston, *op. cit.*, p. 163.

[56] *Encyclopaedia Britannica*, XXIII, 120. According to the United States census of 1850, the population of Vicksburg was 3678.

[57] See Dunbar Rowland: *History of Mississippi*, 2 vols., Jackson (Miss.), and Chicago, 1925, I, 618.

the few mansions of the more prosperous planters, were ugly, cheaply built little cottages, many of them constructed of mud-plastered logs, and most of them without basements. The front yards, even of the middle-class planters, seldom boasted decent coverings of lawn grass. The inhabitants, for the most part, lived on "a diet largely of 'hog and hominy,' " [58] and—if they were literate enough to read at all—knew "no literature but a weekly paper." [58] To Jefferson Davis, frontier cotton planter and politician, the Vicksburg of that day might appear "a wonderful place . . . capital of the rich and fertile county of Warren, the home of noted statesmen and men of affairs"; [59] but to the Massachusetts Yankee, Vicksburg was bound to appear like any other average community in the newer regions of the Deep South: a rather crude, very untidy place where the poor whites lived under amazingly squalid conditions and where the middle-class planters seldom enjoyed "comforts or amenities superior to those of the poorest sort of farmers in the North." [60] Holland must have had Vicksburg in the back of his mind when he wrote in an ostensibly different connection in 1865:

It is very difficult for any one bred in the older communities of the country to appreciate the extreme humility of border life, the meagerness and meanness of its household appointments, and the paucity of its stimulants to mental growth and social development.[61]

As for the Vicksburg public school, we have only to remind the reader that not until 1846 had Mississippi established a state system of elementary education. Hulking boys of twenty, some of them as big as the master himself, undoubtedly sat upon the same benches and conned the same lessons as under-nourished urchins of six. And it must be observed that these children were not the cream of Vicksburg. To call them quite

---

[58] Morison, *op. cit.*, II, 4–5.

[59] Robert W. Winston: *High Stakes and Hair Trigger: the Life of Jefferson Davis,* New York, 1930, p. 33.

[60] Morison, *op. cit.*, II, 4. See also Fish, *op. cit.*, p. 27.

[61] J. G. Holland: *Life of Abraham Lincoln,* Springfield, Mass., 1865, p. 28.

the scum would be unjust and inaccurate; but in Mississippi, as elsewhere in the South, the children of the more favored families were almost invariably educated under private auspices. Then, too, Mississippi had no such cultural traditions as had Massachusetts—or, for that matter, Virginia. During much of its colonial and territorial existence the state had been under French and Spanish rule; and consequently, although a large proportion of its white inhabitants in the eighteen-forties had migrated from older commonwealths of the South [62]—commonwealths which prided themselves at least upon a highly cultivated minority—the average Mississippian of eighty or ninety years ago could hardly have been very school-minded. Certainly he did not look upon the elementary school, as did the average citizen of Massachusetts, as a stepping-stone to the high school, the Latin school, or (perhaps, ultimately) the college. To him an institution that would make his children a little less illiterate than the "Nigger" cotton-pickers was adequate.[63]

To the Yankee doctor-pedagogue, however, such an institution was anything but adequate. If Mississippi was one of the most illiterate states in the Union [64]—and contentedly so—was that any reason why she should remain thus? If Horace Mann could grade the schools of Massachusetts, why could not Josiah Holland grade one school in Mississippi? As a matter of fact, that is precisely what Holland did do: he systematized the curriculum and established what must have been, by a number of years, the oldest graded common school in the Bayou State.[65] What the people of Vicksburg thought at that time of "that damn-fool professor from up No'th" it would be easy to conjecture; but a third of a century later, just after the "professor's" death, one of them was to pay his memory this handsome tribute:

62 For a brief but authoritative sketch of the political, social, and cultural history of Mississippi, see Dunbar Rowland: Article on Mississippi, *Encyclopaedia Britannica*, XV, 602–604.

63 Rowland: *History of Mississippi*, I, 648.

64 Morison, *op. cit.*, II, 15, footnote 2.

65 Plunkett, *op. cit.*, p. 27.

Dr. Holland is remembered here as the principal of our Main Street public school, and as the scholarly preceptor of many of our boys who are now leading citizens of this place. To his administration Vicksburg is now largely indebted for the successful and honored history of this justly celebrated school.[66]

And yet, to tell the truth, Josiah Holland had no such zeal for his teaching as the foregoing tribute might indicate, and he took no particular pride in the results of his labors. The only recorded boast he ever made about his few months' work in Vicksburg was made to a Union veteran after the Civil War, when he declared that he had probably whipped more Southern rebels than had the veteran.[67]

The fact of the matter was that the South gave Holland more education than he gave the South. In this connection, let us visualize the national picture as it was when he arrived in Vicksburg. At that very time President James K. Polk, ably assisted by Generals Zachary Taylor and Winfield Scott, was winding up the job of trouncing Mexico in the war over the possession of Texas, and Uncle Sam was thereby adding hundreds of thousands of square miles to his slave territory.[68] Now most New Englanders believed slavery to be wrong, and Josiah Holland was no exception to the general rule. From his earliest childhood he must have often heard, and as often repeated, pious platitudes against a system which was worthless to the North, but a virtual economic necessity to the South. To call Holland an Abolitionist, however, would be wide of the mark; for militant Abolitionism, even in Massachusetts, had not yet become popular or respectable. To the average New England Yankee of the eighteen-forties, William Lloyd Garrison was a

---

[66] Plunkett, *op. cit.*, p. 193. The excerpt quoted is from the Vicksburg *Sentinel,* presumably a mid-October issue of 1881. Mrs. Plunkett, with her usual propensity for vagueness, fails to indicate the date of the issue; and I have not had access to the files of the *Sentinel.*

[67] See article on Holland, *National Cyclopaedia of American Biography,* New York, 1891, I, 312.

[68] The Mexican War ended with the Treaty of Guadalupe-Hidalgo, 1848. See Casner and Gabriel, *op. cit.*, p. 465.

rattle-brained fanatic,[69] and most of his articulate followers were Unitarian (and therefore heretical) in theology and—well, at least unconventional in moral standards.[70] One of the few outspoken Abolitionists of the time who conformed to the most rigid Puritan ethical and spiritual ideals was that fiery but always saintly Quaker, John Greenleaf Whittier.

In Richmond, where the Negro problem was handled with the minimum of friction, Holland had seen the institution of slavery at its best. So, when he crossed over into the Southwest, he could hardly have been more than lukewarm in his enthusiasm for Abolition.

Just what impressions of slavery he gathered in Mississippi we do not know, but evidently they were not very unfavorable. If the vicinity of Vicksburg boasted no Jefferson Davis—at that time the model plantation owner of Mississippi [71]—neither was it cursed, apparently, with any Simon Legree. If Josiah Holland ever witnessed a slave auction, the experience did not affect him as it did Harriet Beecher Stowe or even Lincoln. All in all, Holland's year and a quarter in the Deep South appears to have given him a sympathetic understanding of the Southern attitude toward the Negro. Provincial and unbending in matters of personal ethics, he could be tolerant regarding large social questions, particularly if tolerance lay—as in this instance—in the direction of conservatism. In short, we may well believe that Holland, during his sojourn in Vicksburg, was far less irritated by the institution of slavery than by the manner in which some of the more vociferous Vicksburgers gloated over the result of the Mexican War.[72]

---

[69] Oliver Johnson: *William Lloyd Garrison and His Times*, London, 1882, p. 273.

[70] See Paxton Hibben: *Henry Ward Beecher, An American Portrait*, New York, 1927, p. 24. See also Lyman Beecher: *Autobiography and Correspondence*, New York, 1863, 1865, II, 53–56.

[71] Allen Tate: *Jefferson Davis: His Rise and Fall*, New York, 1929, p. 71.

[72] According to Professor Morison, the majority of Southern slaves probably "suffered less than any other class" from the institution of slavery. "Their physical wants were better supplied than those of thousands of Northern mechanics." Morison, *op. cit.*, II, 7.

Here we are indulging in no mere idle conjecture. Holland's published writings, from first to last, are singularly free from caustic references to slavery. In one of his essays he complains about the Negro's lack of ethical sense,[73] but nowhere does he burn with indignation over the Southern white man's inhumanity to the black brother. Only in his biography of Lincoln does he speak in praise of the Emancipation Proclamation, and then his words are thoroughly conventional.[74] We are told, on the best authority, that in the years immediately following his sojourn in the South, Josiah Gilbert Holland was "unfriendly" to Abolitionism.[75]

This does not mean that he was learning to be enthusiastic about the South or the Southern people. As a matter of fact, when the novelty of his experience wore off, he doubtless found his surroundings as uncongenial as his work. If the Southerners appeared more polite and hospitable than the people of the Connecticut Valley, they also appeared more shiftless and improvident. If the adherents of Southern evangelical sects were even more ardent in religious expression, even more sound in theology, and even more regular in church attendance than their Yankee counterparts, they appeared better in precept than in ethical practice.[76] Then, too, Josiah and Elizabeth would not have been normal New Englanders if they had not found the Mississippi climate enervating.[77] Holland's enthusiasm for the South and its people may be measured by the attention that he gives to Dixie in his published volumes. In not one of his novels does he take the reader to the Land of Cotton for so much as a single brief scene, and in only one of his poems, *The Mistress of the Manse,* does he deal at all with Southerners. Moreover, he never took the

[73] J. G. Holland: *Every-Day Topics,* I, pp. 159–162.
[74] Holland: *Life of Lincoln,* Chap. XXIII, especially pp. 392–393, 398.
[75] Merriam, *op. cit.,* I, 62.
[76] Morison, *op. cit.,* II, 16.
[77] In 1833 a traveler from the Southeast had reported the whole Yazoo section as "very sickly, though it is very productive." *Papers of Thomas Ruffin,* II, 77. Reproduced by Ulrich B. Phillips: *Life and Labor in the Old South,* Boston, 1929, p. 183.

trouble to publish his *Sketches of Plantation Life* [78] in book form.

When the summer vacation of 1848 arrived, however, the Hollands were glad to accept an invitation to return to their work at Vicksburg for the ensuing year. The work was only a makeshift, but there was no other opening at the time. Thoroughly homesick, and continually anxious about the health of both Mrs. Chapin and Harrison Holland,[79] they would have liked to return to Massachusetts for the vacation. Such a move, however, was impossible; for whether they had taken the all-water route from New Orleans, or the inland Mississippi-Ohio route by way of Cairo and Cincinnati and Pittsburgh, their journey would have consumed a large part of the vacation. And, besides, a trip of fifteen hundred miles and back would have eaten up their combined savings.

But, fortunately for the morale of Josiah at least, a friend—probably a trustee or a patron of the Main Street School—had invited him to visit the former's plantation in Louisiana.[80] Whether or not the invitation included Elizabeth, the records do not state; but it is difficult to believe that either Southern hospitality or Southern chivalry would have permitted a lady to pine in a dull Mississippi village while her husband went gallivanting in another state. It is equally difficult to believe that Josiah Holland's tender conscience would have permitted him to take such a vacation unless his wife could share its pleasures with him. At any rate, we know that when school was out for the summer, Josiah crossed the river into Louisiana and sojourned for a while on one of the largest plantations in that part of the South.[81] Thus, although he got no respite from the hot humidity of the Gulf region, he was afforded at least a change of scene. And certainly it was a real change, not a busman's holiday. In Vicksburg, of course, Holland had learned

[78] See below, p. 34.

[79] Harrison Holland died before the close of 1848. For this information I am indebted to Mrs. Howe.

[80] Plunkett, *op. cit.,* p. 27.

[81] *Ibid.,* p. 27.

more about plantation life through rumor than through observation; he had seen far more of plantation owners than of plantations. In Louisiana he was to see things that apparently interested him much more than anything in Richmond or Vicksburg—things that were to furnish him with the first important literary inspiration of his life. In Louisiana, we may say, Josiah Gilbert Holland was to find his career at last; for here he wrote *Sketches of Plantation Life,* which he sent to the leading newspaper back home, the *Springfield Republican.*[82]

So far as we know, the second year at Vicksburg was uneventful except for two circumstances. One of them was the abrupt manner in which the year's work ended; the other was a family development which we shall mention presently. Early in April, 1849, the Hollands received word that Mrs. Chapin's failing health had passed to the stage of critical illness, and that unless they started homeward immediately, they would probably never again see her alive.[83] Their plans for the coming year were already uncertain. Josiah wished more than ever to obtain a position in the North, preferably Massachusetts. As for Elizabeth, she would not be teaching another year in any event; for it had been known for several months that there was to be an addition to the Holland family.[83] So, when word of Mrs. Chapin's condition reached the young couple, they decided to start for Springfield at once. Following expressions of regret— more, probably, than mere conventional expressions, for the Vicksburg school authorities had apparently come to respect these Yankees and their work—the resignations were accepted, and the long homeward journey was begun. After steam-packet voyages which must have taken them all the way to Pitts-

---

[82] Plunkett, *op. cit.,* p. 27. Mrs. Plunkett says that Holland "sent them" to the *Republican,* but she does not state that they were ever published. Neither Merriam nor Hooker mentions them, and I do not find them in the files of the *Republican.* A biographer of Emily Dickinson states (without direct documentation) that Holland was "engaged in writing" some "stories" of plantation life when Miss Dickinson visited the Hollands at their home in Springfield about 1853. See Josephine Pollitt: *Emily Dickinson,* New York and London, 1930, p. 83.

[83] Plunkett, *op. cit.,* p. 27.

burgh,[84] they made the trans-Appalachian trip by stagecoach and train—chiefly the former, since at that time most of the few railroads were short and unconnected.[84] The Hollands reached Springfield a couple of weeks before the death of Mrs. Chapin.[83] In view of the fact that the Holland infant, Arthur Gilbert, was to arrive in August,[85] the trip had been a bit hazardous; but apparently neither mother nor child suffered ill effects from it.

All the way home from Vicksburg, Josiah was wrapped up in literary plans, which he discussed with the enthusiasm of a teen-aged boy.[86] *Plantation Life* was not the only reason for his enthusiasm. During his stay in the South he had had poems accepted by two of the most popular American magazines of the day, the *Home Journal* and the *Knickerbocker Magazine*. The *Home Journal* poem was a five-stanza lyric entitled "Fleta Gray." [87] Identity of the *Knickerbocker* poem, printed without the author's name, has been lost; but Mrs. Plunkett vouches for the fact that the latter poem appeared.[88]

So, as Josiah neared his native valley, he felt more and more elated over the recognition of his talents as a writer—more and more confident that after years of futile drifting he had found a career.

[83] Plunkett, *op. cit.*, p. 27.
[84] Fish, *op. cit.*, p. 75.
[85] Plunkett, *op. cit.*, p. 27.
[86] See above, p. 10, footnote 36.
[87] See W. H. Judson memorial article on Holland, Chicago *Tribune*, Oct. 22, 1881.
[88] Plunkett, *op. cit.*, p. 27.

III

Sam Bowles and the *Republican*

The modest literary triumphs mentioned in the last chapter fired Holland with the urge to try journalism once more. His failure with the *Bay State Weekly* he ascribed, quite correctly, to lack of financial backing and lack of sagacious business management. His problem, obviously, was to find an editorial opening with a newspaper that was a "going concern."

Early in May 1849, two weeks after his return from Vicksburg,[1] he found, quite fortuitously, just the sort of opening he desired. As a reviewer in the *Independent* has related:

The writer of this notice had from Dr. Holland's own lips the story of his ride up the main street of Springfield in an old and muddy perch-back wagon, with hardly a dollar in his pocket, scanning the signs as he rode in search of an opening for him, till by some guidance of the Providence, in which no man believed more firmly, his eye fell on a sign freshly painted and displayed since the last returning adventurer had passed up that street. It read: *"The Springfield Republican,* Samuel Bowles, Editor." [2]

Mrs. Plunkett tells the story more simply:

The second "Editor Bowles," known the world over as "Sam Bowles," stood in the office door as Dr. Holland drove up the street, and seeing him, said "That is the man I want," while the doctor, pointing to the building, said "That is the place I want." [3]

The interview in Bowles's office must have been as pleasant as it was profitable. Samuel Bowles, Jr., was at that time an enthusiastic, energetic youth of twenty-three [4]—younger than

1 Eggleston, *op. cit.,* p. 163.
2 *Independent,* Vol. XLVI, p. 565. May 3, 1894.
3 Plunkett, *op. cit.,* p. 28.
4 Bowles was born Feb. 9, 1826.

Holland by six or seven years. It is more than likely that he had already formed a highly favorable impression of Holland. If, as Mrs. Plunkett asserts, Josiah had sent his *Sketches of Planta-tion Life* to the *Republican* while still in the South,[5] Bowles would be the first person to have read them. And the *Sketches* might well have attracted the young editor in the first place because Bowles himself had spent the winter of 1844–1845 in Louisiana [6] and had, in all probability, reached much the same conclusions about the South that Holland had reached. More-over, there chanced to be a real opening for Holland at the moment, since the assistant editor of the *Republican,* Sam-uel H. Davis, had died only a few weeks earlier.[7]

The Springfield *Republican* was, of course, a thoroughly "going concern." Founded as a weekly in 1824 by Samuel Bowles, Sr.,[8] it had been converted into a daily twenty years later.[9] And during its first five years as a daily it had, after a somewhat discouraging start,[10] grown phenomenally both in character and in prestige. As the only Massachusetts daily pa-per outside of Boston [11] it had an exceptionally attractive field; and under the editorship of the youthful but brilliant Sam-uel Bowles, Jr., it had reached the enviable position that it probably occupies to this day: that of the most influential small-city newspaper in the United States.[12] For a little over two years, from April 1846 to July 1848, it had had a rival, the Springfield *Evening Gazette;* [13] but it had sucessfully ter-minated that rivalry by absorbing the *Gazette.*[13] Meanwhile its circulation had increased from a few hundred to three or

[5] See above, p. 34.

[6] Merriam, *op. cit.,* Vol. I, p. 22.

[7] *Ibid.,* Vol. I, p. 58. Note, however, that Merriam erroneously gives the year of Davis' death as 1850, instead of 1849. For verification of the 1849 dating I am indebted to Mr. Hiller C. Wellman, City Library Association, Springfield, Mass.

[8] Richard Hooker: *The Story of an Independent Newspaper,* New York, 1924, p. 1.

[9] *Ibid.,* p. 34.

[10] *Ibid.,* p. 41.

[11] *Ibid.,* p. 37.

[12] Merriam, *op. cit.,* Vol. I, p. 179. See also Hooker, *op. cit.,* p. 202.

[13] *Ibid.,* Vol. I, pp. 23–25.

four thousand,[14] and it heavily invaded territory that had previously been monopolized by the Hartford *Courant*.[15] Consequently, when Josiah Holland became assistant editor of the *Republican* he found himself to be an important part of one of the unique and indispensable institutions of western Massachusetts. As Emily Dickinson declared, the advent of the *Republican* was a positive daily thrill to its subscribers. Upon the arrival of an especially interesting issue she says:

> . . . the world grew rounder than it sometimes is, and I broke several dishes. . . . One glimpse of "The Republican" makes me break things again—I read it every night. . . . "The Republican" seems to us like a letter from you [Bowles and Holland], and we break the seal and read it eagerly.[16]

The history of Josiah Gilbert Holland's business relations with the *Republican* may be told very briefly. In the spring of 1849 he was made assistant editor at an annual stipend of $480; in 1851 he was raised to $700; and in 1852 he managed to borrow $3,500 with which to purchase a quarter interest in the paper.[17] The generous lender of the latter amount is said to have been a Dr. Brooks, of Norwich, Connecticut, a Pittsfield classmate of Holland's, the man whom Holland had assisted during the epidemic of erysipelas.[18] Holland retained his financial interest in the *Republican* until the autumn of 1857, at which time he resigned his editorial position.[19] Thereafter, for about seven years, he continued as a more or less regular contributor to the paper whose upbuilding he had so materially aided.[20] And in 1862, when Bowles was traveling in Europe, Holland returned temporarily to his desk to serve as acting editor.[21] The importance of Holland's later connection

---

[14] Plunkett, *op. cit.*, p. 32.

[15] Merriam, *op. cit.*, Vol. I, p. 65.

[16] Letter from Emily Dickinson to Dr. and Mrs. Holland, about 1853. Martha Dickinson Bianchi: *Life and Letters of Emily Dickinson,* Boston and New York, 1924, p. 186.

[17] Plunkett, *op. cit.*, p. 28.

[18] *Ibid.*, p. 28.

[19] See below, p. 46.

[20] Merriam, *op. cit.*, Vol. I, p. 202.

[21] *Ibid.*, Vol. I, p. 315.

with the *Republican*—that is, his connection after 1857—may be seen from the following announcement:

Dr. J. G. Holland ("Timothy Titcomb"), the popular author, continues connected both with the editorial and proprietary departments of the paper, and his pen constantly enriches its columns. In addition to his various editorial articles, he will furnish during the coming year a special series of papers over his own name.[22]

When Josiah Holland first took his chair in the *Republican* office, he and Bowles agreed upon a very definite division of labor, or at least as definite a division as was feasible for a small-town newspaper with its limited staff. By the arrangement Bowles was to continue the writing of the political editorials, since Holland's interest in politics was at that time relatively slight,[23] and his political knowledge perhaps even slighter. Holland, a man of much more literary bent and discrimination than his young chief, was to write the book reviews and to make them much more important and comprehensive than they had theretofore been.[24] Holland was also to add a religious and ethical department, a feature that did not greatly interest Bowles personally, but one whose value Bowles thoroughly appreciated because of its probable wide appeal.[25]

During their years at adjoining desks these two young men had plenty of interesting things to write about, especially as regarded national affairs. Politically there was the aftermath of the Mexican War, with its ever increasing probability of a rupture between North and South. It was during these years that the vacillating President Franklin Pierce—a rather weak specimen of rugged New England Yankeeism—was inadvertently making the line of cleavage sharper and sharper, in-

[22] Springfield (*Weekly*) *Republican,* Jan. 5, 1861. The "special series of papers" mentioned in the item proved to be *Ruminations,* "a series of essays upon human life," which ran in the *Republican* from March 30 to Oct. 5, 1861, and which appeared that same year in book form under the title *Lessons in Life.*

[23] Merriam, *op. cit.,* Vol. I, p. 61.

[24] *Ibid.,* I, 200.

[25] *Ibid.,* I, 64.

advertently forcing such non-Abolitionist papers as the *Republican* into a Free-Soil policy. These were the days of the Kansas-Nebraska Bill, the Dred Scott Decision, and the founding of the Republican party.

In American literature these years witnessed the publication of such notable works as Emerson's *Representative Men* and *English Traits,* Hawthorne's *Scarlet Letter* and *House of the Seven Gables,* Mrs. Stowe's *Uncle Tom's Cabin,* Longfellow's *Golden Legend* and *Hiawatha,* Whittier's *Songs of Labor,* and Whitman's *Leaves of Grass.* They also witnessed the deaths of Cooper and Margaret Fuller, and the waning of the Transcendental movement.

In such volumes as *Plain Talks on Familiar Topics* (1865) and the two series of *Every-Day Topics* (1876 and 1882, respectively) [26] one may find all of Holland's literary comments that he cared to preserve and to offer to the general public. The most significant of these comments I shall discuss in a later chapter. A study, however, of the *Republican* files reveals many interesting data that can most pertinently be discussed here. Most of Holland's literary comments appeared under the heading *Books, Authors and Art,* and much of *Books, Authors and Art* was made up of notices of new books and editions and of the contents of new numbers of magazines.[27] Most of these notices are so objective in tone that they shed little light upon Holland's literary point of view. Here and there, however, one finds paragraphs that are truly revealing. In the following passage, for instance, we can see that Holland was capable of admiring some of the most ephemeral of popular fiction:

Among recent domestic novels we count *The Channings,* by Mrs. Henry Wood, the prolific writer of *East Lynne* and many other popular romances. Mrs. Wood has great readiness of invention, and skill in producing lifelike sketches, and this new story is not inferior in interest to her previous efforts.[28]

[26] For main discussion of Holland's comments upon literature, see below, Chap. V, pp. 68–84.

[27] For example, see issues of the *Republican* for Mar. 2, 1861; Mar. 9, 1861; May 17, 1862; and July 19, 1862.

[28] *Books, Authors and Art,* Springfield *Republican,* May 17, 1862.

But if Josiah Holland, at that period in his career, could stoop to praise a shallow fourth-rate British novelist, he could likewise make truly penetrating criticisms of some of his most prominent American contemporaries. Reviewing Holmes's *Elsie Venner* he says:

The writer does not understand the rural population of New England; he has not even mastered their dialect, and his pictures of country life and character, though with many skilful and admirable touches, are caricatures after all.[29]

And discussing Harriet Beecher Stowe's *Uncle Tom's Cabin* and *Dred,* he has this to remark:

A recent reviewer says of Mrs. Stowe that her descriptions of negro life and character have never been surpassed. This is high praise, but scarcely deserved. The very redundancy of her genius, more creative than imitative, leads her to make of her prominent characters the mouth-pieces to utter her own rich thoughts. She has seized upon the externals of the colored race . . . and breathed through them a vitality not wholly African, but bearing many traces of Anglo-Saxon origin.[30]

It may now be well to consider the relations between Holland and Bowles. These relations, we may say, were always amicable, but never quite cordial. Bowles, though sufficiently upright according to cosmopolitan standards, was hardly a man of Holland's kidney. Unitarian in creed [31] and fairly liberal in ethics, he confessed a moderate fondness for wine,[32] euchre,[32] and the theatre.[32] Moreover, he could mingle freely with publicans and sinners, and he could enjoy their society without showing or feeling the least trace of moral superiority. Holland, on the other hand, was never at ease except in the company of pious Trinitarians of Calvinistic or at least evangelical persuasion. It is, therefore, no wonder that "Holland often thought Bowles irreverent, not to say heathenish, and

---

[29] *Books, Authors and Art,* Springfield (*Weekly*) *Republican,* Mar. 2, 1861.
[30] *Ibid.,* July 19, 1862.
[31] Merriam, *cp. cit.,* I, 12–13.
[32] *Ibid.,* II, 77.

Bowles thought Holland something of a prig." [33] Nor is it any wonder that they were never "Sam" and "Si" to each other; always "Mr. Bowles" and "Dr. Holland." As Mr. Richard Hooker has aptly remarked of the two men: "They remained contrasting personalities, working loyally and well in harness, but never horses of the same color." [34]

In this connection, it is interesting to recall an incident that occurred in 1856 at a time when Bowles happened to be away from Springfield and Holland was temporarily in charge of the paper. An attempt was made to hold a prize fight in the town, and among those who had gathered to witness the affair were a number of socially prominent young men, including some of Mrs. Bowles's relatives.[35] Holland's moral sensibilities being naturally outraged, the good doctor wrote a scathing editorial in which he denounced prize fighting as a most brutal and debasing pastime, and in which he threateningly announced that all who had participated in or patronized the disgraceful affair would be prosecuted and that the *Republican* would give full publicity to the names of all persons implicated.[35] When Bowles returned home he was undoubtedly embarrassed—undoubtedly inclined to feel that the prudish Holland had been a meddling ass. Despite the fact that prize fighting was then illegal as well as disreputable, Bowles himself would have been disinclined to stir up trouble over a matter that did not greatly bother his own conscience, particularly since stirring up trouble would in this case involve some of his "in-laws." But there were several other things to be considered. In the first place, Bowles realized that Holland, without especially trying to do so, had unquestionably voiced the sentiments of most of the *Republican* clientele. In the second place, as a firm adherent of loyalty among colleagues, Bowles considered it his duty to uphold his co-worker unreservedly. Hence he insisted upon publishing the names of the culpable young men—over the protest of Mrs. Bowles.[36]

[33] Merriam, *op. cit.*, I, 63–64.
[34] Hooker, *op. cit.*, p. 51.
[35] Merriam, *op. cit.*, I, 71–72.
[36] *Ibid.*, I, 71–72.

Still, one cannot escape the conviction that Sam Bowles, who was never a prude about his own amusements or a fuss-body about the amusements of others, would have been happy if Josiah Holland had neglected to write that prize-fight editorial.

Holland's longer contributions to the *Republican* during these years were fairly notable. The most ambitious of these was a *History of Western Massachusetts,* begun in 1854 and published in weekly installments over a period of a little more than a year. This work proved to be an almost unqualified success. Historians pronounced it a surprisingly accurate and detailed achievement for a man untrained in the methods of research, and *Republican* subscribers generally found that it awakened in them a new pride in their native counties and native towns. As a result of this *History,* Holland was made a member of the Massachusetts Historical Society,[37] and the circulation of the *Republican* was materially increased.[37]

Close upon the heels of the *History of Western Massachusetts* there followed another Holland serial, *The Bay-Path,* in which the author used material that he had originally gathered for his *History.*[37] *The Bay-Path,* which enjoys the distinction of having inaugurated Holland's career as a novelist, will be discussed in a later chapter. Suffice it to remark at this time that this romance is a tale of seventeenth-century Massachusetts.

A third major Holland contribution to the *Republican* was a series of letters entitled *Max Mannering to his Sister in the Country.*[38] These letters, considered highly ethical and mildly satirical in tone, proved so popular that Bowles suggested to Holland the desirability of a still more extensive series of moralistic essays.[39] As has been previously remarked, Bowles

---

[37] Plunkett, *op. cit.,* pp. 32–33. See also Merriam, I, 100.

[38] Plunkett, *op. cit.,* p. 36. These letters, which were unsigned, are not mentioned either by Merriam or by Hooker. Merriam, however, is apparently referring to them when he speaks (Vol. I, p. 201) of "some series of letters on light social topics."

[39] *Ibid.,* p. 36.

himself was no pietist; but, as has also been pointed out, Bowles was keenly alive to the tastes of the church-going New England villagers and farmers who made up the bulk of the *Republican* subscription list. Of the rigidly moralistic temper of the older *Republican* clientele there can be no doubt. Not until 1878, when Bowles's son, Samuel Bowles III, was the editor, did the paper have the audacity to publish a Sunday edition. And even then, as may be seen from an anecdote told by Mr. Richard Hooker, the venture was a hazardous one. On Sunday morning, September 15, 1878, a prominent Springfield citizen, a survivor of the Holland régime, was horrified to see a Sunday *Republican* lying upon his door-step. When the old gentleman had recovered a little from the shock, he strode to the parlor grate, grabbed the fire tongs, returned to the front door, and picked up the unholy newspaper with the tongs. Then, though clad only in dressing gown and carpet slippers, he marched solemnly around the house to the kitchen door, where he deposited the offending paper in the garbage can. No Sunday newspaper should ever pollute the house or soil the hands of this godly *Republican* reader.[40] It will thus be seen that when Sam Bowles advised Josiah Holland to write another series of moralistic essays, he knew what he was talking about.

The result of Bowles's suggestion was the series of "Timothy Titcomb" letters, which speedily established Josiah Gilbert Holland as a western Massachusetts celebrity and paved the way to his national fame. These letters, arranged in three groups, gave moral advice to young bachelors, young maidens, and young married people respectively.[41] Although the provincial piety of the letters must have alternately bored and amused Bowles, their effect was more far-reaching than either he or Holland could possibly have foreseen. "Timothy Titcomb"—a name perhaps suggested by Thackeray's "Michael Titmarsh"—quickly became a household name throughout the *Republican* territory. Housewives hung upon

[40] Hooker, *op. cit.*, p. 151.
[41] Plunkett, *op. cit.*, p. 39.

the good "Timothy's" words to the neglect of their ovens. Young men ceased sowing modest crops of wild oats. Girls gave up innocuous frivolities. Young married folk on the verge of "agreeing to disagree" decided to make the best of their marriage vows. The circulation of the *Republican* became greater and greater.[41] And Josiah Gilbert Holland, through the aid of a prominent New Englander then resident in New York, gained the ear of one of America's most influential publishers, Charles Scribner. As Mrs. Plunkett tells it:

> Armed with a letter of introduction from George Ripley, Dr. Holland went to the late Charles Scribner and begged the privilege of reading three of the "Titcomb" letters. Mr. Scribner turned the key of his private office and bade the author proceed. At the end of the third letter he said, "I will take the book." [41]

Within a few years thereafter, Scribner was to publish Holland into fame and fortune.

The upshot of the matter was that Josiah Gilbert Holland would soon find Springfield and its *Republican* too straitened a realm to monopolize his activities. A development of 1857 was to hasten that discovery. In the spring of that year Sam Bowles was offered the editorship of the Boston *Traveller,* which had just strengthened its position by absorbing two other Boston dailies, the *Atlas* and the *Telegram and Chronicle*.[42] To the ambitious thirty-one-year-old Bowles, this offer of a chief editor's desk in the New England metropolis was exceedingly attractive—far too attractive, in fact, to be rejected. Much as he was attached to his native Springfield and to the paper which he had virtually created, he could not well forego the tremendous opportunity that now presented itself. He quickly accepted the offer, and in April he fared forth to the big city to take up his new tasks. But with true Yankee caution he retained his interest in the *Republican* and his home in Springfield. In fact, he did not take his family to Boston with him.[42]

41 Plunkett, *op. cit.,* p. 39.
42 Merriam, *op. cit.,* I, 182.

Holland, left in charge of the *Republican,* did not altogether enjoy increased responsibilities, particularly the necessity of writing editorials about matters that did not keenly interest him. To write book reviews and moral aphorisms was one thing; to write leaders on the shortcomings of the Buchanan administration, the struggle for Kansas, and the growing insolence of South Carolina was quite another and much more distasteful thing. It is true that in the conduct of the *Republican* he had two able assistants in the persons of Clark W. Bryan and Joseph E. Hood, both of them capable, sagacious, and experienced newspaper men; [43] but the main responsibility for the paper was Holland's,[44] and this the good doctor must have found bewildering and disconcerting.

Fortunately for Holland, Bowles soon wearied of his Boston job. After a series of disagreements with his colleagues on the *Traveller,* the young editor resigned his new position, packed his carpetbag, and by early autumn was back at his old desk in the *Republican* office.[45] The way was now clear for Holland to step gracefully out of the picture. On October 29, 1857, in a letter to a lawyer friend named Charles Allen, Bowles mentions Holland's determination to resign his editorial position.[45] Soon after that date, Holland sold his interest in the *Republican,* gave up his assistant editorship, and became a free-lance writer. For several years, however, as has been indicated earlier in this chapter, he continued to regard himself as part of the *Republican* family and to furnish plenty of good copy to the paper that had launched him upon his career.

[43] Merriam, *op. cit.,* I, 182.
[44] *Ibid.,* I, 185–186.
[45] *Ibid.,* I, 295.

IV

More Than Local

Forty years ago a reviewer of Mrs. Plunkett's biography of Holland said: "Until . . . 1870, his reputation was hardly more than local. . . . Love for them [his books] was largely an agricultural passion, limited to Western Massachusetts." [1] If the reviewer had said 1858 instead of 1870, he would have been correct; but after the quick success of *Bitter-Sweet*, which appeared in the former year, Holland's reputation was unquestionably far more than local. In fact, it speedily became greater in the wide region beyond the Appalachians than in his native New England.[2]

Before we consider his growing success, however, we may profitably pause to glance at his family life. Holland was fortunate in his marriage. Besides being the typically thrifty, frugal Yankee housewife, Elizabeth Chapin was a good business woman, and she was ambitious for her husband to get on in the world. To keep the growing family budget within bounds, she made her husband's clothing as well as her own and the children's; that is, she did the sewing after the materials had been furnished and cut by the best tailor obtainable.[3] And she had a keen appreciation of the commercial possibilities of her husband's literary wares. She knew, even better than Josiah himself, what his reading public wanted, and she encouraged him to write it. As a biographer of Emily Dickinson well says, Elizabeth Chapin Holland's "strong practical judgment offset . . . her husband's more imaginative temperament." [4]

1 *Independent,* XLVI, 565. May 3, 1894.
2 *Nation,* XXXIII, 315. Oct. 20, 1881.
3 Plunkett, *op cit.,* p. 25.
4 Pollitt, *op. cit.,* p. 83.

Financial considerations were, of course, important; for the Holland family had grown. Arthur, the first-born, had died in early childhood, and a daughter, Julia, had died at birth; but by 1859 there were three other Holland children, Annie, Kate, and Theodore.[5]

Josiah Gilbert Holland, however, was prospering. During his *Republican* editorial days—in 1854,[6] to be exact—he had purchased Buff Cottage, a roomy, wide-porticoed house on a pine-clad slope, with a view to providing for himself and his family a permanent dwelling on a healthful site.[7] But not long after the success of *Bitter-Sweet* (1858) and *Miss Gilbert's Career* (1860), Buff Cottage began to appear far too small and unimposing. The result was the building of the spacious Brightwood, one of the most palatial mansions in the fashionable north end of Springfield, in which the Hollands were to live until their permanent removal from Massachusetts in the late sixties.[8]

The pretentiousness of Brightwood, as well as the growing national fame of its owner, is well revealed in the following letter of a Middle Western admirer who had made a pilgrimage to Springfield:

Let me tell you of "Brightwood," the home of one of . . . our favorites [out here in the Middle West], Dr. Holland. A pretty modern house sitting serenely upon the summit of a hill, half hid by sheltering trees, but sending down to us, as we wound around the hill in its ascent, a cheerful, welcoming look. I wish I was skilled in description, that you might enjoy the exquisite landscape that my eye feasted upon, as I looked from the bay window of the drawing room. Below me the Connecticut river swept by me in its ceaseless course, while the familiar "River road" stretched alongside of its fertile banks, the stately hills towered in the distance, and on either side, through the oak or beech clearings, which seemed arranged with the very "design of accident," the sheen of the river again gleamed through the foliage.

[5] For this information I am indebted to Mrs. Howe.
[6] Bianchi, *op. cit.*, p. 193.
[7] Plunkett, *op. cit.*, p. 70.
[8] See below, p. 165.

Such is "Brightwood" from without. Shall I not be pardoned
if I give you a glimpse from within, and tell you of the pleasant
library where Shakespeare, Dante, and Ruskin preside? A cheerful
room, hallowed by a poet's rhapsodies and an honest man's
reveries.

.   .   .   .

The bright scarlet berries of the Bitter Sweet in delicate vases,
or drooping from picture frames, served as a pretty adornment,
and seemed offering graceful tribute to him who had linked its
wild-wood name with fame.[9]

Any discussion of the Holland family life inevitably involves the element of religiosity; for Holland the benedict
was quite as religious—and as religiose—as Holland the bachelor had ever been. During the score of years that he lived
in Springfield, Josiah was a pillar in two or three Congregational churches—successively, of course, not contemporaneously. Among his churchly activities were singing in the
choir, serving on the official board, acting as Sunday-school
teacher and superintendent, and occasionally filling the pulpit of some absent pastor in or near Springfield.[10] This last-
named activity, together with the persistently homiletical tone
of his writings, led to the oft-repeated but erroneous assertion that Holland was a clergyman.[11] Indeed, it caused even
so well-informed and generally accurate a commentator as
Mr. Carl Van Doren to speak of "the Reverend Josiah Gilbert
Holland." [12] With reference to Josiah's Sunday-school teaching, Mrs. Plunkett declares that the good doctor was sometimes accused of heresy; [13] but it is difficult to believe that he
could ever have been regarded as a very dangerous heretic.

---

[9] Springfield *Illinois State Journal*, June 7, 1865. The name of the correspondent is not given.

[10] Plunkett, *op. cit.*, pp. 112–119. See also Bianchi, *op. cit.*, p. 309.

[11] W. B. Cairns: Article on Holland, *Dictionary of American Biography*, Vol.
IX, p. 147.

[12] Carl Van Doren: *The American Novel*, New York, 1921, p. 122.

[13] Plunkett, *op. cit.*, p. 142.

True, he did object to some details of the Calvinistic creed [14] and—inspired probably by Tennyson's *In Memoriam* and some mildly reckless utterances of the Episcopal clergy—he flirted cautiously with the higher criticism, even going so far as to protest against making a fetish of the Bible.[15] But no intelligent Congregationalist could ever have suspected Josiah Holland of being a wrecker of the faith of youth. Apropos of this matter of religious activity, Noah Porter once thought it worthy of remark that the Holland family prayers were "singularly fervent." [16] And Dr. Porter knew whereof he spoke; for, previously to his long and distinguished career at Yale, he had been Holland's pastor at the South Church in Springfield.[17] Yes, Josiah Holland was an ardently—even an ostentatiously—religious man, and this fact was no small asset to the kind of literary fame that came to him. As word of his Christian endeavor was bruited through the length and breadth of the land, many and many a pious reader must have exclaimed: "I like the books of Dr. Holland; they are the books of a good man!" All this we can record without implying for a moment that Josiah Gilbert Holland was insincere or consciously politic in his religiosity. Josiah *was* a good man —instinctively so—and if goodness happened to be profitable, so much the better for his career.

When the sales of *Bitter-Sweet* began mounting into the thousands, Dr. Holland decided to introduce himself in person to his public by touring the country as a lecturer.[18] The field had already become an attractive one. Authors such as Ralph Waldo Emerson and James Russell Lowell, critics such as George William Curtis and Edwin Percy Whipple, statesmen such as Edward Everett and Charles Sumner, clergymen such as Edwin Hubbell Chapin and Henry Ward Beecher, and reformers such as Wendell Phillips and John B. Gough were reaping handsome rewards—fifty to a hundred dollars

---

14 Plunkett, *op. cit.*, p. 145.
15 *Ibid.*, pp. 143–144. See also below, p. 92.
16 *Ibid.*, p. 75.
17 *Ibid.*, p. 74.
18 *Ibid.*, p. 47.

a night—on widely separated platforms.[19] Why should not Josiah Gilbert Holland appear before a public eager to see and hear him? As early as 1826 Josiah Holbrook, of Derby, Connecticut, had promoted the lyceum idea;[20] and now, a third of a century later, the idea had come to be widely accepted in most of the states north of the Mason and Dixon line.[21] The way was indeed well prepared for Josiah Holland —Josiah, of the imposing presence, the mellifluous voice, and the facile phrase.

Beginning in 1858, and continuing for nearly a score of years—except for the time when he was in Europe (1868–1870)—Holland did more or less lecturing every winter.[22] Especially was he active in this field during the early years of the period mentioned. It was then that he was building his reputation; it was then that he had the most leisure for lecturing; and it was then that—despite the Civil War—public interest in platform oratory was keenest.[23] After 1870, the year in which he assumed the editorship of *Scribner's Monthly,* his time for lecturing tours was considerably limited; but not until about 1877, when failing health compelled him to lead a less strenuous life, did he abandon the platform permanently.[24]

The range of Holland's lecture itineraries was wide—perhaps as wide as that of any platform orator of his day. In a single year, for example, he appeared in as many as ninety different communities,[25] and as early as July 1865 he could boast that he had "been received with favor . . . in nearly every Northern state of the Union."[26]

No definite record of any of Holland's lecture itineraries

---

[19] Fish, *op. cit.,* p. 106. See also Allan Nevins: *The Emergence of Modern America,* New York, 1927, p. 238. See also George William Curtis: "The Lecture Lyceum," *Harper's Magazine,* LXXIV, 823–824. Apr., 1887.

[20] See Fish, as above.

[21] See below, p. 51.

[22] For this information I am indebted to Mrs. Howe.

[23] Plunkett, *op. cit.,* p. 46. See also Curtis, *op. cit.,* p. 823.

[24] For this information I am indebted to Mrs. Howe.

[25] Plunkett, *op. cit.,* p. 47.

[26] Holland: *Plain Talks on Familiar Subjects,* Preface, p. v. New York, 1865.

has been preserved, but a study of newspaper files and other old documents brings some interesting and significant facts to light. It shows, for one thing, that Holland lectured in such widely separated communities as Columbus,[27] Toledo,[28] Norwalk,[28] and Oberlin, Ohio; [28] Adrian, Michigan; [29] Indianapolis and Lafayette, Indiana; and Minneapolis, Minnesota.[30] It shows, for another thing, that he was one of the most popular lecturers, as well as one of the most admired authors, of his day.

His popularity is, for example, well attested by the enthusiasm with which he was received in Columbus on Thursday evening, January 11, 1872. In the *Ohio State Journal* of that date there appeared this glowing announcement:

Josiah G. Holland, who is known throughout the country as Timothy Titcomb, [will speak] at the Opera House tonight. All of our citizens who have read his works will hail this opportunity to hear the great author. The subject of his lecture is "The Social Under-Tow." [31]

In the same issue the *State Journal* took obvious pride in thrilling its readers with the information that Timothy Titcomb was a guest at the Neil House [31] (at that time, and possibly now, the leading hotel of Columbus). The next day the *State Journal* said:

The Opera House was occupied last night by a very large and intelligent audience, who assembled to hear the lecture of Josiah G. Holland, or familiarly known as Timothy Titcomb. The lecture was attentively listened to, and many of its excellent points earnestly applauded. It was replete with fine sentiment and good argument, and was delivered in a manner that did not detract any from its real merit. . . .

Mr. Holland's lecture throughout was solid doctrine, and after it was over, expressions of approbation could be heard from every one.[31]

[27] See below, p. 52.
[28] See *Lorain County* (Oberlin, Ohio) *News,* Jan. 21, Feb. 4, 1863.
[29] See *Education,* Vol. XII, p. 545. May, 1892.
[30] See below, p. 53.
[31] *Op. cit.*

The foregoing passage is an excerpt from a news story almost two-thirds of a column long. In this connection, it is interesting to observe that Mark Twain, who lectured in Columbus six nights earlier, received barely half as much newspaper attention as was accorded Holland.[32]

In that same winter of 1872, the late James Whitcomb Riley, then a youth of eighteen, heard Holland lecture in Indianapolis. In the Hoosier capital, as in the Buckeye capital, Holland's subject was "The Social Under-Tow." [33] That Riley should have recalled this lecture forty years after its delivery is, I think, noteworthy. Holland had, by the way, spoken in Indianapolis at least once before: in 1858,[34] the year of his first extended lecture tour.

Further proof of Holland's popularity as a lyceum orator is afforded by the recollections of a man still living, Dr. William E. Leonard, of Hadley, Massachusetts.

I am sending you [wrote Dr. Leonard recently] the enclosed data from an old diary of 1875, my senior year at the University of Minnesota: "Last night October 29, 1875 I heard Dr. J. G. Holland in the Athenaeum Star Course at the Academy of Music, Minneapolis, on 'Hobby-Riding.' Recall that the Dr. stood to one side of the stairway leading up to the auditorium as the audience filed in, and thus 'sized them up' beforehand." . . . My youthful admiration for Dr. Holland was very considerable, and I read everything he wrote and was very proud of owning and often rereading his 'Mistress of the Manse.' [35]

Among the numerous places that Holland visited during the earlier years as a lecturer, we must make special mention of Lafayette, Indiana. Accessible records do not disclose the exact date of any appearance of Holland at Lafayette, but the following facts have been definitely established: first, Holland visited Lafayette at least once, not later than the winter

---

[32] Columbus *Ohio State Journal,* Jan. 6, 1872.

[33] Marcus Dickey: *The Youth of James Whitcomb Riley,* Indianapolis, 1919, p. 172.

[34] For this information I am indebted to Mrs. Marguerite H. Anderson, Indiana State Library, Indianapolis.

[35] Letter from Dr. William E. Leonard to the author, April 12, 1934.

of 1867–68; secondly, the chairman of the local lyceum committee was Roswell Smith; thirdly, it was in Lafayette that the long and intimate friendship between Holland and Smith began.[36] The story of Josiah Holland's business and social relationships with Roswell Smith, as we shall later observe, is almost a chapter in itself.

One community in which Holland spoke repeatedly was the little college town of Oberlin. Naturally that Western Reserve center of New England Congregationalism would find the good Timothy Titcomb a man after its own heart. In antebellum days, perhaps, Holland's Abolitionism may have been a bit too lukewarm to suit Oberlin;[37] but in most other respects Josiah fitted beautifully into the Oberlin pattern. His meetings with Oberlin's fervently pious president and eloquent evangelist, the Reverend Charles Grandison Finney,[37] must have been a delight to both men. At any rate, Holland is known to have visited Oberlin five times. On his first appearance there, on Friday, November 2, 1860, he lectured on "Work and Play." A little more than two years later, on February 5, 1863, he entertained and edified the townsmen and the gownsmen of Oberlin with a discourse entitled "Fashion." This lecture was so heartily received that near the end of the same calendar year, on December 9, 1863, he was welcomed back to the campus to deliver his timely patriotic oration, "The National Heart." This seems to have marked Holland's last appearance at Oberlin for a decade. During this interim, however, several important things happened: Dr. Finney resigned his presidency to be succeeded by another and perhaps more reticent New England Yankee, Dr. James Harris Fairchild;[38] and Holland himself was busy touring Europe and launching his new magazine. Holland's fourth Oberlin lecture, "Elements of Personal Power," was given on November 20, 1873.[39]

[36] For this information I am indebted to Mrs. George Inness, Jr., daughter of Roswell Smith.

[37] See article on Oberlin, *Encyclopaedia Britannica*, XVI, 668.

[38] See *Universal Cyclopaedia*, IV, 244. 12 vols. New York, 1905.

[39] For notices and reviews of these lectures, see issues of the *Lorain County*

In the autumn of 1875, while returning from a Northwest-
ern tour,[40] Holland stopped at Oberlin to give what proved to
be his final lecture there. That the occasion was notable is
evidenced by the length and enthusiasm of the review given
the lecture by the local newspaper. In the course of over two
thousand words of eulogy and summary the reviewer said:

The second lecture of the course, under the auspices of the
U.L.A., was delivered by Dr. Holland, in the First Church, last
Monday, Nov. 8th, upon the subject of "Hobby Riding." Dr.
Holland's wide reputation as a lecturer secured him a better audience than has been attracted by any previous entertainment of
the season. After prayer by Pres. Fairchild, the President of the
occasion—Mr. E. K. Fairchild—introduced the lecturer, who began his lecture by saying that he had always found the American
people ready to give ear to lessons that would be of use to them
in practical life—suggestions are always in order. . . .

Dr. Holland closed his lecture with some telling arguments
against the growing idea that the two sexes should receive like
courses of education and be equally trained for the work of life.
He said:— "Have women a sphere? I think they have; but we
will compromise and call it a hemisphere. Her mission is to love,
and it argues depravity of soul when a woman pants to enter the
race and contend with man in the labor of life. Her work is to
uplift the world by her refinement and love. The hard work is
to be done by man; woman's apostleship is to cheer him in his
struggle. . . ."

The lecture was one of the Doctor's happiest efforts, and was
listened to by the audience with rapt attention. [41]

It is noteworthy that Holland's lectures were apparently
much more in demand in the West than in his native East,
and that he appears to have lectured far more frequently in
villages such as Oberlin and Lafayette and in relatively small
cities such as Columbus and Indianapolis than in the greater

(Oberlin, Ohio) *News* of the following dates: Oct. 24, 1860; Nov. 7, 1860; Jan.
28, 1863; Feb. 11, 1863; Nov. 25, 1863; Dec. 9, 1863; Dec. 16, 1863; Oct. 23, 1873;
Nov. 13, 1873; Nov. 27, 1873.
[40] See above, p. 53.
[41] Oberlin (Ohio) *Weekly News,* Nov. 18, 1875.

centers of population. The reason why the West of the sixties and the seventies was more eager to hear Josiah Holland than was the East is readily manifest. Whatever may be the truth of the matter today, there can be little doubt that the Corn Belt was then a much more naïve region than the Atlantic Coast; [42] and, as we have said and as we shall have occasion to reiterate, Josiah Gilbert Holland was preëminently the Apostle to the Naïve. To a degree Josiah realized this fact, and, partly for the reason that villages are more naïve than cities, he regarded the former as a more promising field than the latter. Undoubtedly the people of Adrian and Lafayette read his books with more avidity than did their cousins in New York and Philadelphia; so naturally they thrilled more at his presence, hung more upon his words. But Josiah had another good reason for booking the villages.

In the larger cities of the East [he once wrote] the opera, the play, the frequent concert, the exhibition, the club-house, the social assembly, and a variety of public gatherings and public entertainments, take from the lecture-audiences the class that furnishes the best material in the smaller cities; so that a lecturer rarely or never sees his best audiences in New York, or Boston, or Philadelphia.[43]

Now what was true of New York, Philadelphia, and Boston was likewise true, to only a slightly lesser degree, of Chicago, Cincinnati, St. Louis, and Cleveland.[44] Persons more or less accustomed to the robust histrionics of John McCullough and the dulcet warblings of Jenny Lind, before colorful settings and amid ample auxiliary talents, could hardly palpitate at the announcement that Timothy Titcomb would appear (solus)

[42] Nevins, *op. cit.*, p. 159. See also Fish, *op. cit.*, p. 150.

[43] Holland: *Plain Talks on Familiar Subjects*, p. 12.

[44] I have found only two instances of Holland lecture-bookings in large cities, and both of those occurred in the earlier lecturing period—that is, the period antedating Holland's sojourn in Europe. According to the Springfield *Republican* of Nov. 23, 1861, Holland was booked to lecture in Brooklyn within a few evenings of the publication of the item. According to the *Lorain County News* of Feb. 4, 1863, Holland lectured in Cleveland on Friday evening, January 30, 1863.

upon the bare rostrum of the city hall or the First Methodist Church. The village and the small city, then, were preëminently the province of the old-time lyceum lecturer—unless perchance, like the incomparable Dickens, he happened to be an imported celebrity.

Beyond the shadow of a doubt, Holland greatly enjoyed his lecturings. Much as he might complain of days (and nights) in stuffy, sooty day coaches, of other nights on hard hotel and farmhouse mattresses, of poor food and meager food, of missed connections, of long waits in cold and dirty "depots," of stage rides and buggy rides over rutty, muddy, sleety roads,[45] he loved the sound of his own voice, particularly when that voice carried to a hallful or a churchful of admiring auditors. And, like most other public figures, he had no aversion either for fame or for shekels.

That so popular a writer, so imposing an individual, and so silvery an orator as J. G. Holland was one of the salient lecturers of his day there can be no doubt. Thomas Wentworth Higginson has mentioned him as one of the lyceum speakers who had "much formative power over the intellect of the nation."[46]

During these years of public lecturing, Holland appears to have been much in demand as an orator on special occasions and a reader of occasional poems. Indeed, from a letter that he wrote on February 27, 1864, one is led to believe that he was offered more of such engagements than he had the time or the inclination to accept. Here is the letter:

Theodore A. K. Gessler, Esq.,
Dear Sir:

I regret to say that it will be impracticable for me to undertake the writing and delivering of a poem during the coming season, and that I feel compelled to decline the invitation which you have extended to me.

---

[45] Plunkett, *op. cit.*, pp. 47–48.

[46] T. W. Higginson: *Carlyle's Laugh, and Other Surprises,* Boston and New York, 1909, p. 378.

Be kind enough to return my thanks to the Societies you rep-
resent for the unexpected honor they do me,

And believe me,

Yours very truly,

J. G. Holland [47]

It was during these middle years of his career that Holland
was most actively engaged in the writing of essays. Collections
of these essays that followed *Timothy Titcomb's Letters*
(1858), which we noticed in our last chapter, included *Gold-
Foil Hammered from Popular Proverbs* (1859), *Lessons in
Life* (1861), *Letters to the Joneses* (1863), and *Plain Talks on
Familiar Subjects* (1865). Two subsequent volumes, *Every-
Day Topics*, First and Second Series respectively, appeared
during the seventies, the decade in which Holland was editor
of *Scribner's Monthly.*

These essays, all of them markedly didactic in tone, dealt
with such diverse subjects as culture, literature and literary
men, criticism, the popular lecture, preachers and preaching,
Christianity and science, revivals and reforms, personal ethics,
the sphere of woman, amusements, temperance, social inter-
course, town and country, rich and poor, politics and politi-
cians, and American life and manners.[48]

With regard to the tone of these essays, one may get a fair
conception only by reading from them. Here, for example, is
some of Timothy Titcomb's advice to young men:

A clean mouth, a sweet breath, unstained teeth, and inoffensive clothing—are not these treasures worth preserving? Then
throw away tobacco, and all thoughts of it, at once and forever.
Be a man. Be decent, and be thankful to me for talking so plainly
to you. . . . A young man is not fit for life until he is clean—
clean and healthy, body and soul, with no tobacco in his mouth,
no liquor in his stomach, no oath on his tongue, no snuff in his
nose, and no thought in his heart which if exposed would send him
sneaking into darkness from the presence of a good woman.[49]

[47] For the use of this letter I am indebted to Miss Mary A. Benjamin, 501
Madison Avenue, New York City.

[48] For fuller treatment of these essays, see below, Chap. V, pp. 68–102.

[49] Holland: *Timothy Titcomb's Letters,* New York, 1858, pp. 29–31.

And here is an anecdote for the edification of young women:

> I remember once being in the company of a belle—one who had had a winter's reign in Washington. Some kind of game was in progress, when, in a moment of surprise, she exclaimed, "My Gracious!" Now you may regard this as a finical notion, but I tell you that woman fell as flatly in my esteem as if she had uttered an oath.[50]

Comment upon such banalities as these would, of course, be superfluous; they speak for themselves. And, one must add, if this were the tenor and temper of all of Holland's writing, he would hardly be worthy of our consideration—except, perhaps, as a quaint mid-nineteenth-century curiosity.

It is only fair to point out, however, that the foregoing aphorisms were penned early in Holland's literary career—before he had rubbed elbows with scores of widely separated lyceum committees, and, more particularly, before he had sojourned in Europe and resided in New York. In April 1881, in a final preface to *Titcomb's Letters,* he wrote:

> I have taken almost a pathetic interest in going over these pages. The earnestness, directness, frankness, hopefulness, and high purpose, speak to me of a time when life was unchilled by experience, and enthusiasm was unblunted by contact and conflict with the various forms and forces of evil. I am painfully conscious that if I had not written this book when I did, I could not write it today.[51]

And in the same connection William W. Ellsworth remarks:

> Dr. Holland's early *Topics* would not be liked today,—nor would he write them,—but he broadened as the years went on. Life in New York, where he rubbed against all kinds of people, and above all the unconscious, sweetening influence of his young associate, Gilder, did much to change his point of view, opening up the Puritan prison-house which he had built for his soul—at any rate putting a piazza on it.[52]

[50] Holland: *Timothy Titcomb's Letters,* p. 118.
[51] *Ibid.,* pp. v–vi.
[52] W. W. Ellsworth: *A Golden Age of Authors,* Boston and New York, 1919, pp. 43–44.

Although one wishes that Mr. Ellsworth's statement were more completely true than it is, there is a modicum of truth in it. That Josiah Gilbert Holland remained priggish and prudish to the end of his days is all too abundantly attested. His provincial ethical standards; his subconscious Pharisaism; his incorrigible moralizing; his stubborn opposition to woman suffrage; his failure to distinguish between social drinking and debauchery, between light wine and strong whisky, between beer and rum, between the intelligent frankness of Walt Whitman and the vulgar pornography of *The Black Crook*—all these remained almost as irritatingly obtrusive at the end of his career as at the beginning. Typical of Josiah's lifelong views on woman suffrage is the following passage from his essay "The Rights of Woman":

Woman, in my apprehension, is the mistress, not alone of the melody of music, but of the melody of life. Whatever it may be possible to do by cultivation and a long course of development, it is doubtful whether a woman would ever sing bass well. I am aware that she has the right, and the organs, but I question whether her bass would amount to anything—whether it would be worth singing. When women talk with me about their right to vote, and their right to practice law, and their right to engage in any business which usage has assigned to man, I say, "yes—you have all those rights." I never dispute with them at all. Indeed, you see how I have put myself forward as the defender of these same rights; yet I should be sorry to see them exercised by the women I admire and love. It is all very well to say that the presence of woman at the ballot-box would purify it, and restrain the manners of the men around it; but I have seen enough of the world to learn that all human influence is reciprocal and reactionary. Man and the ballot-box might gain, but woman would lose, and men and the ballot-box themselves would lose in the long run. The ballot-box is the bass, and it should be man's business to sing it, while woman should give him home melody with which it should harmonize.

In the matter of rights, I suppose that I should not differ materially with any strong-minded woman; but I have always observed that the most truly lovable, humble, pure-hearted, God-fearing, and humanity-loving women of my acquaintance, never say any thing about these rights, and scorn those of their sex who do. I have never known a woman who was at once satisfied in her affections and discontented with her woman's lot and her woman's work. There is a weak place, or a wrong place, or a rotten place, in the character or nature of every woman who stands and howls upon the spot where her Creator placed her, and neglects her own true work and life while claiming the right to do the work and live the life of man. I will admit all the rights that such a woman claims—all that I myself possess—if she will let me alone, and keep her distance from me. She may sing bass, but I do not wish to hear her. She is repulsive to me. She offends me.[53]

And yet, as Mr. Ellsworth says, Josiah Holland did finally build a piazza to his Puritan prison-house. In his later works, especially his last two collections of essays, we occasionally glimpse the working of the cosmopolitan influence. No longer is Holland certain that all tobacco smokers are reprobates,[54] that the social wineglass leads inevitably to the drunkard's grave,[55] that all theatres are to be shunned,[56] or that the extempore prayers of evangelical preachers are necessarily more edifying than the Episcopal ritual.[57]

And here we find him to be a force of unique value, a prophet to multitudes who could be reached by no other respectable American writer of his day. The good Dr. Holland, paragon of virtue and wholesomeness, could tell his millions of naïve auditors and readers many things that they needed to know, and they would heed his words. He could tell them, as he did tell them, that European travel is more educative than American travel,[58] that European manners are superior to American manners,[59] that revival meetings are of doubtful value,[60] that the Bible is not always to be taken too literally,[60]

[53] Holland: *Lessons in Life,* New York, 1861, pp. 94–95.
[54] In *Miss Gilbert's Career* (1860) Holland becomes positively jocular about the fondness of a New York church worker for tobacco. *Op. cit.,* pp. 375–376.
[55] See Holland: *Every-Day Topics,* p. 247. Second Series. New York, 1882.
[56] See below, pp. 198–199.
[57] See below, p. 92.
[58] *Every-Day Topics,* II, 368–369.
[59] Holland: *Every-Day Topics,* p. 355. First Series. New York, 1876.
[60] See below, pp. 90–92.

and that good paintings and good novels and good plays have
a humanizing effect that is much to be desired.[61] Could Howells or James or Aldrich have told them the same things?
Hardly! For Howells and James and Aldrich were not their
gods; and Howells and James and Aldrich did not speak their
language. Josiah Gilbert Holland was a prophet with honor
among his own people—the naïve—and therein, let it be repeated, lay his unique value.

The attitude of his intellectual contemporaries was a different matter. Emerson apparently never considered J. G. Holland worth mentioning. Longfellow playfully remarked that
the good Dr. Holland was the author of *Bitter-Sweet,* but not
of sweet bitters.[62] Lowell reviewed *Bitter-Sweet* in an almost
insultingly patronizing manner.[63] Whitman, of course, despised Holland—and said so.[64] Aldrich lamented the fact that
Dr. Holland had twenty readers to Lowell's one.[65] Howells was
disgusted with a reading public that would purchase twenty-
five copies of Holland's *Arthur Bonnicastle* to one copy of
Turgenev's *Lisa.*[66] Bret Harte was gleeful over *Nicholas Pep-
permint,* the New York *Sun's* cruel burlesque of Holland's last
novel, *Nicholas Minturn.*[67] Of the major American writers of
the nineteenth century, Whittier alone had unstintingly kind
words for Holland; [68] and Whittier was even more provincial
—at least in contacts and perhaps in other ways—than was
Holland himself.[69]

[61] See below, pp. 68–88, 198–199.
[62] Samuel Longfellow: *Life of Henry Wadsworth Longfellow,* 3 vols. Boston
and New York, 1886, 1891, III, 190.
[63] See below, pp. 107–108.
[64] See below, pp. 191, 195.
[65] Ferris Greenslet: *Life of Thomas Bailey Aldrich,* Boston and New York,
1908, pp. 131–132.
[66] W. D. Howells: *Life in Letters.* Edited by Mildred Howells. Garden City,
N.Y., 1928, I, 197.
[67] Bret Harte: *Letters.* Edited by Geoffrey Bret Harte. Boston and New
York, 1926, p. 52.
[68] See below, p. 205.
[69] The longest trip of Whittier's life took him only as far as Philadelphia.
Will D. Howe: "Whittier," p. 125. Chap. X of *American Writers on American
Literature.* New York, 1931, 1934.

In recounting Josiah Holland's activities during these years between his *Republican* editorship and his European tour, we have said nothing about his relations to the Civil War. As a matter of fact, there is not much to say. That he was whole-heartedly pro-Northern from the moment that news of Fort Sumter reached Springfield may be taken for granted; but that he ever felt the urge to leave his sizable family for the battlefield may be seriously doubted. In this connection, however, we should do Holland a grave injustice if we failed to point out that even had he enlisted he probably could not have passed the physical examination. Strong and rugged as his large, well-shaped body appeared to be, it was afflicted by the most vital of weaknesses: a bad heart, which was ultimately to cause his sudden death.[70] Moreover, in 1861 Josiah Holland was forty-two—older than McClellan or Grant or Sherman, to say nothing of the rank and file. If James Russell Lowell was too old to enlist, his contemporary, Josiah Gilbert Holland, would be too old by the same token.

Holland's three principal works inspired by the Civil War are *The Mistress of the Manse* (1874), a long narrative poem; a memorial address on Lincoln (1865); and a biography of Lincoln (1865). The poem we shall consider in a later chapter. The address and the biography we may appropriately consider here. The address was delivered at a mass meeting in the Springfield city hall on Wednesday, April 19, 1865, the day of Lincoln's funeral in Washington.[71] That Holland should be chosen to make the speech in the western Massachusetts metropolis is not surprising. His seven years of successful lecturing had already earned him a great reputation for eloquence, and his nation-wide fame as a writer of best-selling books had made him probably the most noted citizen of Springfield, if not of all western Massachusetts. Undoubtedly Holland's Lincoln memorial address was a good one of its kind, and un-

---

[70] See below, pp. 203–204.

[71] Plunkett, *op. cit.,* p. 52. For date of Lincoln's funeral, see William E. Barton: *The Life of Abraham Lincoln,* Indianapolis, 1925, II, 361.

doubtedly it made a favorable impression; but one is inclined
to discount Mrs. Plunkett's extravagant statement that by this
address Holland "won an oratorical triumph that surprised
and delighted his most partial friends." [72]

The Lincoln biography, a much more elaborate work, but
as hasty and partial as a campaign biography, was ready within
a few months after Lincoln's death. In order to assemble materials for this book, Holland made a special trip to Springfield, Illinois, where he interviewed many of Lincoln's old-time
friends, particularly Lincoln's law partner, William H. Herndon. As Herndon tells it:

Soon after the death of Mr. Lincoln Dr. J. G. Holland came out
to Illinois from his home in Massachusetts to gather up materials
for a life of the dead President. The gentleman spent several
days with me, and I gave him all the assistance that lay in my
power. I was much pleased with him, and awaited with not a
little interest the appearance of his book.[73]

Since Holland's book was the first full-length Lincoln biography to appear after the Emancipator's death—antedating
the Lamon work by seven years, and the more extensive
Herndon-Weik and Nicolay-Hay works by a quarter of a century—it naturally had a very considerable run. In fact, just
after Holland's death it was widely stated, in newspapers
throughout the country, that the Holland *Lincoln* had
brought its author royalties amounting to some twenty thousand dollars.[74] In recent years, however, few Lincoln bib-
liographers have bothered to list it at all.

As we have already remarked, the Holland *Lincoln* is as
hasty and as partial as a campaign biography. The preface is
dated November 1865; [75] in other words, just seven months
after the assassination. And the book contains 544 octavo pages,
very few of which are devoted to the reproduction of letters

[72] Plunkett, *op. cit.,* p. 48.

[73] William H. Herndon, and Jesse W. Weik: *Abraham Lincoln,* New York,
1888, II, 292.

[74] See Columbus *Ohio State Journal,* Oct. 20, 1881.

[75] See Holland: *Lincoln,* p. 8.

or other documents! As regards the partiality of the work, the author's own words speak for themselves. Says Holland in the preface:

I have not attempted to disguise or conceal my own personal partiality to Mr. Lincoln, and my thorough sympathy with the political principles to which his life was devoted. . . . I have chosen to be a man, rather than a machine; and, if this shall subject me to the charge of writing in the interest of a party, I must take what comes of it.[76]

And near the end of Chapter V:

If this brief statement of his qualities and powers represents a wonderfully perfect character—so strangely pure and noble that it seems like the sketch of an enthusiast, it is not the writer's fault. . . . He [Lincoln] loved all, was kind to all, was without a vice of appetite or passion, was honest, was truthful, was simple, was unselfish, was religious, was intelligent and self-helpful, was all that a good man could desire in a son ready to enter life.[77]

In this connection, it is interesting to observe the manner in which the devout Josiah handles the vexed and vexatious problem of Lincoln's religion:

He was [admits Holland, perhaps a little sadly] not professedly a Christian—that is, he subscribed to no creed,—joined no organization of Christian disciples. He spoke little . . . and always sparingly, of his religious belief and experiences; but [and here the biographer's enthusiasm quickly revives] that he had a deep religious life, sometimes imbued with superstition, there is no doubt. We guess at a mountain of marble by the outcropping ledges that hide their whiteness among the ferns.[78]

In earlier paragraphs of this chapter we have indicated what we consider J. G. Holland's unique value as a writer. We must now add that much of his power lay in his undoubted sincerity. Josiah could be the apostle to the naïve because he himself was one of them; he firmly believed every word that he uttered.

---

[76] Holland: *Lincoln,* pp. 5–6.
[77] *Ibid.,* p. 63.
[78] *Ibid.,* p. 62.

Clever demagogy will hold the mob for a little while, but for only a little while. Even the most gullible of publics, I think, will presently detect any tongue-in-cheek attitude that an author may have. Holland held his large clientele throughout his life—and for a score of years after his death—because of his own lamb-like innocence, his own utter guilelessness. As a writer in the *Nation* declared just after Holland's death:

There was [in Dr. Holland's writings] no deliberate lowering of aim or intellectual standard. He did not make the sad discovery which Goethe and Schiller confided to each other: "We make money by our poor books." Dr. Holland made money by all his books, and not one of them was, from his point of view, a poor one.[79]

And as Hjalmar H. Boyesen has said:

Dr. Holland took the contemptuous treatment of the critics . . . to heart. . . . The tolerant patronage or undisguised sneer of the reviewer remained the drop of gall in the cup of his happiness.[80]

Incidentally, the jealousy with which Holland himself guarded his naïveté was indeed pathetic. At about the end of his editorial career with the *Republican*—in other words, at just about the time when he could first afford a European tour —Noah Porter urged him to go abroad in order to bring himself into contact with foreign peoples, foreign customs, foreign points of view. How eagerly Emerson or Irving or Hawthorne or Longfellow or Lowell would have taken this advice! But Holland demurred. "He had answered that he was afraid he should lose the hold he had upon what he deemed his strength, viz., his New England blood, and his familiarity with the convictions and manners and faith of his own people. These he regarded as his capital."[81] In other words, Josiah Holland refused to play with new ideas for fear he might get burned. He was not yet ready to build a piazza in front of his

79 *Nation*, XXXIII, 315. Oct. 20, 1881.
80 *Forum*, XV, 462. June, 1893.
81 Plunkett, *op. cit.*, p. 101.

Puritan prison-house. Was ever obscurantist more earnest? Not till almost a decade later [82] did he consider his convictions so deep seated that he could risk wholesale contact with the Romanists, the Anglicans, the Lutherans, and the free-thinkers of the Old World. No wonder Josiah Gilbert Holland was the chosen and anointed Apostle to the Naïve!

[82] See below, p. 165.

V

Criticism, Esthetic and Ethical

Dr. J. G. Holland, under the pseudonym of Timothy Titcomb, obtained a wide reputation by truisms insipid enough for a young ladies' boarding school and religious enough for the most bigoted sectarian. All together, nearly half a million copies of the Titcomb letters were sold.[1]

These are the words of Professor Allan Nevins, an outstanding authority upon mid-nineteenth-century American political and social history. Of Holland's wide reputation, as we have already seen, there can be no doubt. Of the correctness of Professor Nevins' circulation figures there can be no doubt either, for such figures are a matter of statistical record. Of the justice of Mr. Nevins' statement regarding Holland's insipid truisms and narrow religiosity we should reserve judgment until we have examined Holland's work more fully. And, in this last connection, perhaps we shall do best to study Holland's seven published volumes of essays.

Josiah Gilbert Holland was a prolific commentator upon books, as well as a prolific maker of books. In his two volumes of *Every-Day Topics* alone there appear no fewer than twenty-four essays devoted directly to literature. Elsewhere, both in these two volumes and in Holland's other five volumes of miscellaneous prose, the allusions to literature are very numerous. Holland cannot, however, be considered a genuine literary critic. Nowhere in his volumes can one find a review of any particular book, and in only three instances does he devote an entire essay to any individual author.[2] Most of his literary

---

[1] Nevins, *op. cit.*, p. 232.

[2] Bulwer-Lytton, Dickens, and Whitman respectively. See *Every-Day Topics*, I, 45–52; *Every-Day Topics*, II, 126–134.

pronouncements, whether sound or unsound, are sweeping generalizations. His statements about books and writers are numerous; his illustrative material is meager. He was, then, a casual observer rather than a penetrating student of literature, an opinionated commentator rather than a true critic.

Nevertheless an examination of Holland's literary dicta will reveal a point of view that is as definite as it is interesting. Among American writers, for example, his prime favorites appear to have been Longfellow, Whittier, Harriet Beecher Stowe, and Mrs. A. D. T. Whitney. Among writers whom he commends, though with a little less enthusiasm, are Bryant, Emerson, Hawthorne, Lowell, and Holmes. Among writers whom he damns with faint praise are Howells and James. Among writers whom he castigates severely are N. P. Willis, Poe, Whitman, and Thoreau.

Speaking of Longfellow, Holland considers his age and country peculiarly fortunate because it "possesses a Longfellow." [3] He finds in Longfellow's "Psalm of Life" "more of the element of ministry . . . than in all that Byron and Poe ever wrote." [4] And, with considerable emphasis, he voices the conviction, "We do not believe the time will ever come . . . when Longfellow's psalms of life will not meet with a response in the souls of the people." [5] Even more glowing are Holland's panegyrics upon Whittier, "our Gabriel in drab—trumpet-tongued for the right, trumpet-tongued against the wrong; loving the poor man more than the rich, loving both more than himself,—loving God more than all." [6] "God," declares Holland, "made Whittier poor, that every son of want, and every victim of wrong should have a sympathizing and ministering brother." [7] Mrs. Stowe evokes Holland's hearty admiration because in her writings "she has incorporated the religion of Jesus Christ, as it is incorporated in her own life and character." [6] He adds to his praise of Mrs. Stowe by bracketing

[3] *Every-Day Topics*, II, 127.
[4] *Ibid.*, p. 137.
[5] *Ibid.*, p. 125.
[6] *Plain Talks*, p. 163.
[7] *Every-Day Topics*, I, 37.

her and Mrs. Whitney as "our best living female writers in America." [8] In connection with the foregoing encomiums, it is a point in Holland's favor that only one of the four writers eulogized in the quoted portions of this paragraph needs any particular introduction to the present-day student of American literature. The reputations of Longfellow, Whittier, and Mrs. Stowe are, of course, thoroughly established. Mrs. Adeline Dutton Train Whitney (1824–1906) will be recalled vaguely as a prolific writer of moralistic fiction that was designed primarily for juvenile readers.

Holland's comments upon Bryant, Emerson, Hawthorne, Holmes, and Lowell are of more than passing interest. All of these writers, with the exception of Emerson and Hawthorne, he finds commendable because they were "men of character." [9] Moreover, he finds Emerson and Holmes and Lowell "readable because of their individual flavor." [10] As regards Bryant, Holland is impressed by that poet's "sweet and solemn voicing of nature's meanings and life's mysteries." [11] As for Hawthorne, Holland is confident that the time will never come when the teller of *Twice-Told Tales* will cease to be interesting for his "interpretations of colonial history," [11] and to be highly significant because "no writer of English stands higher as an artist." [12] To Holland, however, the best thing about Hawthorne is that in *The Scarlet Letter* the author did not permit his lesson to be inferred, "but he put it into words: 'Be true, be true, be true!'" [12] And while we are upon the subject of being true, we may well recall that Holland speaks of Lowell as a writer "whose catholic sympathies and whose quick sense of Christian truth and love and justice are as evident in his 'Biglow Papers' as in his golden 'Vision of Sir Launfal.'" [13]

Holland's brief comment upon William Dean Howells and Henry James is, at first glance, a bit surprising. The best that

8 *Every-Day Topics,* I, 55.
9 *Ibid.,* II, 136.
10 *Ibid.,* I, 13.
11 *Ibid.,* II, 125.
12 *Ibid.,* I, 56.
13 *Plain Talks,* p. 163.

he has to say for their novels is that they "present the lighter social topics and types." [14] To dismiss two of our most intellectual novelists with such feeble praise as that appears rather absurd. It sounds too much like calling Henry Fielding and Jane Austen clever, and letting the whole matter go at that. In the case of Holland and Howells and James, however, it must be remembered that Josiah Holland did not live to see any of Howells' greatest work or much of James's. *A Modern Instance* was not published until the year after Holland's death, and *The Rise of Silas Lapham* and *A Hazard of New Fortunes* came still later. In this connection, the chronology of most of James's major novels is equally significant. *The Portrait of a Lady* appeared in 1881, the year that Holland died; *The Bostonians,* in 1886; *The Wings of the Dove,* in 1902; *The Ambassadors,* in 1903; *The Golden Bowl,* in 1904. This leaves only *Their Wedding Journey* (1872), *The Lady of the Aroostook* (1879), *Roderick Hudson* (1876), *The American* (1877), *The Europeans* (1878), and *Daisy Miller* (1878) as the important Howells and James novels which Holland could certainly have read. And this list is, on the whole, much less impressive than that of the later novels given above. Still, even if one disregards the delicately drawn portrait of Lydia Blood or the touching story of Daisy Miller, one wonders how any critic of real acumen could dismiss Christopher Newman's struggles against the prejudices of an effete Anglo-French aristocracy as one of "the lighter social topics." Perhaps we shall not unduly anticipate some of our further conclusions if we suggest at this point that Howells and James were quite too subtle for the comprehension of so naïve a spirit as Josiah Holland.

Holland is much more positively disrespectful to N. P. Willis than to Howells or James. The two latter writers, as we have observed, he merely dismisses as trivial. Willis, on the other hand, he denounces as one given to "literary coxcombry." [15] Here again Holland is, at first glance, rather aston-

14 *Every-Day Topics,* II, 83.
15 *Ibid.,* I, 22.

ishing; for the indefatigable Nathaniel Parker Willis (1806–1867) was, in his day, as popular as he was prolific and versatile. He was, moreover, a writer who "served a sentimental age" [16] and whose "scriptural poems had made him a national figure." [16] With all his sentiment and his scripture, however, "Willis was a butterfly," [16] who "fluttered in a Byronic way over Europe," [16] "sought the intimacy of noted women, . . . got into quarrels with notorious men," [16] flitted "up and down Broadway with the ephemeral throng," [16] and led altogether an "artificial life." [16] Willis was, in short, a very frivolous person. And, as George S. Hellman truly remarks, he was "inspiring never." [17] For these reasons, apparently, Josiah Holland had no words of commendation for Nathaniel Parker Willis. Furthermore, even as early as the eighteen-seventies it must have been quite evident that Willis had already traveled far on the road that leads to oblivion.

There is nothing at all surprising about Holland's attitude toward Poe. Poe's artistic theory and practice, to say nothing of his personality, were such as could hardly fail to win the almost complete hostility of any man like Josiah Holland. A writer who "had little or nothing to say about the church, the state, the family"; [18] a writer "with no place for high devotion or high aspiration"; [19] a writer who on general principles regarded poetry as having "no concern whatever either with Duty or with Truth" [20]—such a writer was not for Josiah Gilbert Holland. That Poe's art was "clever and graceful," [21] and that its form was "striking," [21] Holland grudgingly admits; but he hastens to add that Poe's verses "did not voice any man's or woman's aspirations or soothe any man's or woman's sorrows. They helped nobody." [22] The reason that Holland gives for Poe's lack of helpfulness is, "His poems are one con-

---

[16] Fred Lewis Pattee: *Century Readings for a Course in American Literature.* Third Edition, New York, 1926, p. 337.

[17] *Cambridge History of American Literature,* 3 vols. New York, 1933, III, 110.

[18] Percy H. Boynton: *Literature and American Life,* p. 425.

[19] *Ibid.,* p. 428.

[20] Poe, "The Poetic Principle." See Shafer, *op. cit.,* I, 580.

[21] *Every-Day Topics,* II, 86, 136.

[22] *Ibid.,* II, 86.

tinued selfish wail over lost life and lost love." [23] It is, however, not merely Poe the artist whom Holland attacks. Poe the man was equally repulsive. "His character," exclaims Holland, "was without value, and nothing of value could come of it." [23] Poe's nature, it appears, was distinctly "not . . . consecrated either to God or song." [22]

Holland gives little attention to Thoreau, but that little is unfavorable. "Of one thing," says he, "we may be reasonably sure, viz., that when the genuine geniuses of this period shall be appreciated at their full value . . . their countrymen will have ceased discussing Poe and Thoreau and Walt Whitman." [24] Holland's objections to Thoreau could hardly have been the same as his objections to the author of "The Raven," for in personal character Poe and Thoreau were about as far apart as the two poles. A man who "drank no wine" [25] and who "never knew the use of tobacco" [25] would, from the standpoint of personal habits, be as attractive to Josiah Holland as the dissipated Poe was repugnant. And yet it is no wonder that Holland could see little value in the work of Henry D. Thoreau. In the eighteen-seventies, when Holland made most of his pronouncements on literature, the Walden philosopher's reputation was at a low ebb. As Professor Pattee has truly observed, Lowell's well-known but unjust essay on Thoreau [26] caused a distinct "decline in interest in the poet-naturalist during the two decades after his death in 1862." [27] Moreover, quite apart from the strictures of Lowell, Josiah Gilbert Holland could never wax enthusiastic over a man who considered his obligation to society "very slight and transient"; [28] a man who "came into this world not chiefly to make this a good place to live in"; [29] a man who would work on the

[22] *Every-Day Topics,* II, 86.

[23] *Ibid.,* p. 136.

[24] *Ibid.,* p. 126.

[25] Robert Shafer: *American Literature,* Garden City, N.Y., 1926, I, 373.

[26] In the *North American Review,* CI, 597–608. Oct., 1865.

[27] Pattee, *op. cit.,* p. 480.

[28] Thoreau: "Life with Principle." Shafer, *op. cit.,* I, 422.

[29] Vernon L. Parrington: *Main Currents of American Thought,* New York, 1927, II, 406.

Sabbath and "keep the rest of the week for his joy and wonder"; [30] a man whose "fellow-townsmen set him down as . . . lazy, selfish, unpatriotic, irreligious." [31] In brief, the one way in which Holland can account for Thoreau's getting any public notice whatsoever may be found in these words: "There is a morbid love of the eccentric abroad in the country which, let us hope, will die out as the love of nastiness has died out." [32]

Holland devotes an entire essay to the work of Walt Whitman—an essay entitled "Is It Poetry?" [33] Holland's answer to his title question is an emphatic negative. Beginning with the statement that magazine editors have a habit of returning Whitman's manuscripts with relentless regularity, Holland explains that this editorial action is not due to personal prejudice—as Whitman and his friends have alleged—but to the conviction that Whitman's stuff is not poetry. Since Whitman's would-be verse lacks rhyme and "numbers," how can it qualify as poetry? Well, if it is not poetry, what is it? For one thing, it is not good respectable prose; for elegant prose is possessed of an evenness, a sustained strength, that is totally lacking in *Leaves of Grass.* By the process of elimination Holland concludes that Whitman's crude attempts at poetry have resulted in what may be termed rhapsodical prose—the kind of prose that Emerson and Carlyle write when they are stylistically at their worst. Whitman's stuff *must* be rhapsodical prose, for in *Leaves of Grass* one finds the most irritating idiosyncrasies of both Emerson and Carlyle: the former's propensity for tedious catalogues, the latter's mania for clumsy involutions of language. About the only difference that Josiah Holland can discern between Whitman verse on the one hand, and bad Emerson-Carlyle prose on the other, is that Whitman begins every line with a capital letter. And yet, admits Holland, Walt Whitman has his redeeming features. He is manly, robust, individualistic, even erudite. He has (thank God!) outgrown the obscenity of some of his ante-bellum *Leaves of Grass.* He is,

<hr>

30 Van Wyck Brooks: *The Flowering of New England,* New York, 1936, p. 288.
31 Shafer, *op. cit.,* I, 378.
32 *Every-Day Topics,* II, 126.
33 *Ibid.,* pp. 126–134.

moreover, *capable* of genuine poetry; for every once in a while
he startles the reader by using an honest decasyllabic line. Yes,
Whitman possesses much of the material of real poetry. But
raw material is not the finished product. The meats in the
butcher's shop and the vegetables at the grocery must be trans-
formed by the fine hand of the chef before they can be served
as a delectable dinner. Holland's conclusion, then, is that
Whitman's verse is not poetry; that Whitman's theories and
performances are radically wrong; that Whitman himself is a
blatant self-advertiser, a vulgar exhibitionist, a shoddy literary
eccentric who neither possesses nor deserves a substantial following.

Holland's estimate of Whitman is, of course, a more illuminating commentary upon Holland than upon Whitman. It
is a still more illuminating commentary upon the age in which
Holland and Whitman lived, for when Josiah Holland dis-
paraged *Leaves of Grass* he was by no means a voice crying in
the wilderness. Other American critics—critics of far more
depth and breadth and acumen than J. G. Holland—agreed
that Walt Whitman was not to be taken seriously as a poet.
Lowell, for instance, declared that Whitman would not do—
that *Leaves of Grass* was "a solemn humbug." [34] Edmund
Clarence Stedman, Charles F. Richardson, and Barrett Wendell, near the end of the century, were just as ungenerous in
their treatment of the Good Gray Poet as was Lowell.[35] Consequently, if posterity has reversed Holland's verdict upon
Whitman, it has likewise reversed the verdicts of abler men
than Holland.

We must turn now to Holland's pronouncements upon the
literature of England. Of the soundness of many of these there
can be no room for doubt. Writing of Shakespeare, our commentator observes: "More than any other man he has drunk in,
assimilated and organized in forms of art the life of the
world." [36] "Simple Bobby Burns," he finds, "goes singing down

<hr>

34 Brooks, *op. cit.*, p. 520 (footnotes).
35 Boynton: *Literature and American Life*, p. 497.
36 *Plain Talks*, p. 293.

the centuries . . . because he was in sympathy with life." [37]
Byron was "stronger in fibre, broader in culture, and bolder
in his vices" [38] than Poe, and he embodied "his character in
verse, with great subtlety and great ingenuity." [38] Browning
and Tennyson our critic finds to be "the two great poets of
England now living." [39] Dickens "had a heart which brought
him into sympathy with all those phases of humanity which
were intellectually interesting to him. . . . Pickwick and David Copperfield are as fresh today as when they were written,
and are sure to be read by many generations yet to come." [40]
As for Thackeray, "We have to thank him for his exposure of
the shallowness and shabbiness of fashionable life which en-
gages his caustic pen." [41] George Eliot, since 1861, "has had no
peer as a literary artist among her sex." [42] Ruskin is "the peerless scholar and Christian leader of art." [43]

With such dicta as these we can have no possible quarrel except that when Holland uttered them they were as obviously
trite as they were sound. It is in his comments upon minor
British authors that Holland is most revealing.

To Josiah Holland, the bright particular stars among
second-rate Victorian writers were George Macdonald, Charles
Kingsley, and Elizabeth Barrett Browning. In fact, so far as
Holland was concerned, these three writers were far too important to be considered second-rate. "If George Macdonald
is not a true artist," exclaims Josiah, "there is no true artist
writing the English language." [42] Charles Kingsley is "a great
Christian genius." [43] Mrs. Browning is "the greatest poetess of
our century, if not all time." [44] Throughout her literary career
she was a poet "who soared and sang as never woman soared
and sang before . . . yet whose heart was the dwelling-place

[37] *Every-Day Topics,* I, 46–47.
[38] *Ibid.,* II, 136.
[39] *Ibid.,* I, 23.
[40] *Ibid.,* p. 47.
[41] *Plain Talks,* p. 158.
[42] *Every-Day Topics,* I, 55.
[43] *Plain Talks,* p. 163.
[44] *Every-Day Topics,* I, 55.

of an all-controlling, all-subordinating Christian purpose." [45]

Holland's comment upon George Macdonald is not intrinsically important. Within a couple of decades after the comment was made, Macdonald had become so negligible that he is not even mentioned in George Saintsbury's detailed *Short History of English Literature* (1898). Prolific as novelist, sermonist, and lyrist, Macdonald undoubtedly enjoyed wide popularity for many years; [46] but to literary critics he never did particularly matter. One wonders just what Holland means by Macdonald's true artistry. W. T. Young, in *The Cambridge History of English Literature,* testifies that Macdonald portrays certain Scottish rural types rather well, "especially simple souls . . . deeply taught in scriptural wisdom, and given to an intense practice of piety." [47] It is to be suspected that although Holland stressed Macdonald's artistry, his real admiration was for the Scotch writer's scriptural wisdom and intense piety.

Charles Kingsley cannot be dismissed so lightly as George Macdonald. Although long since relegated to the ranks of minor writers, Kingsley retains a fairly prominent place in the history of English literature. Holland's estimate of Kingsley, "great Christian genius," is at least one-third correct. Kingsley may have been neither great nor a genius; but there can scarcely be any doubt of that earnest clergyman's Christianity. Indubitably, what appealed to Holland was, in the words of Sir A. W. Ward, "Kingsley's belief that the true task of the [Victorian] age was self-sacrifice in the cause of suffering humanity." [48]

Holland's enthusiasm for Mrs. Browning is entirely comprehensible. As a recent literary historian reminds us, "In religion Mrs. Browning was a devout Christian." [49] And as

[45] *Plain Talks,* p. 162.
[46] See below, p. 186.
[47] *Op. cit.,* XII, 480.
[48] *Cambridge History of English Literature,* XII, 405.
[49] John Buchan (Editor): *A History of English Literature,* New York, 1927, p. 488.

regards Mrs. Browning's literary reputation, there can be no doubt that she was taken very seriously by her contemporaries. "Critics were unanimous, and their praise was pitched high," [50] says Sir Henry Jones with reference to the reception accorded Mrs. Browning's longest poem, *Aurora Leigh*. We twentieth-century readers are much more severely critical of Elizabeth Barrett Browning. If we bother to read her works at all, we are repeatedly annoyed by her unrestraint, her flaws of prosody, her Victorian sentimentalism and didacticism (which Holland undoubtedly admired), and her affectations of diction. Even today, however, there will probably be little inclination to question the following authoritative statement of a present-day commentator: "She was a woman of real genius; her work is pervaded by a noble sincerity and a large and generous human feeling." [51]

One popular English writer whom Holland did not like was Lord Lytton (Sir Edward Bulwer-Lytton). Complaining of Lytton's utter heartlessness, Holland declares: "Lord Lytton is dead, and his works are nearly so. . . . Were it not for two or three plays which still hold to the boards, he, with all his works, would be as dead today as Julius Caesar." [52] Lytton was certainly not the type of man that would strike a sympathetic chord in the soul of Josiah Holland. When we recall that "he cultivated . . . the languor of a dandy and the affectations of a fop" [53] and that he "lived with wasteful violence," [53] we may well assume that Holland despised Lytton for much the same reason that he despised N. P. Willis. The interesting fact is that Holland was as correct about Lytton as he was about Willis. Time has emphatically placed the stamp of approval upon Holland's verdict. As Professor Saintsbury truly remarked, a generation after Holland uttered his prophetic strictures, Lytton's "insincere high-flown Byronic style, . . . after impress-

<hr>

[50] *Cambridge History of English Literature,* XIII, 83.
[51] Buchan, *op. cit.,* p. 489.
[52] *Every-Day Topics,* I, 46.
[53] Edward Garnett, and Edmund Gosse: *An Illustrated History of English Literature,* New York, 1903, 1935, IV, 186.

ing for a decade or two, became the laughing-stock of many decades more." [54]

Two important Victorian writers whom Holland completely ignored were George Meredith and Thomas Hardy. Presumably they were, like Howells and James, too subtle for Holland's comprehension. As a matter of fact, it is scarcely conceivable that Holland could ever have found in Meredith very much worth commenting upon, either favorably or unfavorably. With regard to Hardy, we may suspect that if Holland had lived ten or fifteen years longer he would certainly have denounced *Tess of the D'Urbervilles* and *Jude the Obscure* as unwholesome.

What is the collective significance of Holland's pronouncements upon American and English literature? In this connection, it will be recalled that in an earlier paragraph of this chapter I spoke of the definiteness of Holland's point of view.[55] We have now reached the place where this matter calls for analysis.

In the first place, I believe that it will be agreed that all of the writers whom Holland praises are (or have been) writers of wide popular appeal—writers whose works "meet with response in the souls of people." [55] Certainly Longfellow and Whittier, Burns and Dickens and even the incomparable Shakespeare, have enjoyed a popularity commensurate at least with their merits; and just as certainly Mrs. Browning and Charles Kingsley have basked in the sunshine of a pleasant if ephemeral popularity.

In the second place, however, the mere popularity of an author is not sufficient to win the critical approval of J. G. Holland. If an author is a literary coxcomb (like N. P. Willis) or a heartless and affected fop (like Bulwer-Lytton), he is doomed to ultimate oblivion.[56] In short, if he has no ethical message, no spirit of ministry, no will to make mankind better

[54] George Saintsbury: *A Short History of English Literature,* New York, 1898, p. 687.
[55] See above, p. 69.
[56] *Ibid.,* pp. 71–72, 78–79.

by his writings, he cannot hope to win the good graces of Josiah Holland.

In the third place, the personal character of a writer was as important to Holland as the quality of his work. Holland, as we have observed, particularly admired Mrs. Stowe and Mrs. Browning and Ruskin and Kingsley because they were so "Christian." [57] He detested Poe because the latter's character was valueless.[58] Similarly, Holland could never forget the fact that Byron, for all his strength and magnetism, was a bad man, a horrible example "of the effect of poor or bad character upon art." [59] "Fifty years ago," admits Holland, "he [Byron] was read more than any other poet. Young men drank the poison of his Don Juan with feverish lips." [59] Fortunately, however, the effect of Byron was not lasting. As Holland adds, with grim satisfaction: "The draught over, the book never was taken up again. . . . As a whole, the works of Byron have gone out, and are hardly read at all in these days." [59] In this connection, it must be observed that even some of Holland's favorite authors come in for severe censure on the grounds of deficient personal character. Dickens, for example, was not the man he should have been; for Dickens was not "moved by the spirit of the Master"; [60] he did not "love mankind for His sake." [60] And Dickens was cruel and unfaithful to Catherine Hogarth.

After absorbing the lovely youth of his wife—nay, after having lived with her for twenty years, and seen pillowed in her maternal arms his large family of beautiful children, he decided that her nature was incompatible with his own, and that they must separate.[61]

No, Dickens was not a Christian—not even an Anglican Christian.

[57] See above, pp. 69, 76–77.
[58] *Ibid.*, p. 73.
[59] *Every-Day Topics*, II, 136.
[60] *Ibid.*, I, 49.
[61] *Ibid.*, p. 51.

The Christian element is not to be found in his writings. Christianity is not brought forward, either as a cure or a mitigation of the evils which his eyes are so ready to see, and the woes which touch him with so quick a sympathy. You will find in Dickens travesties of missionary enterprise, and ridicule of various schemes of Christian reform; but nowhere, so far as I can remember, any evidence that he either loves Christianity, or believes in it as his own or the world's consolation and cure.[62]

And Thackeray was found to be deficient on similar grounds. Thackeray, for all his belaboring of English fashionable society, was lacking in spirituality. "He has never, so far as I know, administered any medicine but satire. . . . Image-breaker he may be, but no reformer." [63]

It must not be supposed, however, that Holland was all goody-goody in his attitude toward literature. In his later years he was ready to grant that the picaresque hero might be more fascinating than the paragon of all the virtues. Citing John Hay's Jim Bludso and Bret Harte's heroes and heroines as indubitably colorful characters, he declared, "Wickedness seems to be perennially fresh, as it is proverbially engaging. . . . Some of the most interesting people we ever met were scamps." [64] And by way of explaining this phenomenon he added, "It is the free man who attracts us, and we are not sure that a good deal of the unattractiveness of goodness is not attributable to the impression that it is constrained." [65]

Holland, moreover, went further than that in his rebellion against the utterly goody-good in literature. He even hinted that under certain circumstances a little profanity might be justifiable in the dialogue of fiction.

We venture to suggest [he said] that Mrs. Stowe and Dr. Eggleston and George Macdonald feel the denial of the use of profane language in their novels as a real harm to their art. Men must speak their vernacular or they cannot speak naturally, and

[62] *Plain Talks,* pp. 157–158.
[63] *Ibid.,* p. 158.
[64] *Every-Day Topics,* II, 109.
[65] *Ibid.,* p. 111.

to put "dang it" into a man's mouth when he said something else, or "the deuce" when he said "the devil," is to dodge and palter for the purpose of not giving offense.[66]

Holland's further pronouncements upon literature need not detain us long. In this connection, however, we should tarry for a moment to observe that Holland once offered a formula for novel writing. According to him, the ingredients of an effective work of prose fiction are as follows: first, the romantic love of the sexes; secondly, clearcut characterization; thirdly, conflict between good and evil forces; fourthly, the ultimate triumph of the good.[67] The extent to which Holland practised his formula in his own novels we can best consider in a later chapter.

Before we leave the subject of Holland on literature there remains one other consideration: Holland's criticism of criticism. As we have already noted, Josiah Holland resented the cavalier treatment that his own creative work received at the hands of the critics.[68] And, as we shall note later, Holland did not have to look far in order to find instances of such treatment. The cruel truth of the matter was that the reviewers for leading magazines were, in their estimates of Holland's writings, as unenthusiastic as we have already found a number of his fellow poets and fellow novelists to have been.[69] *Harper's,* the *Atlantic Monthly,* the *North American Review,* and the *Nation*—all of these outstanding periodicals, at one time or another, took occasion to belittle or poke fun at the creative efforts of Timothy Titcomb.[70] No, the critics did not think well of Titcomb—and Titcomb did not think well of the critics. Speaking of critics, Holland remarks: "We do not know why it is that the ordinary courtesies of life are denied to authors more than to painters or sculptors or architects, except, perhaps, that painters and sculptors and architects are not judged

---

[66] *Every-Day Topics,* II, p. 122.
[67] *Ibid.,* II, 96–97.
[68] See above, p. 66.
[69] See above, p. 62.
[70] See below, pp. 111–112, 115–117, 135, 140, 146, 154–155.

by their own co-laborers in art." [71] The implication here is, of course, that the critics of literature, unlike the critics of the other arts, are so circumstanced that they are actuated by motives of professional jealousy. Well, says Holland triumphantly, the public verdict often proves the critics to be dead wrong. To quote his words on the subject, "It is often the case that books which win the widest praise [from critics] find no market whatever, while those which are greeted with critical derision reach no end of editions." [72]

And this brings him to the evidently welcome task of classifying the book reviewers and finding them all a rather shabby lot. According to Josiah Holland's classification, there are eight types of reviewers, all of them sufficiently objectionable. In Class A (the letter being used entirely as a symbol of convenience, not at all as a mark of merit) there is the superficial young man just out of college, the presumptuous young squirt who, with a smattering of textbook learning and no real knowledge of life, makes himself ridiculous by the ignorant, half-baked judgments that he passes upon his elders and betters. In Class B there is the country editor, who, though too busy to read the books that come to his desk, "reviews" them anyhow because he wishes to keep on the good side of the publishers. In Class C there is the sensational editor, who hopes to attract public attention by criticizing books in such a way as to stir up controversy. In Class D there is the dyspeptic reviewer, whose attitude toward a work of literature is determined by the condition of his stomach or his liver. In Class E there is the dyed-in-the-wool partisan, whose every literary pronouncement is colored by political bias. In Class F there is the chronic fault-finder, whose stomach and liver may be in the pink of condition, but who believes on general principles that he should be as derogatory as possible. In Class G there is the pedant, who employs his reviews as vehicles for the display of his erudition. And finally, in Class H there is the ulterior reviewer, who re-

[71] *Every-Day Topics*, I, 69.
[72] *Ibid.*, p. 62.

gards criticism as an instrument of rewards and punishments.[73] In short, so far as Josiah Holland's classification is concerned, there is no such individual as an honest, fair-minded, objective reviewer of books.

As might well be supposed, Holland's pronouncements upon arts other than literature are relatively slight. They are, however, by no means utterly negligible. Next to literature, the art with which Holland was most conversant was music. As we observed in an earlier chapter, Holland was enough of a singer to take his place in the choir; [74] and, as we may see from a careful perusal of his essays, his interest in music extended somewhat further than that. Musicians whom Holland considered worthy of more than passing mention were Jenny Lind, vocalist; Ole Bull and Henri Vieuxtemps, violinists; and Richard Wagner, composer. Of his comments upon these geniuses, two aspects are particularly noteworthy. In the first place, as may be observed from his panegyric upon Jenny Lind, he fully believed that in music, as in literature, the character of the performer is as worthy of consideration as the quality of the performance. Here are his words about the Swedish nightingale: "Thirty years ago Jenny Lind was with us, and with her marvellous gift of song, she brought to us an unsullied character. . . . The noble womanhood which stood behind her voice was an uplifting influence, wherever that voice was heard." [75] In the second place, as may be seen from his dicta about Bull and Vieuxtemps and Wagner, he had scarcely more faith in the musical critics than in the literary critics. Comparing the American tours of Bull and Vieuxtemps respectively, Holland remarks that the latter "was the pet of the musical critics," [76] whereas the former was considered by the critics "a charlatan and a trickster." [76] And the result? Vieuxtemps, the brilliant Belgian technician, was received coldly by the American public; Bull, the soulful Norwegian charlatan, was accorded tremendous acclaim wherever he appeared. As

[73] *Every-Day Topics,* I, 62–66.
[74] See above, p. 49.
[75] *Every-Day Topics,* II, 138.
[76] *Plain Talks,* p. 285.

Holland gleefully puts it, "Vieuxtemps returned across the Atlantic, chagrined and disgusted; Ole Bull remained to win the admiration and the plaudits of a continent." [76] Wagner too, it appears, became the darling of the public while he was still the butt of the critics. "No great musician of the century," says Holland, "has been so persistently sneered at by the critics as Wagner." [77] That fact, however, did not prevent great crowds of enthusiastic music lovers from flocking to Thomas's Garden on a summer evening in the eighteen-seventies to enjoy a symphonic program devoted exclusively to the compositions of the great Bayreuth maestro. As for the poor benighted critics, if they did not like the program, so much the worse for their powers of appreciation. "The critics, in deriding and denouncing it [Wagner's music], simply proclaim their inability to comprehend it." [78]

Holland's interest in music as a profession was evidently a rather late development. In the earlier years of his literary career—perhaps always before his successive protracted sojourns in Europe and New York—he looked with grave disapproval upon music as a public professional career. Writing in 1863 he declared:

There is something very demoralizing in all pursuits that depend for their success upon the popular applause. . . . I never hear of an American girl going abroad to study music, for the purpose of fitting herself for a public musical career, without a pang. A musical education, an introduction to public musical life, and a few years of that life, are almost certain ruin for any woman. Some escape this ruin, it is true, but there are temptations laid for every step of their life. . . . They are constantly acting in operas the whole dramatic relish of which is found in equivocal situations, or openly licentious revelations. . . . I do not read history correctly if it be not true that the artists of all ages have been generally men of many vices. . . . As a class, they have not been men whom we should select for Sunday school superintendents, or as husbands for our daughters. . . . There is no denying the fact that, in the eye of a practical business man, musical accomplish-

[76] *Plain Talks,* p. 285.
[77] *Every-Day Topics,* I, 58.
[78] *Ibid.,* I, 59.

ments in men are regarded as a damage to character and a hinderance to success. . . . I pray that no friend or child of mine may become professionally a singing man or singing woman.[79]

Holland's attitude toward the graphic and the plastic arts calls for no lengthy discussion. There is no evidence, nor is there much reason for supposition, that prior to his two years in Europe and his eleven years in New York, Josiah Holland was art-conscious at all. Virtually everything that he wrote about painting and sculpture is contained in five short essays running consecutively in a volume that went to press the year of Holland's death.[80] These essays, taken collectively, develop three main topics: first, the average American's innate love of art; secondly, the reasons for the comparative poverty of American art; thirdly, the evils of art as a steady diet.

Holland was much impressed by the popularity of the fine-arts exhibit at the Philadelphia Centennial. This exhibit, it appears, drew greater crowds than any other feature of the exposition—greater crowds, even, than the wonders of the Main Building and Machinery Hall. And this phenomenon proved to Holland "that there is an innate love of art—of the beautiful in picture and sculpture—in the average American, from which it only needs time and opportunity to reap grand harvests of achievement and appreciation." [81]

Why, then, had America, up to 1876, produced so pitiably little in the way of noteworthy paintings and statuary? To this question Holland has a fivefold answer: first, the paucity of schools of art in general; secondly, the absence of life-schools in particular; thirdly, the lack of instruction in drawing in the common schools; fourthly, the incompetence and uncharitableness of the critics (a favorite theme with Josiah Holland); fifthly, the tendency of American artists to be petty and over-specialistic. Concerning the inadequacy of American facilities for instruction in art, Holland reminds his readers that a correction of that condition would "result in something far be-

---

[79] J. G. Holland: *Letters to the Joneses,* New York, 1863, pp. 48–56.
[80] *Every-Day Topics,* II, 63–80.
[81] *Ibid.,* II, 64.

yond the picture that hangs on the wall, and the statue that fills the niche"; [82] it would "result in the profitable employment of hundreds of thousands of men and women in producing articles of ornament which we now import." [82] Why, demands Holland, do we Americans make no good chinaware? Why does ninety-nine per cent of our dinner service come from China or Europe? To Holland the answer is simple and obvious: "We do not know enough to make these decorations, and if we could succeed in a clumsy imitation of them, we could design nothing new." [83] As regards the pettiness and over-specialization of American painters and sculptors, Holland makes this complaint:

They know something of a specialty, can do something creditable in it, and can do absolutely nothing out of it. They have no universality of knowledge or of skill. . . . Our "great painters" are our little painters—are the men who plod along in a narrow path, seeing nothing and attempting nothing in the wide field that opens on all sides of them.[84]

In this connection, Holland points out the inferiority of Hiram Powers, the American sculptor, to Titian, the Italian Renaissance painter. The trouble with Powers, it seems, was that he never made a group. "He spent his life on ideal heads, single ideal forms, and portrait busts." [85] As for Titian, on the other hand, he "was one of the greatest portrait painters that ever lived, and he was a much better portrait painter than he would otherwise have been for painting such [comprehensive group] works as 'The Assumption of the Virgin.' " [86]

But J. G. Holland was too much of a Puritan to surrender himself to a whole-hearted love of art. "Art," he warns us, "is a very thin diet for any human soul. . . . For art, it should be remembered, adds nothing to morality, nothing to religion, nothing to science, nothing to knowledge except a knowledge

[82] *Every-Day Topics,* II, 66.
[83] *Ibid.,* II, 66.
[84] *Ibid.,* pp. 71–72.
[85] *Ibid.,* p. 71.
[86] *Ibid.,* p. 72.

of itself, nothing to social or political wisdom, theoretically or practically." [87] Art was powerless to prevent the decline and fall of pagan Greece and pagan Rome; and art has been just as powerless to bring true progress, true civilization, to modern China and Japan.

Japan, in many matters of art, can teach the world, and the same may be said of China. [But] China and Japan are trying to learn everything else of us. They knew little or nothing of science; they had no machinery; their literature was childish; . . . and the word progress was an unknown word in both those vast realms, until daylight shone in upon them from Europe and America.[88]

Turning from literature and the fine arts to other considerations, we are repeatedly reminded of a fact that we have had frequent occasion to note in previous chapters; namely, that Josiah Holland was possessed of an absorbing and abiding interest in religion. Pleasures and palaces never tempted him to roam very far from the spirit of the prayer meeting. Contact with the world of sophistication proved, for the most part, a stimulus to Holland to discuss the problems of the Christian religion in its relations to modern thought and modern life. Thus, in *Every-Day Topics,* we find him dwelling upon such subjects as religion and science, religion and evangelism, religion and ritual, religion and the Bible, religion and popular amusements.

The lifetime of J. G. Holland was, of course, one of the most critical periods in the history of orthodox Protestantism. It was a period when the findings of the scientists compelled educated people to give up one of the most cherished beliefs dating all the way down from the Reformation; namely, belief in the literal inerrancy of the Bible. It was a period when orthodoxy was being jolted not only by men of science like Darwin and Huxley, not only by cultivated critics like Matthew Arnold, not only by popular infidels like Robert Ingersoll; but even by heterodox churchmen like Bishop Colenso. Well

[87] *Every-Day Topics,* II, 78–79.
[88] *Ibid.,* p. 80.

might the pious grow perturbed as obvious discrepancies and misstatements in the book of Genesis were pointed out. Well might they ask: If the Bible is wrong about special creation, how do we know that it is right about anything? Well might they view with fear and trembling each book published, each lecture delivered, by an able and intellectual heretic. Well might the orthodoxly religious, even among our scientists, fight manfully—if vainly—to preserve to the last iota the faith of our fathers. Witness, in this particular connection, the stout insistence of Louis Agassiz upon "the absolute immutability of species" [89]—in other words, upon creation precisely as it is recorded in the first chapter of Genesis!

Of this state of panic among religionists no man was more fully aware than Josiah Gilbert Holland. Speaking in retrospect of a course of lectures delivered in New York by Thomas Henry Huxley in 1876, Holland said: "There was [just before Huxley's coming] an indefinable dread of the man among many religious circles, as if he were not only an enemy, but a very powerful enemy, who was pretty sure to do mischief." [90] Fortunately, added Holland, this dread proved groundless: "For, let it be remembered, the religious mind of the country is not as much afraid of the theory of evolution as it was. . . . It has apprehended and accepted the fact that it takes as great a power to originate an order of beings through evolution as by a direct act of creation." [91] Speaking further of the Huxley lectures, Holland insisted that the English scientist had failed to prove either the *fact* of evolution or the nonexistence of God. As for himself, Holland was willing to admit evolution as a plausible theory, but not as a demonstrated certainty. With reference to God and evolution he declared:

God may work toward creative ends through processes of evolution, or he may not. A horse may have been derived from a three-toed animal . . . or he may not. A man may have descended, or ascended, from a monkey, or he may have been created by a divine

[89] *Universal Cyclopaedia,* Vol. I, 72.
[90] *Every-Day Topics,* II, 41.
[91] *Ibid.,* II, 42.

fiat. It matters very little, so long as God is recognized as the author of life, and the designer of its multitudinous forms.[92]

Writing in another essay with reference to science and religion, Holland reminds the scientists of their everlasting indebtedness to the clergy.

> Christianity is the undoubted and indisputable mother of the scientific culture of the country. But for her, our colleges would never have been built—our common schools would never have been instituted. Wherever a free Christianity has gone, it has carried with it education and culture.[93]

Holland's attitude toward evangelism is, I think, comparable to his attitude toward evolution. Nurtured in an evangelical sect, habituated to annual revival meetings, and, on the whole, intensely loyal to his religious background, Josiah Holland could never dismiss evangelism with a contemptuous sweep of the hand. And yet, as we have already observed, he did modify his views with reference to soul-saving campaigns.[94] By the last decade of his life he was rather thoroughly alienated from the whole tribe of strictly sectarian evangelists. Such men, he felt, had a merely negative message. Their one way of converting worldlings and reclaiming backsliders was to frighten everyone with insistently lurid pictures of hell-fire and brimstone—to cause even the faithful to regard themselves as wretched sinners. The first movement of such revivalists, says Holland,

> . . . is to get the pastor and the pastor's wife and all the prominent members upon their knees, in a confession that they have been all wrong—miserably unfaithful to their duties and their trust. That is the first step, and of course, it establishes Mr. Bedlow [the evangelist] in the supreme position, which is precisely what he deems essential. The methods and controlling influences of the church are uprooted, and, for the time, Mr. Bedlow has everything his own way. Some are disgusted, some are disheartened, a

---

[92] *Every-Day Topics*, II, p. 43.
[93] *Ibid.*, I, 136.
[94] See above, p. 61. See also *Arthur Bonnicastle*, p. 148 *et seq.*

great many are excited, and the good results, whatever they may seem to be, are ephemeral.[95]

And, speaking of the Mr. Bedlows, Holland tartly adds that although their good motives are not to be denied, and although they undoubtedly do a certain amount of good, they are not actuated entirely by Christian altruism. "They seem," as he puts it, "to thrive personally and financially." [95] Moreover, "they are dangerous men." [95]

No, Josiah Holland did not like the Bedlows. He did, however, look with favor upon the Moodys and Sankeys; for the latter held their meetings outside the churches, preached a theology free from strict sectarianism, and encouraged each convert to choose his own denominational affiliations. Such a type of evangelism, declared Holland, promotes harmony and good spirit rather than discord and dissatisfaction within the churches; moreover, it fosters sympathetic understanding between denominations.[96]

Holland's mildly tolerant attitude toward ritual must have been a late development in his career—as late a development as his distaste for the Bedlow type of evangelism. Nothing, either in Holland's religious background or in the documentary evidence, can lead us to suppose that in his early or middle years he had any sympathy for the practices of the ritualistic churches. From what we shall see elsewhere of his general attitude toward Roman Catholicism, we may, I think, assume that the Roman mass could never be other than abhorrent to him.[97] The Protestant Episcopal liturgy, however, came to be a different matter. The dreariness of evangelical prayer meetings was what drove him to tolerance in this particular. Extempore public prayers, especially those delivered by weary and perhaps ignorant brethren at the Wednesday night meetings, became increasingly banal to Holland. To quote his own words:

Spontaneous lay prayers in public are very nice in theory, but in practice, in the main, they are apples that break into ashes on

95 *Every-Day Topics*, II, 17.
96 See *Every-Day Topics*, II, 18–19.
97 See below, pp. 116–118.

the tongue. The opinion seems reasonable to us that any pastor, or body of pastors, who will present to the American churches a liturgy for social use, so genial, so hearty, so full of the detail of common wants, and so appreciative of the aspirations of the people, as to be the best possible expression of social worship and common petitions, will do more to lift the average prayer-meeting out of decrepitude, not to say disgrace, than can be done by any other means. If non-Episcopal Protestants wish to learn why it is that the Episcopal Church makes converts with such comparative ease, they need not go outside of our suggestion for their information.[98]

Holland's attitude regarding evangelism and ritual broadened contemporaneously with his changing attitude toward the Bible. As we have observed elsewhere in this monograph, Josiah Holland arrived at a theological outlook that was definitely removed from fundamentalism.[99] Writing in 1876, in an essay inspired by the preface of Matthew Arnold's *Literature and Dogma,* he protested against "those superstitious notions of the Bible that have made it half-talisman, half-fetich to millions of men, women and children." [100] Calmly admitting that "the old orthodox view of the Bible, as a plenarily inspired book, from the first word of Genesis to the last of St. John's Revelation, is already forsaken by more minds than can be counted," [101] he went on to say: "There is no question that Christianity is as independent of our old ideas of the Bible as it is independent of our ideas of the Koran." [102]

Holland's broadening conception of a Christian's proper attitude toward popular amusements may be definitely traced in his writings. In 1858 he said: "It is probable that the theater is a school of vice rather than of virtue, that the ball-room is a promoter of dissipation." [103] Five years later, however, he did not hesitate to condemn a strait-laced deacon who "opposed a

---

[98] *Every-Day Topics,* I, 155.
[99] See above, pp. 49–50.
[100] *Every-Day Topics,* I, 180.
[101] *Ibid.,* p. 179.
[102] *Ibid.,* p. 181.
[103] *Titcomb's Letters,* p. 79.

harmless dance at a neighbor's house." [104] And by the late eighteen-seventies he could declare:

The card-table, that once was a synonym of wickedness, is [now] a part of the rich man's furniture, which his children may use at will, in the pursuit of a harmless game. A good many manufactured sins have been dethroned from their fictitious life and eminence, and put to beneficent family service on behalf of the young.[105]

And, as we shall see in a later chapter, Holland came to have as tolerant an attitude toward theatre-going as toward dancing and card-playing.[106]

Nowhere, perhaps, is Holland's ethical point of view to be observed to better advantage than in his discussion of social relations. That Holland was interested not only in individual conduct, but also in man as a member of society, is clearly and abundantly manifest. What constitutes a good neighbor? What are the environmental causes and effects of rakes and their progress? What are the moral responsibilities of business and professional men? What attitude should a good citizen have toward capital and labor? These are some of the social questions that Holland answered to his own satisfaction—and, doubtless, to the satisfaction of multitudes of readers.

Three kinds of neighbors who especially incurred Holland's displeasure were the surly neighbor, the confirmed recluse, and the gadabout woman. Of the surly neighbor he says:

In your neighborhood, Mr. John Smith Jones, you are that neighbor. You are always in a quarrel with somebody about a fence. You are always very much afraid that somebody has encroached upon your line, or is about encroaching upon your line. . . . You will join with your neighbors in no effort for beautifying your street. Your consciousness that you deserve ill at the hands of your neighbors leads you to suppose that they are all banded against you, and shutting yourself into your own castle, you look

<hr>

104 Holland: *Letters to the Joneses,* New York, 1863, p. 15.
105 *Every-Day Topics,* II, 344.
106 See below, pp. 198–199.

out upon the little world of neighbors around you in defiance, and full of the spirit of mischief. You do not care how much you annoy them. You would feel uncomfortable if you did not annoy them, and though your dog and your hens are a perpetual plague to them, let but a pet rabbit stray into your enclosure, and down comes your musket, and the pet rabbit dies.[107]

Scarcely less severe is his indictment of the confirmed recluse. In the case of many a recluse, he admits, the "shy manner and reticent mood cover a heart that longs for love and a wealth of conscious intellectual power that would rejoice in recognition." [108] And in so far as the recluse causes merely his own suffering, he is more to be pitied than censured. The really culpable thing about the talented, intelligent recluse, however, is that he does not recognize his social obligations.

You retire into yourself [complains Holland], you take no pains to show that you possess the slightest social value, you do not even exhibit that interest in humanity generally, or in the community in which you live, that leads you to efforts on their behalf, yet, somehow, you feel that society ought to find you out, and make itself agreeable and valuable to you. You may rest assured that society will never do any such thing.[109]

There is, however, such a thing as being too neighborly, too sociable. The gadabout woman is a living witness to that fact. "You," says Holland, addressing this type of woman, "will either have your house full of those who destroy all the sweet privacy and communion of home-life, or you will invade the home-life of some other person." [110] Nor does the fact that many of the Mrs. Gadabouts devote their gadding largely to pious activities exonerate them. They may be running constantly to missionary meetings, or benevolent sewing circles, or funerals, or even hospital wards. But why? Largely, Holland fears, "for the change and excitement which they find in these

107 *Letters to the Joneses*, pp. 326–327.
108 *Ibid.*, p. 299.
109 *Ibid.*, p. 308.
110 *Ibid.*, pp. 258–259.

things." [111] And if change and excitement are their impelling motives, then Holland is inclined to dismiss the whole tribe of them with these words of scorn: "They ought to be at home with their husbands and children." [112]

Holland had very positive ideas upon the subject of rakes' progress. Here is his succinct biography of a typical drunkard.

He drank with his friends occasionally, then he drank with them habitually, then he drank alone to gratify a thirst which drink had created, and which will never die while his vitiated body lives.[113]

And the consequences? "There is but one end to a life of drink, and that is hell." [114] Yet there is an even worse vice than drunkenness; namely, fornication.

Men who drink are sometimes reformed, and if they have not proceeded too far in their vice, they come back to a self-respectful manhood. The taint left upon the morals is not so deep that it cannot be eradicated; but a man who has been debauched by licentiousness is incurable.[115]

The rake himself, however, is not solely to blame for his damnable progress. Society has its grave responsibility in the matter. "Opportunity invites from ten thousand hiding-places." [116]

The community seems to be benumbed, discouraged by its [Vice's] boldness, strength, and prevalence. It literally advertises itself in the public streets, and no man lifts indignantly his voice against it. Ruin and riot thrive. The dram-shop and the brothel are everywhere, and into either of these no man can go without endangering both his body and his soul.[117]

These were Josiah Holland's sentiments in 1863. And, so far as the brothel and its *raison d'être* were concerned, there is no

111 *Letters to the Joneses,* p. 266.
112 *Ibid.,* p. 266.
113 *Ibid.,* pp. 231–232.
114 *Ibid.,* p. 233.
115 *Ibid.,* p. 235.
116 *Ibid.,* p. 234.
117 *Ibid.,* p. 241.

evidence that Holland's point of view ever changed. Speaking in the late eighteen-seventies of a proposal to legalize and regulate houses of prostitution, he declared:

To undertake by law to regulate what we call the social evil . . . is to transform American society, socially the most pure of any on the earth, into the semblance and substance of that which prevails in Paris, Vienna, and Berlin. . . . We call upon all good people to oppose as they would oppose fire, or plague, or invasion, every attempt to give us the regulative laws that have debased all Europe.[118]

His attitude toward alcoholic drinks, on the other hand, became somewhat modified. He himself remained a strict teetotaler, and he steadfastly refused to serve wine to his guests; [119] but after several years' residence in New York he was willing to make this admission: "We do not suppose that a very large number of drunkards are made by wine drunk at the table, in respectable homes." [120] He hastened to add, however, that if ever the curse of drunkenness is removed from the land, the reform will be accomplished by teetotalers; for "it is only the total abstainer who can be relied upon to work for temperance." [120]

Holland's opinions regarding business and professional ethics do not call for lengthy discussion. His remarks about unethical tradesmen, preachers, doctors, and lawyers are not directed at the obvious malefactors—the cheats, the hypocrites, the quacks, and the shysters—but rather at men who, though keeping strictly within the law and the pale of respectability, do not quite play fair with the public. For example, Holland does not like the too "promising" shoemaker. Such a shoemaker, although both his materials and his workmanship may be first-rate, is a disgrace to his craft and his community. Merely for the sake of keeping his customers in a good humor, he lies about the time that it will take him to do a piece of

<hr>

118 *Every-Day Topics,* II, 306–307.
119 See below, p. 191.
120 *Every-Day Topics,* II, 247.

work; he makes glib promises that he knows he cannot keep.[121] Then there is the hidebound minister—the minister who is more concerned with doctrine than with conduct. Such a minister, says Holland scornfully, is everlastingly wondering "not whether I am a Christian man, loving and serving God and men, but whether I am orthodox." [122] And such a minister is a menace rather than a blessing. As for the physician, he may have the best of training and the greatest of skill. If, however, he is closed-minded, he is both unscientific and unsocial. Contempt for quackery is all very well, but when such contempt degenerates into bigotry it becomes thoroughly reprehensible.

> Why [asks Holland, addressing a closed-minded doctor] should you and your associates set up for exclusive possessors of medical wisdom? You know very well that medicine has made advances only by empiricism. . . . Almost every system of quackery has been found to have in it . . . some valuable power or principle, which it has always been the business of the regular profession to seek out and incorporate into their system.[123]

Just as bad as the competent but intolerant doctor is the reputable but unscrupulous lawyer. Such is the lawyer who is habitually "confounding that which is right with that which is legal." [124] Such is the lawyer who is a chronic "promoter of litigation." [124] Such, above all, is the lawyer who talks by the hour "to demonstrate the innocence of a man whom . . . [he knows] to be guilty." [125]

As might be supposed, Holland's pronouncements about capital and labor are neither startling nor profound. In fact, about all that they show is that Holland was conscious of a capital-labor problem. The merits of the capitalistic system were, or course, taken for granted by Holland, as by nearly all of his articulate American contemporaries. Holland did not live to witness the nomination of the first national Socialistic

---

121 *Letters to the Joneses,* pp. 57–70.
122 *Ibid.,* p. 145.
123 *Ibid.,* pp. 289–290.
124 *Ibid.,* p. 199.
125 *Ibid.,* p. 190.

ticket in this country,[126] and there is no evidence in his writings that he had ever read Karl Marx's *Das Kapital* or any other anti-capitalistic political treatise.

A man has a right to get rich [declared Holland, with characteristic simplicity] . . . The desire for wealth is a legitimate spur to endeavor, a good motive to the exercise of wholesome economy, and a worthy incentive to honest and honorable work. . . . There always will be rich men and there always ought to be rich men.[127]

Assuming, then, that capitalism is a good thing and that it is here to stay, Holland concerns himself with such problems as the stewardship of rich men, the relations of mistresses and servants, and the relations of industrialists and employees.

Too many successful business men, in Holland's opinion, take the wrong attitude toward their families and toward the community. They are not niggardly with either, but they are indiscreet with both. They may have the best of intentions, but their judgment is poor. They are generous to a fault —or, rather, they have a mistaken kind of generosity. Having been trained in the school of privation and severe manual labor, they are doubly determined that their children shall never be subjected to the hardships that they themselves were forced to endure.

Permit me to ask [says Holland to such men] what harm those early hardships of yours inflicted upon you. Was it not by the means of these hardships that you learned to achieve your successes? . . . Money won without effort is little prized, and you may be sure that you will get few thanks from your children for releasing them from the necessity of industry.[128]

The problem of the rich man in relation to his community is very similar.

It is right [says Holland in this connection] that you, who have been so abundantly prospered, should be abundantly charitable.

---

[126] In 1892. (See P. L. Haworth: *Hist. of U.S.*, N.Y., 1920, p. 265.)
[127] *Every-Day Topics*, I, 320.
[128] *Letters to the Joneses*, pp. 161–162.

. . . The real danger with you is, that you will give in such a way as to relieve others of the burden of duty which they should carry.[129]

And speaking further in the same strain he declares:

The greatest kindness you can show to the poor is to give them employment, and to pay them for it well and promptly. No matter if you do not really need their service. If they need your money, make a service for them.[130]

Does this mean that rich men are to refrain entirely from giving away money? Not at all.

The superfluous wealth held in this country would found ten thousand scholarships in the various colleges of the United States for the poor, furnish every town with a respectable library and reading-room, give sittings in churches to ten millions of people who have none, and found hospitals and funds of relief for labor to meet all emergencies.[131]

The American servant problem is, in Holland's opinion, a peculiar one. Social, economic, and religious circumstances tend to make it so. And the well-to-do American housewife who forgets or ignores these circumstances is bound straight for trouble. In Europe a mistress may lord it (or lady it) over a servant with impunity, for long-established class stratifications, together with a glutted labor market, compel the servant to take her humble lot for granted. Once a chambermaid, always a chambermaid! In America, however, both social and economic conditions are very different. Socially we have no class stratification—in theory, at least. Moreover,

Labor [in this country] is everywhere in demand, and no girl ever steps out of your door without knowing that, within a short space of time, she can easily find another place, with a chance at least for better treatment than you give her.[132]

[129] *Letters to the Joneses*, pp. 163–164.
[130] *Ibid.*, p. 168.
[131] *Every-Day Topics*, I, 324.
[132] *Letters to the Joneses*, p. 93.

But the social and economic factors are not the only difficulties with the American servant problem; there is the religious factor. To quote Holland,

You [Mrs. Well-to-do Housewife] are a Protestant, as the majority of Americans are, and you know that servants . . . are Catholics. It is notorious and incontrovertible that your servants are taught to consider you a heretic—a person who has no religion, and who is bound as directly for hell as if she were a murderess. It is cruel to teach these ignorant women such horrible stuff, but they are taught it. The Irish girl in your kitchen . . . regards you and the whole community of American Protestants with contempt, as the accursed of God, and of those whom she supposes to be His representatives on the earth. . . . Consequently, you, and every Protestant mistress in America, must necessarily labor under disadvantages in the management of servants.[133]

In brief, as a matter of self-interest (if for no more altruistic reason), the well-to-do American housewife is obliged to deal courteously and considerately with her servants.

Somewhat different, but just as perplexing, is the problem of the industrialist and his employees. Capital, all too frequently, forms pernicious combinations to the detriment of the laborer and the consumer. Labor retaliates by organizing trade unions and fomenting strikes. And the result is movement in a vicious circle, in which the behavior of both capital and labor is "unnatural and outrageous and tyrannical." [134] Well, what is the remedy? The remedy is a spirit of coöperation. Let the workingman remember that "the assumption of the same business risks to which capitalists expose themselves, and the exercise of the same business capacity, can alone give to labor all the wealth which it produces."[134] Let the capitalist, meanwhile, remember that the workingman is a human being, not a machine. Let him pay a living wage for work done under conditions as safe and sanitary as possible. Let him endow scholarships and libraries and hospitals. "Nay,

[133] *Letters to the Joneses*, pp. 94–95.
[134] *Every-Day Topics*, I, 321.

what is more, and in some respects better . . . [let him] lend
in many instances to labor the capital necessary to secure the
profits upon its own expenditures." [135]

Having examined Holland's dicta touching art and morals
generally, we are ready to return to a question that we left
unanswered in the first paragraph of this chapter: Is Professor
Nevins right in declaring that J. G. Holland's writings are
made up of truisms insipid enough for a young ladies' boarding school and religious enough for the most bigoted sectarian? If in his assertion Professor Nevins has reference to
the *Letters* of 1858 alone, or to *most* of Holland's dicta in the
other essays, the answer to our question must obviously be
a decided affirmative. If, on the other hand, Professor Nevins
means *everything* that Holland said prominently, then we
must qualify our answer a great deal.

By "bigoted sectarians," Professor Nevins clearly means orthodox members of American evangelical Protestant denominations. He means the rural and the small-town pillars in
such churches as the Methodist, the Baptist, the Christian
(Campbellite), the Presbyterian, and the Congregational. He
means the people who, whatever may be their disagreements
concerning predestination, immersion, formal creeds, and
church polity, are a unit in their beliefs about the funda-
mentals of faith and morality—the people who speak with
one voice in their unqualified denunciation of higher criticism, evolution, Catholicism (Roman or Anglo-), vestments,
printed prayers, dancing, playing cards, theatres, alcoholic
beverages (heavy or light), and tobacco (particularly ciga-
rettes). Would such people agree that "a man may have descended, or ascended, from a monkey," [136] that American
churches need "a liturgy for social use [or *any* use]," [137] or that
Christianity is "independent of our old ideas of the Bible?" [138]
Would they grant that there can be such a thing as "a harm-

[135] *Every-Day Topics,* I, 324.
[136] See above, p. 89.
[137] See above, p. 92.
[138] See above, p. 92.

less dance," [138] or that the card-table can ever be "put to beneficent family service," [138] or that "not . . . a very large number of drunkards are made by wine drunk at the table, in respectable homes?" [139] Would they admit that profanity is ever justifiable on the printed page or that a colorful rogue can possibly be more engaging than a paragon of all the virtues? [140] Would they concede that Josiah Holland (or any other Christian) has any right to be even mildly interested in secular things so utterly lacking in utilitarian value as "fiddling" and painting and sculpture? [141] The proper replies are as obvious as they are uniform. The person who would hesitate to answer any or all of these questions with an emphatic negative simply does not know our "most bigoted sectarians" of Colonial American descent.

Yes, Josiah Holland was both truistic and religiose, and he could hardly have offended even the mildest and most timid liberal of evangelical persuasion. Manifestly, however, he outgrew the "most bigoted sectarians." Passing years and cosmopolitan contacts broadened him—if ever so little.

[138] See above, p. 92.
[139] See above, p. 96.
[140] See above, pp. 81–82.
[141] See above, pp. 84–88.

VI

Poems

It is significant, perhaps, that J. G. Holland's first published work was a poem; that the heroes of his two longest poems are both of them poets; and that his one work which has enjoyed a more lasting renown than any of his five novels is his poem *Bitter-Sweet*. It is, I think, equally significant that up to the last decade of his life, Holland's efforts in the realm of creative literature were predominantly poetic.

If it be asked why a man as eager for fame and remuneration as was Josiah Holland should have turned to verse-writing in preference to novel-writing, the answer is not difficult. Up to and including the time when J. G. Holland's literary career was getting under way, this country had produced only two really notable novelists, Cooper and Hawthorne. Charles Brockden Brown, William Gilmore Simms, John Neal, and John Pendleton Kennedy had written more or less prolifically; but their novels had certainly been less important than the best of Cooper's and Hawthorne's, and—among the discriminating at least—they had attracted considerably less attention. Harriet Beecher Stowe and Bayard Taylor had yet to win their publics.[1] As for Herman Melville, he was destined to lie in his grave for many years before discriminating readers would recognize him for the genius that he was.[2] As Mr. Carl Van Doren points out, "The rise of the great Victorian novelists in England was not paralleled in America." [3] And, as Professor Fish reminds us, Amer-

---

[1] With *Uncle Tom's Cabin* (1852) and *Hannah Thurston* (1863), respectively.

[2] Halleck's *American Literature* (1911) gives Melville three lines (p. 407). Boynton's *American Literature* (1919) does not even mention Melville. Boynton's *Literature and American Life* (1936) gives Melville 16 pages (pp. 461–477).

[3] Van Doren, *op. cit.*, p. 67.

ican public taste was keen for poetry and didactic essays before it "changed . . . to romances and stories of adventure and travel." [4] In this country, at about the middle of the nineteenth century, "there was less of critical interest manifested in fiction than in poetry. The serious reviews rather looked down upon the novel." [5] There was, to be sure, a great deal of novel-reading—a fact of which the magazine writers took full cognizance.

We must remember, however, that when the [mid-nineteenth century] critics talk about fiction-reading in America they are talking mainly about the reading of novels produced abroad, for the greater part of the novels turned out by American presses were English, French, German, and (in Fredricka Bremer's case) Swedish. [5]

Meanwhile, the country had witnessed the great success of such poets as Bryant, Lydia Sigourney, Whittier, Longfellow, Poe, Holmes, and Lowell. Not until the Reconstruction period ushered in such novelists as Mark Twain, William Dean Howells, and Henry James did the novel come to be the salient form of American literature. In ante-bellum days our American publishers were not particularly eager for the manuscripts of native novelists. [6] Why should they have been, when—thanks to the lack of an international copyright law —any publisher in this country could freely pirate the novels of Dickens, Thackeray, George Eliot, Trollope, and Reade? True, our more substantial publishers were too ethical to take full advantage of this situation, [7] but certainly the piracy of British fiction was waged on a large enough scale to discourage, if not utterly to dishearten, American talent. These being the circumstances, it is no wonder that poetry was Josiah Holland's first love.

In a previous chapter we have mentioned the fact that even

[4] Fish, *op. cit.,* p. 255.
[5] Frank Luther Mott: *A History of American Magazines, 1741–1850,* New York and London, 1930, p. 415.
[6] Fish, *op. cit.,* p. 248.
[7] *Ibid.,* p. 249.

before his *Republican* days Holland had had a few short lyrics accepted by nationally circulated periodicals.[8] We have likewise mentioned the success of his first long poem, *Bitter-Sweet* (1858).

Fortunately for Holland, he had succeeded in placing this poem with Charles Scribner, one of the foremost American publishers of that day and of a much later day as well. Scribner, although only thirty-seven years old—two years Holland's junior—had been in the publishing business for twelve years and already enjoyed a prestige equal to that of any New York publisher.[9]

The popular success of *Bitter-Sweet* was almost instantaneous, and it continued great for many years. Reprintings of the poem were made in 1867, in 1881, in 1886, in 1909, and in 1923,[10] the last printing being therefore nearly two-thirds of a century later than the first, and more than twoscore years after Holland's death. By 1894 some ninety thousand copies of the poem had been sold, "notwithstanding it was savagely attacked by some of the critics." [11]

The poem covers about two hundred pages, mostly in blank verse, but occasionally in varied lyrical measures. Although it is in dialogue, it is in no legitimate sense a drama, for it involves little action, and it is divided into "movements" rather than acts. The scene of the entire poem—or, as the author puts it, the "locality"—is the interior of a New England farmhouse.

A brief synopsis will give the reader a fairly adequate idea of the general content of the work.

Israel, a patriarchal New England farmer, lives with his youngest daughter, Ruth, who has served as his housekeeper since the death of her mother. His other three children have married and left home; but at the end of the story they have

---

[8] See above, p. 35.

[9] For short biographical sketch of Charles Scribner (1821–1871), see *Universal Cyclopaedia*, X, 395.

[10] For this information I am indebted to Mr. J. H. Poli, Production Department, Charles Scribner's Sons.

[11] Plunkett, p. 48.

returned with their families to spend Thanksgiving at the old red farmhouse. Present also is Mary, an adopted daughter who, after a miserable existence with a drunken husband, has come back to the shelter of her foster father's roof.

The festivities begin quaintly with a lengthy theological discussion about the ways of Providence. Ruth, who is a skeptic, asks why a good God—if good God there be—should permit sin and sorrow in this world. The pious Calvinistic Israel, shocked at what he considers his daughter's irreverence, sternly commands the young woman to hold her peace. But David, Israel's only son-in-law, who is a poet and a liberal Christian, calmly endeavors to justify the ways of God to Ruth.

Later in the evening David's wife, Grace, has a long private conversation with Mary. Knowing something of Mary's misfortune, Grace declares that she herself has been living under the cloud of a great sorrow. She says that her marriage to David has not been at all the happy affair that it appears to be. She says that David, for all his pious speeches and his uplifting verses, is a wicked philanderer—that he has a mistress whose identity is unknown to her. Mary, apparently shocked at this revelation, repeats the story of her own unfortunate marital experience. She concludes by telling how, when despair had driven her to the verge of madness, she was brought back to her best self by the kindly ministrations of a Christian young man whose name she does not reveal.

At this juncture in the story, a wailing human voice penetrates the stormy, wintry night outside the farmhouse. Israel's sons and his son-in-law, responding to the voice, bring in a strange man who is half dead from an enfeebled physical condition and from exposure to the storm. The stranger, stretched upon a settle, is soon identified as Mary's erstwhile reprobate husband, Edward. The dying man explains that although he is a physical wreck he has been spiritually redeemed by the grace of Jesus Christ, and that he has come to beg the forgiveness of the woman whom he has wronged so grievously. Mary tearfully grants Edward's petition, and at the same time she reveals the fact that David is no hypo-crite, no philanderer, but her blessed rescuer—that she her-self is the woman whom Grace wrongly supposed to be David's mistress.

Thus, by the revelations of a single evening, the ways of God are justified to Ruth, to Grace, and to the entire com-pany. As David points out, much so-called evil is only appar-ent evil; and much real evil may be turned to good account.

Only one influential periodical took the trouble to review *Bitter-Sweet* upon its first appearance; but that one periodical happened to be the peerless *Atlantic Monthly*, which, al-though only in its second year at the time, had already estab-lished a reputation as enviable as it enjoys today.[12] The review, written by the *Atlantic's* distinguished editor, James Russell Lowell,[13] is as follows:

"Bitter-Sweet" is truly an original poem—as genuine a product of our soil as a golden-rod or an aster. It is as purely American—nay, more than that, as purely New English, as the poems of Burns or Scott were Scotch. We read ourselves gradually back to our boy-hood in it, and were aware of a flavor in it deliciously local and familiar—a kind of sour-sweet, as in a *frozen*-thaw apple. The family party met for Thanksgiving can hit on no better way to be jolly than in a discussion of the Origin of Evil, and the Yankee husband (a shooting-star in the quiet haven of village morals) about to run away from his wife can be content with no less cometlike vehicle than a balloon. The poem is Yankee, even to the questionable extent of substituting "locality" for "scene" in the stage directions; and we feel sure that none of the characters ever went to bed in their lives, but always sidled through the more decorous subterfuge of "retiring."

We could easily show that "Bitter-Sweet" was not this and that and t'other, but, after all said and done, it would remain an obstinately charming little book. It is not free from faults of taste, nor from a certain commonplaceness of metre; but Mr. Hol-

---

12 Arthur Bartlett Maurice: "Literary Magazines," p. 471. Chapter **XXXIV** of *American Writers on American Literature*. See also Boynton: *Literature and American Life*, p. 459.

13 See Plunkett, p. 135.

land always saves himself in some expression so simply poetical, some image so fresh and natural, the harvest of his own heart and eye, that we are ready to forgive him all faults in our thankfulness at finding the soul of Theocritus transmigrated into the body of a Yankee.

It would seem the simplest thing in the world to be able to help yourself to what lies all around you ready to your hand; but writers of verse commonly find it a difficult, if not impossible, thing to do. Conscious that a certain remoteness from ordinary life is essential in poetry, they aim at it by laying their scenes far away in time, and taking their images from far away in space —thus contriving to be foreign at once to their century and their country. Such self-made exiles and aliens are never repatriated by posterity. It is only here and there that a man is found like Hawthorne, Judd, and Mr. Holland, who discovers or instinctively feels that this remoteness is attained and attainable only by lifting up and transfiguring the ordinary and familiar with the *mirage* of the ideal. We mean it as very high praise when we say that "Bitter-Sweet" is one of the few books that have found the secret of drawing up and assimilating the juices of this New World of ours.[14]

To the present-day American, who thinks of the last Thursday in November as a time when one gorges one's self upon roast turkey, spends the afternoon at a football game or a "bargain" matinée, and devotes the evening to a supper dance or a bridge party, *Bitter-Sweet* could hardly be more than a quaint curiosity. That reunited relatives, brought together for a single day, should waste precious social hours in drab theological discussions appears incredible to us. But Calvinistic New Englanders of eighty years ago knew something that we have had abundant opportunity to forget; they knew the solemn purpose for which William Bradford had created Thanksgiving. In general theme, therefore, *Bitter-Sweet* is not absurd; it is realistic. And, despite the fact that its general poetic level is not high, it contains more than a few genuinely good passages. Take, for example, these lines from the introductory "Picture":

<hr>

14 *Atlantic Monthly,* III, 651–652. May, 1859.

Across the swale, half up the pine-capped hill,
Stands the old farm-house with its clump of barns—
The old red farm-house—dim and dun tonight,
Save where the ruddy firelights from the hearth
Flap their bright wings against the window-panes,—
A billowy swarm that beat their slender bars,
Or seek the night to leave their track of flame
Upon the sleet, or sit, with shifting feet
And restless plumes, among the poplar boughs—
The spectral poplars, standing at the gate.[15]

Perhaps the most objectionable feature of *Bitter-Sweet* is its plot. We may grant that David's wife might jealously suspect him of philandering; but we find it difficult to believe that she would fail to identify his "mistress," especially in view of the fact that she had spied upon David to the extent of seeing him in Mary's company. Moreover, the manner of Edward's appearance at the farmhouse does not quite ring true; it smacks too much of the clumsily arranged coincidence to be good art. But Josiah Holland's public were, on the whole, not the kind of public to insist overmuch upon verisimilitude. What they insisted upon were simplicity, and sentiment, and an outcome in strict accord with the most immediately obvious poetic justice.

Holland's second long poem, *Kathrina,* another Scribner publication, made its appearance in 1867, near the very end of Holland's long residence in his native Massachusetts. Although it did not quite repeat the long-lived success of the earlier poem, it scored an even greater immediate popular triumph. "It rapidly reached a sale of a hundred thousand copies—and to this day [1894] has had a steady sale." [16] It was, in fact, in sufficient demand to have been reprinted in 1868, 1881, 1895, 1910, and 1917.[17]

As may be noted from a brief recital of the synopsis, the

15 Holland: *Bitter-Sweet,* New York, 1858, 1873, p. 11.
16 *Plunkett,* p. 73.
17 See above, p. 105, footnote 10.

plot of *Kathrina* is much more discursive than that of *Bitter-Sweet*.

Paul, the hero of the poem, lives with his widowed mother in a beautiful village of western Massachusetts. His childhood is clouded by the fact that his father, though once the richest man in the town, committed suicide through fear of impending financial ruin. This unhappy circumstance causes the boy to grow up in the bitter conviction that there is no just God in the universe. Out of deference to his devout, affectionate mother, however, he pays lip-service to religion. Near the end of his senior year at college, he is summoned home by the serious illness of his mother. Her illness proves to be mental rather than physical, and shortly after the young man's arrival home she does what her husband did years earlier—takes her own life. Paul, who has long cherished the ambition of becoming a great and famous author, is now more determined in his ambition than ever before; but he is also more bitterly determined than ever that God—if God there be—shall have no share in his plans.

One Sunday morning about a year after his mother's death Paul is taking a stroll near the village church. Attracted by the sweetness of a feminine voice which rises above the others in the singing of a hymn, he wanders into the church and joins the worshippers. He soon observes that the owner of the voice is a very pretty girl whom he has never seen before. Late in the service the girl is baptized and received into the fellowship of the church. At the conclusion of the service Paul lingers at the door and sees the girl coming out of the church with an elderly woman whom he recognizes as an old friend of his mother's. The woman greets him, commiserates him upon his bereavement, and introduces the girl as her orphan niece who has come to live with her. To Paul's great delight, the old lady cordially invites him to call upon her and her niece. The young man loses no time in accepting the invitation, and a courtship is speedily begun between him and the lovely girl. At first he has doubts as to whether he could be happy with an ardently religious wife, but he soon dispels these doubts with the thought that religious women make more dependable mates than do giddy pleasure lovers. The rather odd courtship of the young couple is replete with lengthy arguments concerning the true function of art. Paul maintains that art is sufficient as an end in itself; Kathrina contends that the ultimate purpose of art should be Christian and altruistic.

In the autumn Paul and Kathrina are married. Inspired by his new happiness, Paul blossoms into one of the most successful authors in the land. Multitudes buy and read his books. At first, after his success is well established, the critics praise his writings unreservedly; but as time goes on they suggest that his work, for all its excellent technique, is somehow lacking in soul. Paul's triumphs grow more and more hollow to him. To add to his unhappiness, a mortal illness lays its hand upon Kathrina. On her deathbed she reiterates what she has often declared: that Paul's success has proved a mockery because the aim of his art has been utterly selfish and worldly. Begging Paul to become a Christian, she insists that only by yielding himself to Christ can he achieve the peace and joy for which he has hungered all his life. The sorrowing husband heeds his wife's plea at last, and she dies with a smile of joy upon her lips. Kneeling devoutly in the death chamber, Paul consecrates his talents to the service and betterment of his fellow men.

The *Atlantic Monthly* for December 1867, by this time edited by James T. Fields,[18] deals very severely with *Kathrina*. The reviewer, after cynically wondering why Dr. Holland has had the audacity to call his work a poem, and why the heroine has not laughed in the face of the hero when the latter has persisted in reading her his atrocious verses, comments upon the character of Kathrina herself. "She is," he declares, "herself scarcely other than a name for a series of arguments, with little of the flesh and blood of a womanly personality." [19] And of the poem as a whole he says: "It appears to us puerile in

---

[18] Boynton: *Literature and American Life,* p. 884.
[19] *Atlantic Monthly,* XX, 763–764. Dec., 1867.

conception, destitute of due motive, and inartistic in treatment." [19]

Harper's for the same month is decidedly more generous.

"It is," says the reviewer, in speaking of *Kathrina*, "pleasantly, carefully, earnestly told. The singer evidently believes what he sings, and he evidently thinks everybody else ought to believe it too." [20] But the reviewer emasculates his praise by paying this left-handed compliment to Holland's literary reputation:

It is a peculiar reputation; almost a rural and provincial reputation. . . . The chief literary tribunals, which are, of course, in the larger cities, deliver judgment upon Mr. Titcomb in a rather supercilious tone, and . . . he has not yet conquered a place in the general estimation among the representative American authors.[20]

Harper's for January 1869, reviewing the 1868 illustrated edition of *Kathrina*, is positively enthusiastic.

Mr. Holland [says the reviewer] is a genuine poet. More perhaps than any other American writer he grapples with the deepest problems of our interior life. The secret battles of the soul he depicts always graphically. He is sometimes morbid, but he is rarely, if ever, weak. Whether it is desirable to tell the story of such a life as he has undertaken to describe in *Kathrina* we seriously doubt. But no one can doubt that it is powerfully done.[21]

The majority of twentieth-century readers will doubtless feel that the *Atlantic* reviewer was much nearer the truth than his *Harper's* rival. That the story of *Kathrina* is puerile in conception and bad in motivation may be seen from the most cursory reading of the synopsis. The manner of the courtship alone is quite sufficient to damn the narrative. In the midst of a typical love scene Kathrina speaks these words in defense of Christian art:

[19] *Atlantic Monthly*, XX, 763–764. Dec., 1867.
[20] *Harper's Monthly*, XXXVI, 126–127. Dec., 1867.
[21] *Ibid.*, XXXVIII, 274. Jan., 1869.

> If from out my book
> I gather that which feeds me, and inspires
> A nobler, sweeter beauty in my life,
> And give my life to those who cannot win
> From the dim text such boon, then have I borne
> A blessing from the book, and been its best
> Interpreter.[22]

Surely no heroine, even in the eighteen-sixties, ever met the amatory advances of her wooer with such words as these. And surely there is no evidence that any work of art was ever made the greater by the leaven of Calvinistic or evangelical religiosity. Even *Paradise Lost* and *Paradise Regained* and *Pilgrim's Progress,* sole Calvinistic masterpieces of the first order, are far greater because of their imaginative qualities than because of their theology or, for that matter, their moral earnestness.

It is unfortunate that we cannot forget the parochial thesis, the feeble plot, and the banal dialogue of *Kathrina;* for the poem unquestionably has its merits. Possibly no minor American poet of the middle nineteenth century wrote more competent blank verse than did J. G. Holland. And some individual passages in *Kathrina* are as rich and varied in imagery and as felicitous in tropes as they are sound in prosody. Let us take, for example, these lines:

> We often left the village far behind,
> And walked the meadow-paths to gather flowers
> And watch the ploughman as he turned the tilth,
> Or tossed his burnished share into the sun
> At the long furrow's end, the while we marked
> The tipsy bobolink, struggling with the chain
> Of tinkling music that perplexed his wings,
> And listened to the yellow-breasted lark's
> Sweet whistle from the grass.
>
>   Glad in my joy,
> My mother smiled amid these scenes and sounds,
> And wandered on with gentle step and slow,

[22] Holland: *Kathrina,* New York, 1867, 1872, pp. 99–100.

> While I, in boyish frolic, ran before,
> Chasing the butterflies, or in her path
> Tossing the gaudy gold of buttercups,
> Till sometimes, ere we knew, we stood entranced
> Upon the river's marge.[23]

This is far from being great or distinguished poetry, but at least it is genuine poetry. Here are concreteness and charm, as well as movement and music. Such phrases as *chain of tinkling music* and *tossing the gaudy gold of buttercups* are not merely competent and adequate; they are inspired. After all, the *Harper's* reviewer was partly right in his estimate.

The third and last of Holland's major poems, *The Mistress of the Manse,* came off the press in 1874. This piece, as we observed in an earlier chapter, is a tale with a Civil War background. Its plot is simple—almost, one might say, obviously hackneyed.

At the beginning of the story, Philip, a young Northern minister, has just brought Mildred, his Southern bride, to her new home, a New England manse.

For a number of years their lives are destined to be idyllically happy. Philip is a scholarly, an eloquent, and a highly respected preacher. Mildred, in her saintly mode of living and in her unostentatious ministrations to the unfortunate and the needy, is an ideal pastor's wife. The union of the couple is blessed with a large and an admirable family.

But after these placid years the clouds of war hang more and more heavily over the nation—clouds of civil war between Philip's native section and Mildred's. Philip is now torn between duty and love. Though he hates to wound his devoted Mildred, he feels that he would be unworthy of his sacred calling if he did not raise his voice in the condemnation of slavery and threatened disunion. Mildred also is torn between duty and love. She thinks of her dear Southland, of her gallant brother, and of her indulgent father, the kindly master of happy slaves. With horror she envisages her brother

---

[23] Holland: *Kathrina,* p. 15.

and her husband pitted against each other in mortal combat. But she thinks also of her vows of faithfulness to a truly Christian husband. And with Mildred, as with Philip, the call of duty is even stronger than the call of love.

Fort Sumter is fired upon, and the men rush to arms. Philip, the shepherd of souls, becomes a leader of soldiers. Mildred's brother, heeding the call of his native South, dons a uniform of gray.

One night a sick, disheveled man seeks admittance to the manse. It is Mildred's brother, who has presumably escaped from a Northern prison. What can Mildred do to give him comfort, shelter, and a hiding place? Sisterly devotion affords the only answer to this question.

Meanwhile Philip has been fatally wounded at the Battle of Gettysburg, and he is being brought home to die. He arrives in time to greet and embrace Mildred with words of affection and to exchange words of respect and love for his dying Confederate brother-in-law.

The coffins of the two soldiers are placed side by side in the same grave. The twice-bereaved widow is comforted by the fact that her eldest son, grown to young manhood, is ready to step into his father's shoes as pastor of the church and master of the manse.

The Mistress of the Manse, like *Bitter-Sweet* and *Kathrina*, scored a quick popular success. Soon after its publication a prominent Middle Western daily hailed it as "the fall sensation in literature." [24] Eastern metropolitan critics, however, gave the poem a frigid reception. The *Atlantic Monthly* did not deign to review it because—as its then editor, William Dean Howells, explained in a letter to Edmund Clarence Stedman—the *Atlantic* could find no competent reviewer who "would promise to praise it or even to spare it." [25] *Harper's* damned the poem with faint praise in these words:

The Mistress of the Manse, by J. G. Holland, is valuable rather for the high and pure moral tone which is characteristic of all

[24] Columbus *Ohio State Journal*, Oct. 14, 1874.
[25] Howells, *op. cit.*, I, 197.

its author's writings than for poetic genius; . . . rather for the sentiment which it will enkindle . . . in many hearts . . . than for originality of thought or rare felicity of utterance.[26]

Strangely enough, a really reputable authority of a generation later, James L. Onderdonk, spoke much more favorably of the poem.

It is [declared Onderdonk] decidedly among the best narrative poems of the Civil War. A tender, grave, and patriotic spirit characterizes the work throughout. It failed of the popular success attained by the earlier poems [*Bitter-Sweet* and *Kathrina*], perhaps because there was not enough of preaching to satisfy the poet's former admirers, and not enough of poetry to please those of a more critical judgment.[27]

Onderdonk is too generous. *The Mistress of the Manse* possesses neither the distinctive atmosphere of *Bitter-Sweet* nor the occasional, sporadic charm of *Kathrina*. Its stanzaic form is, in fact, the one feature that raises it at all above the level of mediocrity. Most of its stanzas are five-lined iambic tetrameter groups with a rhyme-scheme of *ababa*. This is a novel arrangement, and it is, on the whole, ingeniously handled.

The only other Holland poem that calls for extended notice is *The Marble Prophecy* (1872). This poem, one of the inspirations of Holland's European tour in the late sixties, has modern Rome for its setting. Approaching St. Peter's cathedral to witness one of the great ceremonial processions of the Church, the poet pauses in the Cortile del Belvedere to contemplate the celebrated Laocoön statue. Presently, as he watches the parade of gorgeously panoplied soldiers and ecclesiastics, he begins to compare and contrast the simplicity of primitive Christianity with the sensuous gaudiness of the "brave pageant" now being unfolded before him. And as the Holy Father appears, borne upon the shoulders of his stalwart guards, canopied by golden tapestries, and wearing

---

[26] *Harper's*, L, 289. Jan., 1875.

[27] James L. Onderdonk: *History of American Verse*, Chicago, 1899–1901, pp. 204–205.

the triple crown, the poet recalls that eighteen hundred years earlier the founder of Christianity rode upon an ass. Disgusted by the elaborate ostentatiousness of the Papal procession, the bard avers that modern Rome, like ancient Laocoön, is held in the grip of serpents—ecclesiastical serpents that prey upon her and rob her of her freedom and her self-respect.

Harper's for February 1873, in commenting upon the poem, says:

> Dr. J. G. Holland's *Marble Prophecy* is almost an invective against the Church of Rome. Its biting sarcasm consorts not well with the spirit of poetry, hardly with the spirit of Christianity. . . . In the opening description of the festival of St. Peter's Chair . . . its spirit of contempt for the "brave pageant" is almost painful.[28]

One wonders why the reviewer calls the poem *almost* an invective. As a matter of fact, it is a downright, unqualified invective. It is, however, precisely the sort of thing that one would expect from a man of Josiah Holland's background and prejudices. A rural New England Congregationalist who was afraid to go to Europe lest he lose some of his sectional naïveté could hardly be expected to show much sympathy or even tolerance for the Roman Catholic church.[29] In this connection, too, it must be remembered that by the third quarter of the nineteenth century the waves of Irish and French-Canadian immigration into the industrial centers of lower New England had already reached sufficient proportions to cause a widespread and ugly antipathy between the old Puritan stock and the Celtic newcomers. Even as early as the middle of the century, as Professor Fish points out,

> . . . the Roman Catholic Church was becoming more distasteful to the [native American] majority as it became more important. The feeling toward it was not merely religious but political, for it was considered as an extension of the great estab-

---

[28] *Op. cit.,* XLVI, 458.
[29] See above, pp. 66–67.

lished church of Europe, monarchical in its own organization and the chief prop of civil monarchy as well. When, therefore, the first Catholic church arose in the Irish [or other foreign] quarter of city or town, the combination was regarded as a menace.[30]

Nor was this the only aspect of Roman Catholicism that caused it to be viewed with grave apprehension. Speaking of the period between 1865 and 1878—the period in which *The Marble Prophecy* was written and published—Professor Nevins says:

Much needless worry was caused among the religious [of the older native stocks] by the "Continental Sabbath," one of the results of the immigrant invasion. Still more alarm was felt among Protestants over a supposed intent of the Catholic Church to gain control of education, or to obtain a share of the public-school funds for its parochial schools.[31]

Naturally, therefore, Dr. Holland's clientele uttered many a hearty "amen" to the sentiments expressed in *The Marble Prophecy*. These were the sentiments of a good Yankee rustic, spoken to a multitude of equally good Yankee rustics from Goshen, Massachusetts, to Clay Center, Kansas. Again, however, it must be remembered that Josiah Holland was not consciously politic when he made this highly popular appeal to geographical, racial, and religious prejudices. He sincerely believed every word that he uttered. Although he may have added a piazza to his Puritan prison-house—a piazza upon which Unitarians [32] and Episcopalians [33] might bask at rare intervals—he had no room, no nook, no resting place for the Scarlet Woman of the Tiber.[34]

The one sustained merit of *The Marble Prophecy*, as of

[30] Fish, *op. cit.*, p. 114.

[31] Nevins, *op. cit.*, p. 346.

[32] According to Roswell Smith, Holland was at least once suspected of *being* a Unitarian. See Plunkett, *op. cit.*, p. 163.

[33] For Holland's mildly tolerant attitude toward Episcopalianism, see above, pp. 91–92.

[34] For Holland's strictures upon Roman Catholic intolerance of Protestants, see above, p. 100.

Kathrina, is the craftsmanlike quality of the blank verse. That J. G. Holland could write respectable unrhymed heroics there can be no doubt. And, what with the problems of the light stress, the initial trochee, the internal anapest, the terminal amphibrach, the masculine caesura, the feminine caesura, and the enjambment, this is not so mean an achievement as foolish people have often supposed.

Of Holland's numerous short lyrics a few merit brief attention. "Wanted," a peculiar sonnet with a rather clumsy rhyme-scheme—*aabcbcdedeffgg*—was an outstanding favorite because of its earnest pleading for clean politics and incorruptible statesmen. It is, I believe, still quoted by the older clergy; but the only genuinely poetical line that I have ever been able to discover in it is this:

Tall men, sun-crowned, who live above the fog.[35]

"Albert Durer's Studio" and "The Old Clock of Prague" are pretty ballads in the manner of Longfellow. "Gradatim" is a respectable didactic poem somewhat suggestive of Holmes's "Chambered Nautilus." "Verses Read at the Hadley Centennial" (June 9, 1859) is a tolerably good occasional poem. "The Mountain Christening" is a pleasant little tale of one of the sunnier aspects of New England Colonial life—a fresh, spontaneous poem that is agreeably free from its author's rather common habit of sanctimonious didacticism. *The Puritan's Guest,* which is the title piece of a small volume issued in 1877, is a ballad whose uncanny supernaturalism is more reminiscent of some of Hawthorne's *Twice-Told Tales* than of any well-known American poem. "There's a Song in the Air" is a graceful, better-than-average Christmas carol that still has some vogue.

Garnered Sheaves is the title that Dr. Holland gave his complete poetical works, an illustrated edition published in 1873. An enlarged *Garnered Sheaves* appeared late in 1879.

[35] *The Marble Prophecy, and Other Poems,* p. 79.

The earlier edition contains seventeen illustrations, including an autographed frontispiece portrait of the author. The enlarged edition has all of the original illustrations and eight additional ones.

Probably no present-day anthologist has included any of J. G. Holland's poems in his work; yet as recently as 1900 Edmund Clarence Stedman reproduced four of Holland's poems in his *American Anthology*,[36] which is still the most representative and most famous anthology in its field.

Holland's verse means little to us of the twentieth century. But in its day it served an invaluable purpose: it brought the muse to multitudes of persons who scarcely knew even Longfellow or Whittier.[37]

How shall we account for the tremendous appeal of Holland's poetry to the readers of his time? The answer to this question is, I think, not so difficult as it might appear. Speaking of the most popular major American poet of Holland's generation, Professor Howard Mumford Jones says: "Lucidity, gentleness, musicality—these are the essential qualities of Longfellow's poetry." [38] Now it may readily be seen that Holland, an ardent admirer of Longfellow, had much in common with that well-beloved bard.

For one thing, Holland had musicality. Upon the competence of his craftsmanship I have already commented. And if there is any remaining doubt as to his capability of combining smooth numbers, easy rhymes, and pleasant imagery, one has only to read such stanzas as these from his lyric "Words":

> The robin repeats his two musical words,
>   The meadow-lark whistles his one refrain;
>   And steadily, over and over again,
> The same song swells from a hundred birds.

---

[36] *Op. cit.*, pp. 233–235, 588.
[37] See Bloom, *op. cit.*, p. 97.
[38] H. M. Jones: "Longfellow," p. 108. Chap. IX of *American Writers on American Literature*.

Bobolink, chickadee, blackbird, and jay,
Thrasher and woodpecker, cuckoo and wren,
Each sings its word, or its phrase, and then
It has nothing further to sing or to say.[39]

For another thing, Holland had gentleness. No characters, for example, could be more sweet-spirited than David in *Bitter-Sweet* or Kathrina in *Kathrina*.[40] But let us carry this matter of gentleness a little further. Let us note the manner in which Professor Jones defines it with reference to Longfellow: "a serene faith in goodness." [41] Well, as we have already seen, every one of Holland's major poems is replete with just such a faith. Every one of them concludes with the triumph of good as Holland sees it. In *Bitter-Sweet* all of the virtuous characters are made happy at the end, and even Edward the reprobate is spiritually redeemed. In *Kathrina* the poet-hero is ultimately converted to Christianity—and hence to "the peace and joy for which he has hungered"—through the noble example and the tender pleadings of his saintly wife. In *The Mistress of the Manse* two Christian soldiers, though enemies in the war, "exchange words of respect and love" on their deathbeds, and they go to adjoining graves to await the same undoubted resurrection in heaven—all of which is a supremely beautiful consolation to the good Christian woman who happens to be the wife of the one soldier and the sister of the other. This serene faith in goodness comes very close to what one authoritative critic has called the mainspring of sentimentalism; namely, "confidence in the goodness of average human nature." [42] And this sentimental-moralistic attitude "hit exactly the current taste" [43] of the "uncritical and unsophisticated generation" [43] in which Longfellow and Holland flourished.

Finally, Holland had lucidity. In a sense, in fact, he had

[39] *The Marble Prophecy, and Other Poems*, p. 36.
[40] See above, pp. 125–126, 130–131.
[41] Jones, *op. cit.*, p. 111.
[42] Ernest Bernbaum: *The Drama of Sensibility*. Quoted by G. R. Coffman: *Five Significant English Plays*, New York, 1930, p. 146.
[43] Parrington, *op. cit.*, II, 439.

lucidity to an even greater degree than Longfellow. As Samuel Bowles's biographer, George S. Merriam, declared just after Holland's death:

He [Holland] could think the thoughts and speak the speech of the common people. He represented that democratic quality in literature which our social conditions demand, and are only beginning to get. Take from your shelf at random a standard author other than a novelist, and read a page to the first man you chance to meet. Ten to one, he listens with a sort of uncomprehending look; the voice comes to him muffled, as of someone speaking in the next room, for most authors write out of a mental habit and equipment which is unfamiliar to the common people; they use a literary dialect—the dialect of a class, as much as is the dialect of science or theology. But take almost any book of Dr. Holland, and read it to any man or woman of common intelligence: the eye responds, they understand what he means; they agree or deny; they comprehend, they are moved, influenced. He was a man of the people, and the common people heard him gladly.[44]

When Merriam speaks of the difficulty that the common people have in comprehending the works of standard authors, he is obviously referring to such authors' penchant for out-of-the-way allusions. Now even Longfellow did not entirely avoid such allusions. Such references as "Orestes-like" (in the last stanza of "Hymn to the Night"), "O Philhellene" (in the second sonnet of "Three Friends of Mine"), "errands of the Paraclete" (in "Giotto's Tower"), and "the young Endymion" (in the sonnet on Keats) mean little or nothing to the reader devoid of classical background. The poetry of Holland, on the other hand, is almost totally free from such allusions. Holland's most recondite references are to Rhode Island Greenings, Baldwins, Flyers, Merinoes, and Carters,[45] —which, however, are perfectly comprehensible to any Yankee reader who knows apples and potatoes. Virtually the only old book to which Holland refers in his poetry is the Bible;

[44] Plunkett, *op. cit.,* pp. 34–35.
[45] *Bitter-Sweet,* pp. 76–79.

and, for the most part, his biblical allusions are the simplest,
the most obvious,—such as "Eden's fallen lord," [46] "the great
Immanuel," [47] and "the Apostolic Twelve." [47] It is, then, not
surprising that Holland's poetry found many readers, including readers on too low a cultural level to appreciate the best
efforts of the simple but cultivated Longfellow.

[46] *Bitter-Sweet,* p. 46.
[47] *Ibid.,* p. 91.

VII

Five Novels

At the beginning of our last chapter we cited a few of the handicaps that confronted the American novelist during the early and middle years of the last century. A further handicap now demands consideration; namely, the attitude of substantial Americans in general and moralists in particular toward fiction.

The dullest critics [says Mr. Carl Van Doren] contended that novels were lies; the pious, that they served no virtuous purpose; the strenuous, that they softened sturdy minds; the utilitarian, that they crowded out more useful books; the realistic, that they painted adventure too romantic and love too vehement; the patriotic, that dealing with European manners, they tended to confuse and dissatisfy republican youth.[1]

All middle-aged Americans who were reared in evangelical faiths have a distinct recollection of the annual revival meetings with their inevitable fulminations against dancing, card-playing, and theatre-going. And our septuagenarian and octogenarian elders can remember a fourth object of the revivalist's wrath: they can remember when all works of fiction—at least, of prose fiction—were denounced as unqualifiedly and indiscriminately as were plays and players. For the moralist of our grandfathers' day, the mere fact that a novel dealt with characters and incidents literally untrue to actuality was quite sufficient to damn it. In point of actual fact, no young lady by the name of Clarissa Harlowe ever had an affair with a young man by the name of Lovelace; therefore it was a lie, an abomination unto the Lord, for Richardson to report that she did. Seldom did the moralist bother about

1 Van Doren, *op. cit.*, p. 3.

the more important but more subtle fact that through bad motivation, overemphasis upon romantic love, and an illogical ending, a novel might present a distorted picture of life. Still less was he concerned with the distinction between truthfulness and factuality; for that distinction, vital as it is, was quite beyond his simple comprehension. General Grant, in the second chapter of his *Memoirs,* sorrowfully confesses that in his youth he read many novels, and his sorrow is apparently not mitigated by his further statement that most of these novels were of the sort rated as classics rather than trash.[2]

Speaking of conditions during the early years of our national existence, Professor G. Harrison Orians has this to say:

Novels, it was maintained, were subversive of the highest moral principles or, in short, were the primer of the Devil. In New England and Pennsylvania, moreover, novels were objected to, not only because of their fruits, pragmatically considered, but because they were fiction: they related that which had not occurred and had no basis in actual happening; they were bundles of *lies* and therefore not to be countenanced.[3]

That the conditions mentioned by Professor Orians continued for many years there can be no doubt. Ample documentary evidence, in fact, shows that they continued until at least the middle years of the nineteenth century. For example, the *Democratic Review* of May 1847 quotes with apparent approval the following remarks of a Bible Society agent about an old man addicted to novel-reading:

What will he do with his passion beyond the grave? Can he throw aside God's truth, and have fiction in heaven? Can he have it in hell? though more fitting there than in any other department of eternity![4]

2 U. S. Grant: *Personal Memoirs,* New York, 1885, I, 39.

3 G. H. Orians: "Censure of Fiction in American Romances and Magazines, 1789–1810," pp. 210–211. *Publications of the Modern Language Association,* LII. March, 1937.

4 *Op. cit.,* XX, 462.

More satiric, but no less severe, is an engraving by W. T. Matteson in the November 1847 issue of the *Union Magazine*.[5] This engraving is described as follows by the leading historian of American magazines:

[It] represents a woman sitting at an uncleared breakfast table reading a novel: the dog is at the meat, the cat is in the milk, the baby is crying, the husband is scolding, the daughter is pleading, the butcher-boy is waiting at the door; but the woman reads on serene and untroubled.[6]

Three or four years later an influential religious periodical lamented the fact that a newly established American monthly of high standing would consent to publish fiction at all:

Were it not for the occasional works of fiction to which the pages of the Magazine [*Harper's*] give currency . . . our commendation would be absolutely unqualified.[7]

From what we have already observed of the early life of Josiah Holland we may safely conclude that novel-reading formed no part of his childhood or youthful recreations. To the family of Harrison Holland a work of prose fiction must have been considered as defiling as a pack of cards. As has been suggested in an earlier chapter of this monograph, it is probable that not until Josiah entered the household of Judge Dewey at Northampton did he ever read a novel.[8]

Many years later, when Holland himself began writing novels, he felt called upon to apologize for doing so—or, at least, to justify the art of fiction on moral and religious grounds. In the preface of his first novel he said:

Fiction, though much abused by those who write it, and persistently traduced by those who do not comprehend its true mission, has always been a favorite mode of communicating truth, and has, for its support, the highest sanctions of Christianity. The author of the Christian system spake evermore in parables in the

---

[5] *Op. cit.*, Vol. II.
[6] Mott, pp. 417–418.
[7] *Methodist Quarterly Review*, XXXIII, 186. Jan., 1851.
[8] See above, p. 10.

illustration of important practical truth. In fact (let it be reverently uttered), the great principle of human nature which called Him into the world is identical with that on which the claims and power of legitimate fiction rest. He came to embody abstract truth in human relations, and the naked, incomprehensible idea of God, in the human form. He came to exhibit, in human development, the true nature of the divine life, and to demonstrate, in human experience, under the influence of legitimate human motives, the beauty of holiness. It was upon this principle that his wonderful parables were based. The necessity was to exhibit truth in its relations to the feeling, thinking, acting soul; and, in order to meet that necessity at that day, it was requisite that the case should be imagined and the relations created. In the birth of new questions, in the revolution of opinions, and in the shifting aspect of affairs, the great necessity becomes perpetual, and the requisites for its satisfaction remain the same.[9]

Holland's career as a novelist began fortuitously. When he was collecting material for his *History of Western Massachusetts* it evidently occurred to him that his native region was as interesting a field for historical romance as was Scott's Scotland or Ainsworth's England. The result was *The Bay-Path*, published in 1857 by Scribner.

This novel, founded upon historical incidents and concerned largely with historical characters, marks Holland's only venture into the realm of the historical romance. Its plot may be related briefly.

William Pynchon, chief magistrate of the settlement of Agawam (Springfield) on the Connecticut River, is a man revered in the settlement for his justice and mercy. His patience with heretics, however, is sternly disapproved by the Agawam minister, the Reverend George Moxon, a rigid and none-too-tolerant Calvinist. Particularly annoying to Mr. Moxon is Squire Pynchon's leniency toward John Woodcock, a ruffianly, defiant man who has stubbornly refused to repent of his sins and join the church.

Mr. Moxon has Woodcock haled before the magistrate

---

[9] *The Bay-Path,* pp. vii–viii.

upon various charges, the most serious of which is that Woodcock and his motherless little daughter Mary have practised wizardry and witchcraft upon the Moxon children. In each instance Squire Pynchon deals as gently as possible with Woodcock, his theory being that the ruffian is far more likely to be reformed by moral suasion than by persecution. And, to aggravate the situation in the eyes of Mr. Moxon, the squire's grown daughter Mary befriends the unfortunate little Woodcock girl in many ways.

Finally Mr. Moxon succeeds in making Agawam so uncomfortable for Woodcock that the latter leaves for parts unknown. Mary Woodcock is left at the settlement in charge of the Pynchons—or, rather, in charge of Mary Pynchon, who has married Elizur Holyoke, the upstanding young son of one of Squire Pynchon's old friends in the Massachusetts Bay colony.

Mary Woodcock grows to womanhood and is wedded to Hugh Parsons, an industrious, self-respecting youth of her own humble class. But Mr. Moxon is relentless in his determination to make trouble for her, and eventually his persecutions drive her to such violent insanity that she murders her own baby. For this act of infanticide the young woman is placed upon trial and sentenced to death.

Meanwhile Squire Pynchon is having trouble of his own. He has published a theological book which is much too liberal for the Massachusetts of his day, and he is summoned to appear before the General Court in Boston to answer to the charge of heresy. Firm in the conviction that he has done no wrong, the squire valiantly defends himself; but after a time, wearied to the point of physical illness, he is browbeaten into making a recantation. He is then permitted to return to Agawam and resume his duties as chief magistrate.

The downfall of Mary Woodcock, the virtual exile of her father, and the discomfiture of Squire Pynchon fail to bring real happiness to the Reverend George Moxon. He leads, in fact, a most miserable life. His daughters, although now at the age of womanhood, are stunted in mind and body. He himself is oppressed by melancholia. He is regarded with increasing disfavor by the members of his flock. Indeed, even among the most orthodox, he is less revered, less loved, than the heretical but kindly Squire Pynchon. There comes a time when Mr. Moxon is glad to escape to England.

Squire Pynchon is also obliged to leave the colonies. When the authorities in Boston learn that he still holds to his heretical views, he is summoned to reappear before the General Court. Disregarding his second summons, he departs for the mother country. But he does not go away friendless. On the contrary, he is bidden an affectionate Godspeed by the entire populace of Agawam.

On shipboard he is joined by John Woodcock, whose years of exile from Agawam have been spent among the Indians. Woodcock, now a chastened, God-fearing man, becomes the loyal, devoted follower of the man who has shown him so many kindnesses.

Back at Agawam the affairs of the settlement are placed in the hands of Squire Pynchon's son John, his son-in-law Elizur Holyoke, and a highly respected deacon named Samuel Chapin.

The book takes its title from the name of the path or trail leading from the old Massachusetts Bay settlement to the newer settlements on the Connecticut River.

The Bay-Path evoked favorable comment from at least one prominent periodical, the *North American Review*.

Not everyone [said its reviewer] who is skilled in antiquarian research, and able to compile a good history, succeeds in writing an historical novel. In the work before us, however, Mr. Holland has proved that the gifts of the novelist and the historian are not incompatible. The characters of his tale are well conceived and well sustained, and the story . . . is interesting from beginning to end. The descriptions of scenery are those of a careful observer, and the exhibition of opinions, dogmas, and religious differences, as they were two centuries ago, shows that the author's sympathies are large, generous, and catholic. . . . Mr. Holland, as it seems to us, has not been equally successful in reproducing the manners or the conversation of the Puritan age in Massachusetts. The language which his men and women use is not the traditional language of the early settlers, or such as is left to us in the private journals or the printed sermons. . . . It may be said, however, that adherence to the ancient dialect in such a story would make its conversations insufferably tedious.[10]

There is little reason to quarrel with this enthusiastic review; for, on the whole, its points are well taken. Both as a narrative and as a historical picture *The Bay-Path* is at least the equal of most of the popular romances that flooded the market during the historical-novel craze at the beginning of our own century.[11] Doubtless its theological discussions would weary the average present-day reader, but even these are less obtrusive than might be supposed. And, as the reviewer has truly pointed out, "the author's sympathies are large, generous, and catholic." In this connection, we have observed elsewhere that Holland, in middle and later life, was by no means an utter bigot in his theology.[12] In this same connection, it is important to remember that by the middle years of the nineteenth century the liberal influence of the Unitarian movement extended far beyond the relatively small membership of the Unitarian denomination.[13] What with the eloquence, the sweet reasonableness, and the enlightened humanitarianism of such preachers as James Freeman Clarke and such lecturers as Ralph Waldo Emerson, Unitarianism inevitably leavened orthodox thought; it inevitably left its mark upon many a pious individual who would have been horrified at the appellation *Unitarian*—including such individuals as Josiah Holland.

So far as lack of accurate dialect in *The Bay-Path* is concerned, it must be remarked that Josiah Gilbert Holland was never a student of linguistics. Of the history of New England idiom and pronunciation he could hardly have known much.

---

[10] *Op. cit.,* LXXXV, 258–259. July, 1857.
[11] Van Doren, *op. cit.,* pp. 248–255.
[12] See above, pp. 49–50, 92.
[13] Fish, *op. cit.,* p. 187.

Indeed, at the time *The Bay-Path* was written, his knowledge of dialects must have been limited to a superficial observation that the Southern speech of his own day differed markedly from that of western Massachusetts.

It cannot be said that *The Bay-Path* earned for its author a national reputation. That feat, as we have seen, was to be accomplished by *Bitter-Sweet* a year later. Indeed, *The Bay-Path,* although perhaps the least faulty of Holland's novels, was at the same time probably the least popular. True, it was reprinted in 1882, in 1885, in 1909, and in 1914; [14] but these reprintings may be ascribed more to the general popularity of the author than to any particular demand for his earliest and least-heralded novel.

Miss Gilbert's Career (1860) had the good fortune to come off the press while people were still talking enthusiastically about *Bitter-Sweet.* Consequently, Scribner doubtless accepted its manuscript with few misgivings.

Miss Gilbert's Career, as may be noted from a synopsis, is as thoroughly contemporary in setting as *The Bay-Path* is historical.

Theophilus Gilbert, physician and leading citizen of the village of Crampton, New Hampshire, has a talented and ambitious daughter, Fanny, of whom he is exceedingly proud. Although Miss Fanny is but sixteen years old, she is about to complete a romantic novel.

Next door to the Gilberts lives the Widow Blague with her two sons, one of them a young man of eighteen, the other an infant in arms. Now that Mrs. Blague has become widowed, it becomes necessary for her elder son, Arthur, to secure steady employment. Accordingly Dr. Gilbert finds a position for Arthur in a small textile mill near Crampton. Old Ruggles, proprietor of the mill, is a vulgar, overbearing man who browbeats and underpays his employees and who has dealt harshly and unjustly with the late Mr. Blague; but since the Blagues are sorely in need of an income, the bright,

14 See above, p. 105, footnote 10.

capable, and refined Arthur swallows his pride and goes to work at the mill.

Here Arthur meets Mary Hammett, a pretty, well-mannered, and surprisingly well-educated girl of twenty-two, whose past life is a mystery. An accident to Old Ruggles at the mill necessitates Arthur's taking temporary charge of the establishment and staying at the Ruggles residence. He is thus compelled to endure the unwelcome society of Mrs. Ruggles and her daughter Leonora, who prove to be quite as vulgar as Old Ruggles himself.

Since Arthur can no longer be at home, he wishes to find a suitable person to stay with Mrs. Blague and her infant son. Fortunately at this very time the Crampton village school is in need of a mistress, and it occurs to Arthur that Mary Hammett would be ideal both as schoolmistress and as lodger at the Blague home. Arthur loses no time in communicating his thought to Dr. Gilbert, who happens to be president of the school board. Although the doctor is at first reluctant to consider a millgirl about whose family connections he and Crampton know nothing, an interview with the young woman quickly convinces him that Arthur's judgment in the matter is entirely sound. Accordingly Miss Hammett leaves the mill for the much more desirable surroundings of Crampton school and the Blague residence.

Meanwhile Miss Gilbert has completed her novel and has had little difficulty in persuading her father to seek a publisher for it. Since letters fail to bring satisfactory results, the doctor decides to make a special trip to New York to interview publishers personally. In the office of Kilgore brothers, Dr. Gilbert is rebuffed by the haughty Mr. Kilgore, senior member of the firm. Mr. Kilgore, however, makes a disparaging comment upon a young publisher named Sargent, a former clerk of his, and this chance remark inspires the doctor to try the firm of Sargent. The younger publisher, after some hesitation, accepts the manuscript.

Dr. Gilbert, back at Crampton, grows lonely in his widowerhood and falls in love with the mysterious Mary Hammett. He proposes and is rejected. Arthur Blague likewise loves the attractive young teacher vainly. Miss Gilbert comes to look upon Miss Hammett as a wise and kindly but sometimes painfully frank older sister. When Fanny discusses her novel with Mary and mentions the name of Mr. Sargent, Mary displays such emotions as to convince the reader that Mr. Sargent must have played an important part in her mysterious past. Fanny's novel, upon publication, is not at all the success that the girl had dreamed of. The only important critics who review it declare what Mary Hammett has already suggested: that its young author is too immature, too ignorant of life, to achieve anything approaching a masterpiece.

The appearance of Dan Buck, a dissolute New Yorker, at Crampton brings important matters to a crisis. Buck comes ostensibly to work for Old Ruggles, but spends much of his time forcing unwelcome attentions upon Mary Hammett. It now becomes evident to the reader that Buck is fully acquainted with Mary's past and that he purposes to expose it.

Soon Old Ruggles suffers from a series of calamities. Dan Buck elopes with Leonora Ruggles; the Ruggles mill is burned to the ground; and Old Ruggles commits suicide.

Mr. Kilgore, of New York, now appears mysteriously at Crampton, in angry pursuit of Mary Hammett, whose whereabouts he has evidently learned from Dan Buck. It now transpires that Miss Hammett is really Miss Kilgore, daughter of the great publisher, and that she fled from home because her father would not permit her to marry young Sargent. Miss Kilgore seeks refuge in the home of Dr. Gilbert, whither her irate father pursues her. At the Gilbert residence Mr. Kilgore is stricken with a sudden illness so serious that he is unable to leave the place. His daughter dutifully nurses him back to health, and a complete reconciliation is effected between father and daughter. Young Sargent comes from New York and marries Mary Kilgore—with the blessing of her father.

Arthur Blague, now out of steady employment and unable

to afford a college education, prepares himself at home for the ministry of the Gospel, and serves very ably as an occasional supply preacher. Much of his time, however, is devoted to caring for his little brother, who has become a permanent cripple and imbecile as a result of an accident encountered on Mary Kilgore's wedding day.

Fanny Gilbert blossoms into a brilliant young woman and a highly successful novelist and often visits at the delightful home of the Sargents in New York, where she receives the admiring attentions of many distinguished personages. As time goes on, however, she finds less and less satisfaction in the plaudits of the world, and more and more satisfaction in the friendships of her simple intimates at Crampton. Arthur Blague's consecrated and self-sacrificing life wins her respect and then her love. And Arthur, perceiving Fanny's feelings, loves her in return.

Through the quiet efforts of Mary Sargent, Arthur is surprised to find himself called to the pastorate of a fashionable New York church, of which the Sargents are leading members. Although delighted at the wonderful opportunity, Arthur hesitates, because of his younger brother, to accept the call. The death of the poor little cripple soon leaves Arthur free to marry Fanny Gilbert and go to the metropolis.

Other interesting characters in the story include Aunt Catharine, Dr. Gilbert's housekeeper and sister-in-law, a plain-spoken but admirable and affectionate old lady; Tom Lampson, an uncouth but warm-hearted and diligent village lad, who becomes a successful railroader; and Fred Gilbert, Fanny's intelligent and amiable but rather weak brother.

The *Atlantic Monthly* gave *Miss Gilbert's Career* a moderately laudatory review.

The volume [said the *Atlantic* critic] adds to vivacity and interest vigorous sketches of character and scenery, droll conversation and incidents, a frequent and kindly humor, and, underlying all, a true, earnest purpose, which claims not only approval for the author, but respect for the man.[15]

15 *Op. cit.,* VII, 125–126. Jan., 1861.

But the critic adds:

That any clever girl will be kept from the perilous paths of authorship by the warnings . . . of any novel whatever, we are not prepared to assert; we venture to say no one will be deterred by the history of Miss Fanny Gilbert.[15]

At least one British periodical, the London *Athenaeum,* took notice of *Miss Gilbert's Career.* The *Athenaeum* review was summarized as follows by a writer in the Springfield *Republican,* apparently Holland himself:

The London *Athenaeum* speaks of Dr. Holland's story "Miss Gilbert's Career" as a work of talent, good sense and good feeling, illustrative of American life, but that [*sic*] the figures are hard and stiff, and that it is the author, after all, who makes the speeches.[16]

In short, then, the *Athenaeum* critic found characterization to be the weakest feature of *Miss Gilbert's Career.*

The twentieth-century reader, however, is likely to find more glaring faults. For instance, a study of the plot of this novel will reveal plenty of bad motivation. The mysterious past of Mary Hammett, the unmitigated villainy of Dan Buck, and the entire manner in which Mary's mystery is cleared and her domestic problems are solved—these, of course, are melodrama of the most patent sort. The romantic way in which Arthur Blague is rewarded by a fashionable New York pastorate is likewise claptrap.

Nevertheless *Miss Gilbert's Career* has much to commend it—more, I suspect, than commentators on American literature have generally recognized. The setting of the book, as we have observed, is contemporary. And in many important particulars it is authentic. The pictures of Old Ruggles' mill,[17] of mid-nineteenth-century modes of travel,[18] and even of publishers' offices in New York [19] are more than ordinarily

15 *Op. cit.,* VII, 125–126. Jan., 1861.
16 *Books, Authors and Art, op. cit.,* March 9, 1861.
17 *Op. cit.,* pp. 44–45, 57–59.
18 *Op. cit.,* pp. 140–148.
19 *Op. cit.,* 149–159.

well drawn; they are good bits of local color. Dr. Theophilus
Gilbert is, on the whole, a successful portraiture; and Aunt
Catharine and Tom Lampson are certainly better than mere
types. As for Miss Fanny Gilbert, if she herself is not quite
convincing, her early aspirations and experiences are fully
conceivable if not exactly probable. In other words, Josiah
Gilbert Holland produced a realistic novel—at least a super-
ficially realistic novel—a full decade before any of the so-
called pioneer American realistic novelists began to publish.[20] To mention Holland in the same category with Mark
Twain and Bret Harte, Howells and James, would, of course,
be utterly preposterous. But Holland, none the less, anticipated these much abler and more penetrating realists. Nor
need we be greatly perturbed by the fact that Josiah Holland
as a realist built better than he knew or intended. What if he
did have an axe to grind? What if his main purpose was to
prove that young ladies have no business with careers? The
fact remains that he did achieve the semblance of a realistic
novel. And in the United States of 1860 that was no mean
accomplishment. Incidentally, *Miss Gilbert's Career* was reprinted as late as 1909,[21] almost half a century after the appearance of the original edition.

For over a decade after the appearance of *Miss Gilbert's
Career*, Holland wrote no more novels. During the interim
he was busy lecturing, writing essays, touring Europe, launching his new magazine, and trying—not quite successfully—to
repeat the triumph of *Bitter-Sweet*. In the autumn of 1872,
however, the doctor's numerous admirers were greeted by a
pleasant surprise. The November issue of *Scribner's Monthly*
contained the first installment of a new Holland novel,
Arthur Bonnicastle. Further installments followed in the

[20] According to Professor Quinn (*American Fiction*, p. 257), "realism came
into its own" in the work of Howells, whose first novel was *Their Wedding
Journey* (1871). Much earlier, of course, there had been sporadic examples of
realism—for example, Caroline M. S. Kirkland's *A New Home—Who'll Fol-
low?* (1839) and A. B. Longstreet's *Georgia Scenes* (1835). (See Quinn, *op. cit.*,
p. 100). Neither of these works, however, is a novel.

[21] See above, p. 105, footnote 10.

next eleven issues, so that the serial was completed in October 1873. To add to the attractiveness of the new novel, each installment was introduced by a drawing from the pencil of Mary Hallock. Miss Hallock, at that time a girl in her twenties, had already established herself as one of America's most popular illustrators. Subsequently, as Mary Hallock Foote, she was to win greater renown in the field of fiction; but it was as an illustrator that she first gained recognition.[22] *Arthur Bonnicastle* was published in book form in 1873 without the illustrations. It was republished in 1882, in 1901, in 1905, in 1908, and in 1922, a fact attesting to its great and fairly enduring popularity. Here is a synopsis of *Arthur Bonnicastle*.

Mrs. Sanderson, a wealthy and eccentric elderly widow in a small New England industrial city, becomes interested in a distant relative, Arthur Bonnicastle, the little son of one of her tenants, and offers to adopt him. Arthur's father, an affectionate parent, is loath to part with the boy, but being a poor man with a large family and realizing that Mrs. Sanderson can give the boy the best of educational and social advantages, he finally consents to the proposed adoption.

Arthur is sent to "The Bird's Nest," a boys' boarding school conducted by a Mr. and Mrs. Bird, an amiable and highly idealistic couple. At school he becomes intimate with Henry Hulm, a very manly lad who bears a striking resemblance to a portrait which Arthur has seen at Mrs. Sanderson's, but about which the old lady has been extremely secretive. At vacation time Henry is invited to accompany Arthur home, but for some mysterious reason, the former chooses to visit the latter's parents rather than Mrs. Sanderson. At the Bonnicastle home Henry becomes interested in Arthur's pretty sister Claire. Meanwhile Arthur becomes interested in Millie Bradford, the winsome child of a philanthropic gentleman who has shown the Bonnicastles many kindnesses.

<hr>

[22] For short biographical sketch of Mary Hallock Foote (1847–   ), see *Universal Cyclopaedia*, IV, 439.

After finishing their course at "The Bird's Nest," Arthur and Henry are admitted to Yale, where they spend four years. At college Henry proves to be a much more diligent student than his companion. Arthur, more eager for social prestige than for academic attainments, cultivates the acquaintance of a gay young man named Livingston, scion of a wealthy and fashionable New York family. Accompanying Livingston home for a Christmas vacation, Arthur drinks his first glass of wine and falls into evil ways. In fact, while making New Year's calls he becomes inebriated and disgraces himself. Finally he is sobered and humiliated by the discovery that he is calling at a home where Mr. Bradford and his daughter Millie are guests. Wondering whether the Bradfords can ever forgive his shocking behavior, he vows that he will never touch liquor again.

When Arthur graduates from college without honors, Mr. Bradford, Mr. Bird, and Mr. Bonnicastle hold a serious conference. They decide that Arthur has had more money than is good for him, particularly since the youth has never had to earn a penny.

During Arthur's college years his guardian has felt increasingly the infirmities of old age and has, from time to time, sought the invigorating air of a seaside resort. On one of her sojourns at the resort she has found a much-needed companion and nurse in the person of a refined middle-aged woman named Mrs. Belden. During a later sojourn of the old lady's, Arthur persuades Henry Hulm to stay with him at the Sanderson mansion, and on this occasion great excitement occurs. The mansion is invaded by robbers; and Henry, while bravely repulsing the marauders, sustains a broken leg. It is thereupon decided that Henry must remain at the mansion during his convalescence, and that Mrs. Sanderson and Mrs. Belden must be summoned home. The return of the two women adds another mystery to the story, for Mrs. Belden greets young Hulm with truly maternal affection.

An earnest conversation between Arthur and Mr. Bradford now clears two mysteries so far as Arthur and the reader are concerned. The portrait at the mansion is that of Mrs. Sanderson's son, who turned out to be a ne'er-do-well, was disowned by his mother, and died in poverty far from home, leaving a wife and one son. The hapless man's widow, a total stranger to Mrs. Sanderson, wrote an appealing letter to the old lady and was denied all aid. The widow, who subsequently took the name of Belden, was Henry Hulm's mother; and Henry is therefore Mrs. Sanderson's rightful heir. Mr. Bradford now intimates that Arthur is morally obligated to apprise his guardian of the facts and to renounce all claim to the Sanderson estate.

At about this juncture Livingston, the gay young New Yorker, turns up in the little city. Meeting Arthur on the street, he refuses to explain his mission in the town, but it soon transpires that he has come to get better acquainted with Millie Bradford, who greatly attracted him on the occasion of the memorable New Year's call in New York. Arthur now feels that his own cause with Millie is more hopeless than ever; for Livingston's secure social position, handsome person, and charming manners seem quite sufficient to allure any young girl such as Millie. Moreover, Livingston's sobriety and dignity on the fateful New Year's day, in contrast to Arthur's shameful condition, must have made an indelible impression upon Millie.

Everything, however, turns out well. Arthur, of his own initiative, bravely surrenders his place to the rightful heir, and thus wins the respect and love of Millie, who finds Livingston to be a shallow pleasure seeker and a snob. Henry Hulm, heir to unexpected wealth, decides to live altruistically by becoming a minister of the Gospel. Arthur becomes a successful lawyer and an upstanding Christian layman and citizen—and, of course, marries Millie. Henry marries Claire Bonnicastle.

Apart from the main plot the book contains several memorable characters. There is, for example, Mrs. Bonnicastle, an efficient and conscientious housewife, but a chronic pessimist. There is Jenks, Mrs. Sanderson's man-servant, an ignorant and illiterate but warm-hearted and highly imaginative old man. And there is Peter Mullens, who, both as Yale divinity student and as pastor, is notable for his dowdy dress and his everlasting propensity for sponging upon his friends.

As has been the case with nearly all of J. G. Holland's works, the critics took much less kindly to *Arthur Bonnicastle* than did the public.

> We believe [said the *Harper's* reviewer] that the novel was designed to have a good influence . . . but we doubt the propriety of indulging in unsatisfactory discussions of religious principles among fictitious incidents.[23]

The *Nation* was more severe.

> What the novel undertakes to show [declared its reviewer] is, apparently, the injurious effects of wealth and self-indulgence on the young. . . . Poor Arthur's little frigid temptations are hardly more than the outbreaking of his petty, priggish nature. He is the most colorless hero ever known. In fact, the whole book, while written with the best intentions in the world, is too pallid, too lifeless to deserve praise.[24]

Thirty years after Holland's death, however, Professor Reuben Post Halleck, an outstandingly authoritative commentator upon American literature, called *Arthur Bonnicastle* "the best" [25] of Holland's five novels. And a much more recent authority agrees that "Holland's masterpiece is undoubtedly *Arthur Bonnicastle*." [26]

Not much can be said for the plot of *Arthur Bonnicastle*. For the most part it is a clumsy combination of the stereotyped and the far-fetched. Even the element of suspense, elaborately as it has been worked out, does not grip the mentally alert reader; for the solution of every "mystery" is patent from the beginning. In this particular, Josiah Hol-

23 *Op. cit.*, XLVII, 777. Oct., 1873.
24 *Op. cit.*, XVII, 277. Oct. 23, 1873.
25 Reuben Post Halleck: *History of American Literature*, New York, Cincinnati, Chicago, 1911, p. 406.
26 Bloom, *op. cit.*, p. 101.

land might well have taken a leaf from the notebook of one of his British contemporaries, Wilkie Collins. The latter, although often crude, melodramatic, and sensational, knew how to keep his readers guessing to the very end. In fact, his *Moonstone* and *Woman in White* are still capable of keeping readers guessing. It is difficult to believe, however, that many intelligent readers, even sixty years ago, were greatly fooled by the "mysteries" of *Arthur Bonnicastle*.

The characters of this novel are not much better than the plot. None of them, I think, is the equal of Dr. Gilbert or Aunt Catharine, in *Miss Gilbert's Career;* and most of them are indistinct or unconvincing puppets. Arthur may not be the most colorless hero ever known, but he is surely one of the most colorless of heroes; and Henry Hulm, for all of his alleged virtues, is not a whit more appealing than Arthur. The waxen Mrs. Sanderson might have stepped out of almost any of the novels of Mary J. Holmes, Mrs. E. D. E. N. Southworth, or Augusta J. Evans Wilson. Mr. Bird is somewhat more human; but despite Professor Paul Monroe's assertion that in the Bird's Nest "the New England private school receives probably the most attractive treatment given to a school in American literature," [27] one cannot escape the feeling that Bird's establishment is a rather dull affair. Jenks the servant is mildly amusing at times, but he seems far more an emasculated Dickens character than a flesh-and-blood American. Livingston, the gilded youth from New York, is fairly well drawn, and he has probably won more sympathy from the upper strata of Holland's readers than his creator ever intended him to have. Perhaps the most successfully portrayed character in the book is the Reverend Peter Mullens. Unfortunately, however, Mullens is not essential to the plot, and his portrait is often botched by a superfluity of inane expository comment.

The redeeming feature of *Arthur Bonnicastle* is its comparative wealth of really memorable incidents. The New

---

[27] Paul Monroe: "Education." Chap. XXIII of *The Cambridge History of American Literature,* III, 416.

York scenes, particularly the Episcopal service [28] and Arthur's New Year inebriation,[29] are well done as far as they go. So are the parts relating to the New England revival meeting.[30] The scenes at Yale are, for the most part, not so good; for J. G. Holland's acquaintance with college life was, of course, both scant and indirect. In this connection, however, we must make one happy exception. The scene in which Peter Mullens' fellow students surprise that mendicant young man with a "shower" of their cast-off clothing [31] is as entertaining and as credible as anything in the book. After all, college pranks remain pretty much the same from generation to generation. Some college alumnus must have suggested the Mullens "shower" to Dr. Holland, and Holland evidently made good use of the suggestion.

Arthur Bonnicastle being the first Holland novel that was both widely and unfavorably reviewed, its author undoubtedly experienced many unhappy hours during the year 1873. Some authors consider it better to be damned than to be ignored, but this was not true of Josiah Holland. He craved recognition; but he wanted plaudits, not cat-calls. Much as he might protest to his friends that a large and enthusiastic reading public meant more to him than all the comments of the penny-a-liners, the shafts of the critics struck home. As Professor Boyesen has pointed out, J. G. Holland was too thin-skinned, too confident of his literary gifts, to laugh good-naturedly at the slings and arrows of outrageous critics.[32] But the persevering Timothy Titcomb was ready to try again— and again.

In the twelve issues of *Scribner's Monthly* for 1875 will be found the installments of Holland's *Sevenoaks*. The twelve illustrations are by a little-known artist and engraver, one

[28] *Op. cit.,* p. 241.
[29] *Ibid.,* pp. 245–247.
[30] *Ibid.,* pp. 148–151, 156–157, 161–168.
[31] *Ibid.,* pp. 259–267.
[32] See above, p. 66.

J. P. Davis. This novel was issued in book form a short time before the appearance of the last serial installment.

Sevenoaks, like Holland's earlier novels, has a small Yankee community for its principal locale. It does, however, involve New York far more extensively than any of the author's previous fictional efforts.

The plot of *Sevenoaks* is concerned mainly with the activities of Robert Belcher, millionaire manufacturer, who is virtual owner of the small northeastern industrial town of Sevenoaks.

By the double means of wealth and a vulgarly assertive personality, Belcher holds the whip hand over almost the entire population of the community. Among the many persons whom he has browbeaten and defrauded is one Paul Benedict, an inventor, who now languishes in the insane ward of the county poorhouse, just outside Sevenoaks. Years earlier, Benedict has invented a rifle of incalculable value in warfare; but Belcher, having cheated him of the patent rights, has dubbed the invention the Belcher rifle and has amassed a fortune upon its manufacture and sale. With Benedict in the poorhouse lives his little son Harry. Mrs. Benedict is dead.

Jim Fenton, unlettered woodsman and trapper, erstwhile companion of Benedict, effects the escape of Benedict and the boy from the place of their incarceration. Belcher, hearing of the escape, offers a handsome reward for their apprehension; but they are not found, and Paul Benedict is given up for dead. Living at Fenton's secluded place in the woods, Benedict speedily recovers his physical and mental health.

The greedy Belcher, turning his energies to new fields of conquest, interests the people of Sevenoaks in some worthless Pennsylvania oil stock and greatly enhances his fortune at the expense of numerous persons. Discovery of the fraudulent character of this enterprise will inevitably make Sevenoaks an undesirable place of residence for Mr. Belcher, but the shrewd manufacturer has already laid careful plans to meet that contingency. He purchases a princely mansion in New York, removes with his family to the metropolis, and plunges into a whirl of high society and high finance. In the course of his social rounds he becomes infatuated with a Mrs. Dillingham, a brilliant and beautiful widow.

Meanwhile, a summer vacationist at Jim Fenton's northern woodland camp is a prominent New York lawyer named Balfour. The latter, who is already on intimate and friendly terms with Jim, becomes deeply interested in Paul Benedict and his case; and it soon becomes evident to the reader that in due time Mr. Balfour will seek legal redress for the grievous wrong that Belcher has done Benedict. Before he leaves the summer camp, Mr. Balfour has arranged with the reluctant but grateful Mr. Benedict that little Harry Benedict shall accompany Mr. Balfour to New York, live temporarily with the Balfour family, and enjoy the best of metropolitan educational and social advantages.

Soon after Harry Benedict's arrival in New York, Mr. Belcher recognizes the boy and lures him to the Belcher mansion for the purpose of learning whether Paul Benedict is alive and, if so, where he is hiding. The lad, however, escapes Belcher's clutches and, of course, reports his harrowing experience to Mr. Balfour. The immediate upshot of this affair is a letter of rebuke and stern warning from Mr. Balfour to Mr. Belcher.

But Belcher is a persistent man. He puts detectives upon the trail of Paul Benedict and, in this connection, he seeks the aid of Mrs. Dillingham. That worldly lady, apparently willing to assist Mr. Belcher in his nefarious scheme, gets in touch with the Benedict boy, wins his confidence, and sets out to obtain the information that Belcher so eagerly desires. The winsome, confiding child, however, quickly gains the genuine affection of Mrs. Dillingham, and the woman turns traitor to the rascally Belcher—to whom, by the way, she owes nothing. In her new determination to side with the Benedict boy, she is powerfully aided by the unwitting Mr. Belcher himself, who is so madly, recklessly in love with her that he fully and brazenly reveals to her the history of his persecution of Paul Benedict. In fact, not until he has tried vainly to win Mrs. Dillingham as his paramour does he begin to suspect that he may have overshot his mark.

Mr. Belcher's plunges into the high finance of Wall Street include the purchase of majority stock in the Crooked Valley Railroad, a run-down property which he purposes to rehabilitate on so grand a scale as to make himself America's foremost capitalist. At first his plans move so successfully that he is hailed on the Street by the proud title of "General." Before long, however, his reckless and unscrupulous tactics hasten his railroad to the brink of ruin. Meanwhile he has failed utterly to bring Paul Benedict out of hiding.

The psychological time has now arrived for Mr. Balfour to bring suit in behalf of his outraged friend and client, Mr. Benedict. In the trial, which is a spectacular one, the lovely Mrs. Dillingham appears as a highly effective surprise witness for the plaintiff. Belcher is proved to be a forger as well as a cheat, and Benedict is at last accorded the rich fruits of his patience and ingenuity. Belcher, deserted by his friends, with whom he has never been capable of dealing fairly, flees ignominiously to Canada in order to escape the penitentiary.

Paul Benedict and his son now settle down to a pleasant life at the former Belcher mansion in Sevenoaks. Mr. Benedict's charming hostess is Mrs. Dillingham, who—the reader has been surprised to learn—is the inventor's sister. Years earlier the haughty woman snobbishly turned her back upon her brother because he was regarded as the family ne'er-do-well and because he married beneath the Benedict social level. But, in the words of the master dramatist, "All's well that ends well." Mrs. Dillingham's spiritual regeneration began at that fateful moment when her heart went out to little Harry Benedict.

In the concluding chapter the reader is given to understand that Mr. Benedict is quietly providing a modest but adequately comfortable income for Belcher's unfortunate wife and children. The story closes with a happy gathering at the Benedict mansion. Of course the Balfours are there, and so is Jim Fenton, that brave and warm-hearted wood-man who started Mr. Benedict upon the road to health and prosperity. Jim, by the way, is now the proprietor of a flourishing summer hotel and the husband of one of the most estimable women in Sevenoaks. The last rumor concerning the inglorious Belcher is that he has become a bartender on a St. Lawrence River boat.

Prominent critics were by no means slow in telling what they thought of *Sevenoaks;* and most of their comments, as will be observed, were unenthusiastic.

The book [said the reviewer for the *Atlantic*] is a satire on the life of a coarse man who becomes wealthy and enters into successive deliberate frauds . . . until he overreaches himself. . . . Yet it is not so much a satire as a rebuke; for Dr. Holland has hardly the patience with wrong-doing which is requisite to satire. . . . The novel is readable, has the advantage of being based on sound morality, and contains considerable humor. But it is very far from being a true work of the imagination.[33]

Robert Belcher [protested the reviewer for *Harper's*] is too coarse and vulgar a rascal to be a centre piece, and too exceptionally so to be a truly artistic piece of character-drawing.[34]

But this critic admitted:

The action of the story is rapid . . . and the trial scene is . . . original . . . and managed with very decided artistic skill.[34]

Dr. Holland's instrument [declared the critic for the *Nation*] is not so much the lyre as the melodeon, as he proceeds to narrate the infamous life of just such a rich manufacturer, speculator, and "railway king" as is known to readers of the newspapers of the period.[35]

At this point, however, it is only fair to add that a very recent and highly authoritative critic, Arthur Hobson Quinn, has spoken more generously of *Sevenoaks.* According to Professor Quinn, *Sevenoaks*

<hr>

33 *Op. cit.,* XXXVII, 117–118. Jan., 1876.
34 *Op. cit.,* LII, 467. Feb., 1876.
35 *Op. cit.,* XXI, 374. Dec. 9. 1875.

. . . is a better novel [than *Arthur Bonnicastle*], for the plot
is more thoroughly worked out. . . . Belcher's final catastrophe,
brought on by his forgery of Benedict's transfer of his patent
rights, and the gradual breaking down of his character through
his dissipation, are . . . well portrayed. He comes near to being
a great portrait of a moral failure, and if Holland had not
stopped so often to preach, the effect would have been greatly
strengthened.[36]

Sevenoaks, we may suppose, was J. G. Holland's most ambitious novel. Certainly its plot is more elaborately developed
than that of any other Holland narrative, and its major developments are less easily anticipated than are those of *Arthur Bonnicastle*. Its action too, as the *Harper's* critic pointed
out, is rapid—sufficiently rapid, indeed, to hold the interest
of any present-day reader. Unfortunately, however, it has the
besetting weakness of all of Holland's plots: it will not hold
water. That the villainous Robert Belcher might get his just
deserts is entirely believable. That Paul Benedict might re-
gain both his health and his legal rights is conceivable if not
probable. But the most important means by which these ends
are consummated are wholly unconvincing. Jim Fenton and
Mr. Balfour are much too convenient accessories; they over-
tax the reader's credulity at every turn. And Balfour, by the
way, is utterly colorless; he never quite comes to life. Then,
too, the sudden transformation of Mrs. Dillingham from a
beautiful villainess into a virtuous and devoted sister is quite
beyond the belief of even the most gullible reader. Such a
transformation might be acceptable in Elizabethan drama,
but in a modern novel it will not do.

As regards the element of character, *Sevenoaks* is probably the weakest of Holland's novels. Belcher, as the *Harper's*
critic has said, is too coarse and vulgar a rascal to be an
artistic piece of character-drawing. And Belcher is, by wide
odds, the dominant character of the book! The only characters in *Sevenoaks* who furnish much human interest in
themselves are Jim Fenton and the eccentric spinster who be-

[36] Quinn, *op. cit.,* p. 191.

comes his wife. And both of these characters are dragged in; they do not belong except by arbitrary fiat of the author.

Sevenoaks, like *Arthur Bonnicastle,* has its memorable scenes. One of these is the trial scene,[37] the originality of which was praised by the reviewer for *Harper's.* Another is the New York harbor scene [38] in which Belcher makes a futile attempt to escape to Europe prior to his successful flight into Canada. And still other scenes that remain in the reader's imagination are the majority of the scenes in which the town of Sevenoaks furnishes the background. The following passage at the very beginning of the book will serve as well as any to illustrate this point:

Everybody has seen Sevenoaks, or a hundred towns so much like it, in most particulars, that a description of any one of them would present it to the imagination—a town strung upon a stream, like beads upon a thread, or charms upon a chain. Sevenoaks was richer in chain than charms, for its abundant water-power was only partially used. It plunged, and roared, and played, and sparkled, because it had not half enough to do. It leaped down three or four cataracts in passing through the village; and, as it started from living springs far northward among the woods and mountains, it never failed in its supplies.

Few of the people of Sevenoaks—thoughtless workers, mainly —either knew or cared whence it came, or whither it went. They knew it as "The Branch"; but Sevenoaks was so far from the trunk, down to which it sent its sap, and from which it received no direct return, that no significance was attached to its name. But it roared all day, and roared all night, summer and winter alike, and the sound became a part of the atmosphere. Resonance was one of the qualities of the oxygen which the people breathed, so that if, at any midnight moment, the roar had been suddenly hushed, they would have waked with a start and a sense of suffocation, and leaped from their beds.

Among the charms that dangled from this liquid chain—depending upon the vest of a landscape which ended in a ruffle of woods toward the north, overtopped by the head of a mountain—

[37] *Op. cit.,* pp. 381–407.
[38] *Ibid.,* pp. 436–442.

was a huge factory that had been added to from time to time, as
necessity demanded, until it had become an imposing and not
uncomely pile. Below this were two or three dilapidated saw-
mills, a grist-mill in daily use, and a fulling-mill—a remnant of
the old times when homespun went its pilgrimage to town—to
be fulled, colored, and dressed—from all the sparsely-settled
country around.

On a little plateau by the side of The Branch was a row of
stores and dram shops and butchers' establishments. Each had a
sort of square false front, pierced by two staring windows and a
door, that reminded one of a lion *couchant*—very large in the
face and very thin in the flank. Then there were crowded in,
near the mill, little rows of one-story houses, occupied entirely by
operatives, and owned by the owner of the mill. All the inhabitants, not directly connected with the mill, were as far away
from it as they could go. Their houses were set back upon either
acclivity which rose from the gorge that the stream had worn,
dotting the hill-sides in every direction. There was a clumsy
town-hall, there were three or four churches, there was a high
school and a low tavern. It was, on the whole, a village of importance, but the great mill was somehow its soul and centre.
A fair farming and grazing country stretched back from it east-
ward and westward, and Sevenoaks was its only home market.[39]

On the other hand, the metropolitan scenes, with the exception of the two already cited, are disappointing. After a residence of four years in the great American metropolis, Josiah
Holland should have been far more alive to its colorfulness
and individuality than he really was. He tells us of mansions
on the avenue and of offices in the financial district, but he
does not really help us to visualize these places. If he had had
as keen an eye for cosmopolitan Manhattan as he had for
Sevenoaks, what vivid pictures he might have given us of
Fifth Avenue and Broadway and the Battery, of Central
Park and the Astor House and old Trinity! But if we want
rich and unforgettable pictures of nineteenth-century New
York, we shall not find them in *Sevenoaks;* we shall do far
better to turn to Howells' *Hazard of New Fortunes,* James's

[39] *Op. cit.,* pp. 1–2.

Washington Square, and any one of a dozen of Mrs. Wharton's novels and novelettes.

After all, however, the most important fact about *Sevenoaks* was its huge popular success. Critics might laugh the book to scorn, but the public bought it and read it. Ladies' reading circles discussed it as solemnly as if it had been *Hamlet* or *Vanity Fair* or *Adam Bede.* Speakers at teachers' institutes referred as reverently to its author as if he had been a genius of the first water.[40] Scarcely a middle-class home was without it.[40] Those of us whose memories go back to the days of bangs and bustles will recall that *Sevenoaks* was almost as inevitable a parlor adornment as was the whatnot, the large seashell, the stereoscope, or the plush photograph album. Yes, Josiah Holland had really triumphed this time. Whatever the penny-a-liners might say, he had written the best-selling American novel of its year. How the good doctor's dark, childlike eyes must have twinkled at the happy realization! How his benign mouth must have smiled beneath the luxuriant walrus mustache that he wore in his later years! Just how many copies of *Sevenoaks* were ultimately sold I do not know, but I have no doubt that this novel outsold all of Holland's other works with the exception of the Titcomb letters and the poems *Bitter-Sweet* and *Kathrina.*[41] As recently as 1903, 1906, 1909, and 1922 [42] Scribner's still found it worth their while to make printings of *Sevenoaks.*

Undoubtedly the swift action of this novel, together with the beautifully naïve poetic justice of its dénouement, was what kept the book alive for half a century; but timeliness was a most important factor in giving the novel its initial success. The "rich manufacturer, speculator, and railway king" referred to by the *Nation* reviewer was Jim Fisk, the most notoriously disreputable American financier of the early seventies. The murder of Fisk, in January 1872, at the hands

40 See below, p. 207.

41 Before the end of 1861 the 26th edition of the Titcomb letters and the 15th edition of *Bitter-Sweet* were issued. See publisher's advertisement in the Springfield *Republican,* Nov. 23, 1861.

42 See above, p. 105, footnote 10.

of a defrauded erstwhile business associate, was still very fresh in the public mind when the first installment of *Sevenoaks* appeared; and despite the fact that Jim Fisk never lived to escape to Canada, the public had no difficulty in recognizing the piratical, blackguardly Robert Belcher as a thinly veiled portrait of Fisk.[43] Hence *Sevenoaks* was—to use a Browning expression—"piping hot." The knavish Jim Fisk had come to a richly merited evil end. All that remained was for some popular novelist to give a few of Fisk's hypothetical victims a handsome reward for their virtue. No wonder Josiah Holland's large public was delighted with *Sevenoaks*!

Holland lived to write one more novel, *Nicholas Minturn*, the eleven installments of which appeared in *Scribner's Monthly* beginning with December 1876 and concluding with October 1877. Charles Stanley Reinhart did the illustrations for this third and last of Holland's serials. Reinhart, a Pittsburgher with Munich and Paris training, was at that time and for some twenty years thereafter one of our foremost magazine illustrators. Before his death in 1896, at the age of fifty-two, he was to become internationally famous as a genre painter.[44]

The plot of this final Holland novel is as complicated as the author ever devised.

Nicholas Minturn, a wealthy but lonely orphan in his twenties, has just embarked upon a European voyage. On shipboard he meets several interesting persons, including the elderly Mr. Benson, the latter's ward Grace Larkin, Mrs. Coates, and Miss Jenny Coates. Mr. Benson is a prominent and highly respected New York banker, a pillar in his church, a "model" man—but, from the very first, Nicholas does not quite like him. Miss Larkin is a beautiful but fragile young creature, apparently doomed to a life of hopeless invalidism. Mrs. Coates is an impulsive, warm-hearted, ungrammatical

---

[43] For short biographical sketch of James Fisk (1834–1872), see *Encyclopaedia Britannica*, IX, 330. See also Plunkett, *op. cit.*, p. 91.

[44] For short biographical sketch of Charles Stanley Reinhart (1844–1896), see *National Cyclopaedia of American Biography*, VII, 465–466.

woman of considerably more wealth than culture. Her daughter Jenny is a pretty, vivacious, and sufficiently refined girl. In mid-ocean the ship is wrecked in a collision. The panic-stricken Mr. Benson, unmindful of anything but his own safety, leaves Miss Larkin to the impossible task of shifting for herself. Nicholas heroically rescues the ladies, and the survivors are brought back to New York in another boat.

Shortly after Nicholas' return his home on the Hudson River is visited by a trio of robbers, who secure, among other articles, some bonds of large denomination. Nicholas, who has become much infatuated with Miss Larkin, goes to New York to the Benson home for the ostensible purpose of asking Mr. Benson's advice about the stolen bonds. Since Nicholas has apparently lost his memorandum of the serial numbers of the bonds, Mr. Benson does not offer him much hope that the bonds can be recovered.

Soon afterward Mr. Benson is visited by a ruffian who wishes to borrow money, and who offers some excellent bonds as collateral. Mr. Benson, certain that the ruffian is a criminal and probably Nicholas Minturn's robber, threatens to call the police if the scamp does not immediately surrender the bonds and make a quick departure. Rid of his uninvited guest, Mr. Benson puts the bonds quietly away until such time as Nicholas can positively identify them.

Having found country life boresome, Nicholas takes an apartment in New York for the winter. In the metropolis he can have excitement, and he can frequently enjoy the society of the lovely Miss Larkin. Early in his metropolitan sojourn he is visited by three swindlers who fleece him out of a neat sum of money. Their conquest, however, is short-lived; for, aided by a one-armed popcorn vendor named Timothy Spencer, he tracks the rascals to their lair, a lower East Side saloon, and offers them their choice between going to jail and reforming under his tutelage. Through the aid of a New York lawyer friend, Montgomery Glezen, Nicholas finds honest employment for the erstwhile swindlers, and they willingly walk the path of rectitude. A little later Nicholas, seeking a worthy manner of employing his own talents and energies, founds a social settlement; in this enterprise he has the whole-hearted coöperation of the three men whom he has be-friended and reformed, and the generous but rather cynical aid of his lawyer friend Glezen.

Hard times are meanwhile falling upon the country and its metropolis. Mr. Benson, finding himself and his bank in straitened circumstances, yields to the temptation to use the hidden bonds as collateral on a loan. The relief that he thus secures is but temporary. There is a run on the Benson bank, and Mr. Benson faces financial ruin and social ostracism.

The receipt of an anonymous letter, obviously written by an illiterate ruffian, now makes Nicholas virtually certain regarding the recent whereabouts of the stolen bonds. Against Glezen's advice, Nicholas broaches the subject in an indirect manner to Mr. Benson. The only satisfaction that he gets from the banker is a thinly veiled threat of prosecution for libel; for, it must be recalled, Nicholas apparently does not have the serial numbers of the bonds. But soon after the interview between Nicholas and Mr. Benson, the memorandum of the bonds is discovered—in the pocket of an old overcoat that Nicholas has given to one of the former swindlers.

Mr. Benson, already on the brink of financial and social ruin, is threatened with a prospective visitor: the irate ring-leader of the bond thieves. Benson manages to commit sui-cide just in time to escape meeting his unwelcome visitor, and he performs the deed in such an ingenious way as to make it appear certain that he has been murdered by the bond thief.

During these exciting months, the love affair between Nicholas Minturn and Grace Larkin has progressed steadily, but not quite so rapidly as Nicholas has desired. As long as the young lady has believed herself to be a hopeless invalid, she has been reluctant to do Nicholas the injustice of accept-ing his serious attentions. And Nicholas, loath to place Miss Larkin in the embarrassing position of accepting him out of gratitude for his having rescued her from a watery grave, is hesitant to propose marriage. But Miss Larkin begins to recover her health and strength with surprising rapidity. Once out of the clutches of Mr. Benson—whose house she has left some weeks before his inglorious death—she becomes a new creature. In this connection, she finds the pleasant society of Nicholas Minturn, Montgomery Glezen, and the vivacious Jenny Coates a wonderful stimulus. Mrs. Coates, upon learning that Nicholas Minturn and Grace Larkin are about to be married, can ill conceal her disappointment; for the impetuous old lady has somewhat too patently set her cap— or, rather, Jenny's cap—for the wealthy and thoroughly eligible Nicholas. The sensible Jenny, however, has comprehended and fully accepted the situation from the very start. And when the mischievous Montgomery Glezen informally announces his engagement to Jenny by kissing her in the presence of her mother, the old lady is adequately consoled—even though she has repeatedly voiced a prejudice against "perfessional" men.

The only really interesting character not heretofore mentioned in this synopsis is the amiable Mr. Coates. That self-made merchant is obviously of as humble origin as his wife; but he has the saving graces of modesty, good sense, and shrewd humor. And he speaks with a quaintly amusing and positively ingratiating stutter.

Only one prominent periodical considered it worth while to review *Nicholas Minturn;* and that periodical, the *North American Review,* attacked the book savagely.

He has in this novel [said the critic] introduced several characters not uncommonly met with in fiction,—a guardian of the godly sort, but wicked at heart and fraudulent; a young and beautiful ward; a young man, Nicholas Minturn, who combines all the virtues of both sexes, and who in the end exposes the guardian's infamy and marries the ward. . . . When we close the volume, no room is left for doubt as to who are bad and who are good; and there is no haziness as to the dividing line between vice and virtue. . . . We can cordially recommend *Nicholas Minturn* to either the infantile or senile public. The very young or the very old may be trusted with it without fear of the results. With adults the consequences cannot be predicted with absolute certainty.[45]

The plot of *Nicholas Minturn* is, of course, rather trashy. As a rescuer, Nicholas is great beyond all belief. The manner in which the stolen bonds are recovered, first by Mr. Benson, and then by Nicholas, is exciting, but not at all credible; it is almost ingenuously disingenuous in its entire conception; it depends absolutely upon a series of convenient but virtually impossible coincidences. And the episode of the three swindlers is not much better; the reformation of these rascals is much too rapid, much too thorough, for the credence of anyone but the devotee of third-rate fiction.

For all that, however, *Nicholas Minturn* is far from being a wholly bad piece of work. Indeed, one is not certain, even, that discriminating readers of its day were right in assuming it to be the worst of Holland's five novels. Benson, for example, is a much better creation than the ruffianly Belcher in *Sevenoaks*. As Professor Quinn says (with obvious reservations):

[Holland] did have an ability to draw characters, and he had studied Dickens carefully and learned to a certain degree how to incarnate hypocrisy and dishonesty as in Benson, the banker of *Nicholas Minturn*.[46]

Of course Benson is too sharply etched, and he does several impossible things; but at times he is a remarkably human hypocrite. The manner in which he rationalizes himself into condoning his most shameful conduct is psychologically good. One is almost tempted to give Benson ranking with the immortal Pecksniff; but unfortunately Benson, like Pecksniff, is presented largely by exposition, and of course Holland's exposition is uniformly duller, flatter, and less piquant than

[45] *Op. cit.*, CXXV, 589. Nov., 1877.
[46] Quinn, *op. cit.*, p. 192.

Dickens'. But even so, Benson is a notably successful creation; and incidentally he everlastingly dispels the notion that his creator always stood in awesome respect of the pillar in the right kind of church. And there are other good portraitures in *Nicholas Minturn.* The whole Coates family group, for example, is particularly well done.

From the standpoint of local color, *Nicholas Minturn* is about the equal of *Sevenoaks*—no better, no worse. In his last novel, as in the one immediately preceding, Holland had a wonderful opportunity to depict New York; and, in the later work as in the earlier, he muffed his opportunity. Except for an occasional vague reference to Broadway, *Nicholas Minturn* offers nothing that would particularly individualize Manhattan. Only a few scenes linger in the memory. One of these is the scene in which Nicholas embarks upon his ill-fated voyage.[47] Another, a better one, takes us to the Crown and Crust, the lower East Side saloon in which Nicholas apprehends the three swindlers.[48] This resort, with its red-curtained stalls and its gaudy barmaids, is so colorfully presented that one wonders whether Josiah Holland ever visited its counterpart.

Considered as a popular success, *Nicholas Minturn* must be rated an anticlimax. It sold well at first, and it was reprinted in 1882, in 1904, in 1906, and in 1914;[49] but it never approached the vogue of *Sevenoaks.* The scorn of the critics, of course, had little to do with the comparative popular failure of *Nicholas Minturn.* Relatively few of J. G. Holland's numerous clientele knew what the anemic intellectuals were saying—and still fewer cared. The trouble with *Nicholas Minturn* was that it had no particular timeliness. Mr. Benson was no such public figure as was Robert Belcher. There may be Bensons in every sizable Christian congregation, but the Bensons are not spectacular in their misbehavior; the nefarious deeds of a whole company of Bensons look pale beside

[47] *Op. cit.,* pp. 20–25.
[48] *Ibid.,* pp. 211–213.
[49] See above, p. 105, footnote 10.

the devilry of a single Belcher. And, besides, Belcher was Jim Fisk; Benson was legion.

In our rapid survey of Holland's novels, we have noticed that they have a number of qualities in common. We have noticed that their plots, for example, are generally so ingenious as to hold the not-too-exacting reader in a desirable state of suspense, but that these plots are seldom notable for their verisimilitude. We have noticed, from the synopses, that Holland's conception of poetic justice is as simple, as naïve, as sentimental in his novels as in his narrative poems; true to the Anglo-Saxon moralistic tradition, Holland invariably shapes his events in such a way that ultimately the virtuous are rewarded and the wicked are chastised. We have noticed, further, that Holland's heroes and heroines are, for the most part, either colorless nonentities or namby-pamby prigs; that his unusual characters are more likely to be caricatures or stock types than pulsating human beings; and that it is only in an occasional Dr. Gilbert or Mr. Benson that the characters rise to anything approaching distinction. We have noticed, finally, that although Holland's novels are none too rich in local color, their author often became so much interested in his setting that he gave the reader some truly memorable pictures.

Of the contemporary popularity of Holland's novels, let us repeat, there can be no doubt. All of them, with the possible exception of *The Bay-Path,* enjoyed their days as best-sellers. The intelligentsia of the *North American Review,* the *Atlantic Monthly,* the *Nation,* and *Harper's* might decry them or ignore them; but the plain American people everywhere read them with avidity. Members of the Lotos Club or the Harvard Club, sipping their whisky-and-sodas or puffing their Havanas, might chuckle superciliously at the fatuities of *Sevenoaks;* but plenty of small-town reading clubs no doubt hailed the creator of Robert Belcher as the great American Dickens. And, by the way, Holland was not without his loyal champions on the printed page; for provincial newspapers from New London and Albany to Milwaukee and San Francisco praised him unstintingly.[50] In village book-stores, in circulating libraries, and even in the majority of college libraries the novels of J. G. Holland were undoubt-edly in constant demand.[51] Solid business men and profes-sional men, impressive in their General Garfield beards, their frock-coats, their baggy striped trousers, and their square-toed congress boots, undoubtedly read *Arthur Bonnicastle* and *Nicholas Minturn* aloud to their delighted families. Clergy-men and lecturers and legislators, we may well imagine, sen-tentiously quoted the ennobling aphorisms of Arthur Blague or the wise drolleries of Mr. Coates. Sharp-tongued maiden aunts and gruff bachelor uncles, we may assume, declared that what Miss Gilbert should have had was not a career but a spanking—a sentiment obviously shared both by Arthur Blague and by Josiah Holland. Six years after Holland's death, Edwin Percy Whipple, himself a tremendously popu-lar essayist and lecturer, could truthfully say:

J. G. Holland has succeeded in everything he has undertaken, whether as a sort of lay preacher to the young, as an essayist, as a novelist, or as a poet. It is hardly possible to take up any late edition of any one of his numerous volumes without finding "fortieth thousand" or "sixtieth thousand" smiling complacently and benignly upon you from the title-page.[52]

At the end of his career as a novelist, in short, J. G. Holland was as widely read, as widely discussed, as any author in the United States.[53]

Several aspects of Holland's novels need yet to be consid-ered. The importunate religiosity already remarked in his

[50] See publishers' advertising pages between the text and the back cover of Plunkett. Here Holland and his novels are eulogized by such newspapers as the New London *Telegram*, the Albany *Argus,* the Milwaukee *Evening Wisconsin,* and the San Francisco *Alta-California.*

[51] For example, in the libraries of Ohio University and Hiram (Ohio) College respectively, all copies of Holland's five novels have a well-worn ap-pearance, despite the fact that in recent years they have seldom been drawn.

[52] E. P. Whipple: *American Literature and Other Papers,* Boston, 1887, p. 127.

[53] See above, p. 2, footnote 4.

essays and in his poems is no less prominent in his novels. *The Bay-Path,* as we have seen, has its main concern in New England Calvinistic theology. *Miss Gilbert's Career* has a preacher for its hero. *Arthur Bonnicastle* edifies the reader with the Damon-and-Pythias friendship of a young minister and a very Christian young layman whose intimacy was formed in the school of an extremely religious pedagogue. It is in *Arthur Bonnicastle,* too, that the author, in a characteristically Puritan spirit, takes a sly dig at Episcopalianism by having a presumably good Episcopalian, young Livingston's father, get boozy at Christmas.[54] In *Sevenoaks* the villainous Robert Belcher is quite as much a scamp for his irreligiosity as for his cruelty and his dishonesty. And, finally, *Nicholas Minturn* has to do with the wrong kind of church pillar on the one hand, and the right kind of social settlement on the other. The missionary efforts of young Minturn and Jenny Coates are primarily evangelistic; only secondarily are they humanitarian.

Possessed of such a fervor for homilies and homilists, Josiah Holland naturally did a great deal of preaching in his novels —quite as much as in his verse; almost as much, in fact, as in his essays. And to say merely that he loitered too much upon his scenes, making himself annoyingly conspicuous, is not telling the whole truth. That is merely stating that Holland's novelistic technique, what there is of it, is the technique of the mid-Victorian English novelists. Dickens and Thackeray and George Eliot, as every student of literature knows, interspersed their novels with voluminous editorial comments. In fact, no English novelist before Hardy, no American novelist before Howells, displayed an objectivism comparable to that of Flaubert or Turgenev. As a twentieth-century British critic has said:

The novelist is able, if he chooses, to supplement it [the concrete presentation of life] by direct personal commentary and explanation. He can, as it were, step before the curtain, elucidate

54 *Op. cit.,* p. 239.

the action, discuss the characters and their motives, and generalise on the moral questions suggested by them.[55]

Yes, the novelist is able to do all that, and do it effectively— *if* he is a genius. But Josiah Holland was not a genius; his preachments are almost invariably more tiresome than are those of Thackeray, Dickens, or even George Eliot. Objectively considered, Thackeray is a bad technician; but the cultivated reader will pardon, even delight in, Thackeray's lengthy expoundings because they so frequently possess the intimate charm of a brilliant and urbane gentleman and citizen of the world. Dickens, at his best, has the saving grace of inimitable humor. As for George Eliot, although she is often tedious, she has something eminently worth saying; seldom does she dispense mere platitudes. The trouble with J. G. Holland is, frankly, banality. Too rarely are his ideas either fresh or important. The following passages from *Sevenoaks* —all of which Josiah doubtless considered to be utterances of great pith and moment—will serve to illustrate this point:

Robert Belcher knew that the woman before him was fearless and incorruptible. He knew that she despised him—that bullying and brow-beating would have no influence with her, that this ready badinage would not avail, and that coaxing and soft words would be equally useless. In her presence he was shorn of all his weapons, and he never felt so defenceless and ill at ease in his life.[56]

He had no culture, but his nature was manly. He had little education, but his heart was true, and his arm was strong. Compared with Mr. Belcher, with all his wealth, he was nobility personified. Compared with the sordid men around her, with whom he would be an object of supercilious contempt, he seemed like a demigod. His eccentricities, his generosities, his originalities of thought and fancy, were a feast to her. There was more of him than she could find in any of her acquaintances—more that was fresh, piquant, stimulating, and vitally appetizing. Having once

[55] William Henry Hudson: *An Introduction to the Study of Literature,* Revised Edition. Boston, New York, Chicago, 1913, p. 219.
[56] *Op. cit.,* pp. 9–10.

come into contact with him, the influence of his presence had remained, and it was with a genuine throb of pleasure that she found herself with him again.[57]

In the great house, there is a happy woman. She has found something to love and something to do. These were all she needed to make her supremely self-respectful, happy, and, in the best degree, womanly. Wilful, ambitious, sacrificing her young affections to gold at the first, and wasting years in idleness and unworthy intrigue, for the lack of affection and the absence of motive to usefulness and industry, she has found, at last, the secret of her woman's life, and has accepted it with genuine gratitude. In ministering to her brother and her brother's child, now a stalwart lad, in watching with untiring eyes and helping with ready wit the unused proprietor in his new circumstances, and in assisting the poor around her, she finds her days full of toil and her nights brief with grateful sleep.[58]

It will thus appear that in many respects Holland is a rather atrocious novelist. Why, then, all this pother and palaver about his work? Is he worthy of serious or detailed consideration? In a sense, J. G. Holland might be bracketed with Harold Bell Wright and the two Porter women (Pollyanna and Limberlost); that is, the lineal descendants of the Holland cult are now perhaps, to a considerable extent, the devotees of the aforementioned trio of twentieth-century fictionists. But this, if true, is only a half-truth; and, like most half-truths, it is dangerously misleading. The other half of the truth is that Holland's appeal occasionally reached up into the higher cultural levels. True, all of the best critics of his day belabored Holland roundly, but at least they took the trouble to notice him. Would any reputable later-day critic bother about Harold Bell Wright, except possibly to consider him as an amazing and amusing phenomenon? [59] The point is that not all of Holland's readers, by any means, were

[57] *Op. cit.,* p. 177.

[58] *Ibid.,* p. 452.

[59] No mention of Harold Bell Wright, Eleanor H. Porter, or Gene Stratton Porter is made by either of the two recognized authorities on the history of American prose fiction: Van Doren and Quinn.

innocent rustics or even untraveled villagers. As editor of one of the few indubitably first-rate magazines, Josiah Gilbert Holland, during the last decade of his life, was in a position of peculiarly great influence. Many substantial people, as was remarked earlier in this chapter, read him and enjoyed him and quoted him. And this respectable following continued loyal for at least a decade or two, perhaps a quarter of a century, after his death. Apropos of this circumstance, a middle-aged Ohio man writes:

In the little college community in which I was born and reared —a community that has produced one eminent Harvard economist, one conspicuously original American poet, and one of the two professor-Presidents of these United States—Timothy Titcomb was a household name. Looking back upon my childhood in the dying years of the last century, I can recall no professorial home—not even that of our free-thinking Natural Science professor—in which the works of J. G. Holland did not occupy a prominent place upon the library shelves. And in comparing experiences with my contemporaries who were brought up in more pretentious, less provincial academic communities, I have discovered that my little college town was no anomaly. Until about my sixteenth year—the year that Queen Victoria and President McKinley died,—I fully supposed that *Arthur Bonnicastle* was a worthy companion for *David Copperfield*. Indeed, when I was in my early teens, two of my best-loved cronies were a blue-bound *Arthur* (Illustrated Edition) which stood beside a green-bound *David* (illustrations by "Phiz") on a familiar shelf in my father-professor's study.[60]

The long and short of the matter is that if we are to compare the appeal of J. G. Holland with that of any twentieth-century American fictionist, we shall do much better to compare Holland with Booth Tarkington than to compare him with Harold Bell Wright. (This we may say without implying for a moment that Holland was ever as good as Tarkington or that Tarkington is ever as bad as

[60] Letter to the author, Sept. 6, 1933. At the correspondent's request, his name is withheld.

Holland.) In other words, if Josiah Gilbert Holland never quite qualified as one of James Russell Lowell's writers whose appeal is both to the few and to the many, he did, at any rate, appeal in his time to many of the few and to most of the many.

What is the significance of all this to the literary historian? We have, I think, an adequate answer to this question. There are some novelists who are so utterly bad that they make no artistic contribution either directly or indirectly; they have no appeal either for persons of taste or for persons capable of acquiring taste. There are other novelists who are so good or so nearly good—in spots—that the intelligent reader takes the trouble to read them and to wish that they were better. In this latter class belongs J. G. Holland. If he never quite wrote a good novel, he at least wrote novels with so much of good in them that educable people could read them with some degree of pleasure. If he never quite wrote a realistic novel, he at least wrote novels with so much of the semblance of realism in them that many of his readers acquired a taste for genuine realism. The first readers of *Arthur Bonnicastle* and *Sevenoaks* and *Nicholas Minturn* were the readers of the old *Scribner's*. In the *Scribner's* they found not only the fiction of Holland but also that of George W. Cable and that of Bret Harte.[61] And many of the *Scribner's* readers were no doubt *Harper's* readers as well. In *Harper's* they found the novels of William Black, Constance Fenimore Woolson, and, better still, Thomas Hardy and William Dean Howells.[61] J. G. Holland was, in short, a good enough novelist to give the better portion of his clientele a taste for something really meritorious—something superior to what he was capable of writing himself. Pious persons started with Holland, for if they had conscientious scruples touching the ethics of novel-

---

[61] Among the novels appearing serially in the old *Scribner's* were Cable's *The Grandissimes* (XIX, 97 *et seq.*) and Harte's *Gabriel Conroy* (XI, 16 *et seq.*). Among novels running at about the same time in *Harper's* were Black's *Macleod of Dare* (LVI, 401 *et seq.*), Mrs. Woolson's *Anne* (LXII, 28 *et seq.*), Hardy's *Return of the Native* (LVI, 415 *et seq.*), and Howells' *Indian Summer* (LXXI, 261).

reading in general, they knew that Josiah Holland was so godly a man that he would never offend or corrupt even the most innocent of their children. Presently many of the more intelligent ones must have turned eagerly from Holland to more artistic and significant fiction. Ultimately, perhaps, a few of them read even James and Meredith.

As Professor Quinn has truly said:

Holland's novels will remain important documents to the social and economic historian. . . . His merit can best be appreciated when he is compared with such a novelist as the Reverend E. P. Roe who began in 1873 to pour forth a series of absurd productions which sold widely and preached plentifully the special form of sentimental Evangelicalism to which Roe belonged. The closing scenes of *Barriers Burned Away* (1873) . . . are so bad that the critical judgment which confuses Holland's work with Roe's is unfortunate. His popularity emphasizes the service of the better novelists of this transition [in the eighteen-seventies] in raising the taste of the audience above the stilted conversation and the nauseating pietism of the type of fiction Roe represented.[62]

Some day, we may be sure, other literary historians will take cognizance of these facts, and then they will accord Holland the same honor that they now accord his friend Edward Eggleston.[63] They will hail Josiah Gilbert Holland not as a great novelist or yet as a good novelist, but as a tremendous, an invaluable, a truly unique influence in the realm of prose fiction.

[62] Quinn, *op. cit.*, p. 192.

[63] For example, Professor Boynton, in his *Literature and American Life* (pp. 597, 845) comments briefly but favorably on the work of Eggleston. He makes no comment upon the work of Holland. Mr. Van Doren states (p. 122) that Holland's poems *Bitter-Sweet* and *Kathrina* "probably caught more readers than any of his tales in prose," but he does not name a single Holland novel by specific title.

VIII

The Old *Scribner's*

Late in the spring of 1868 the Hollands packed their trunks, found a desirable renter for Brightwood, and embarked upon a leisurely European tour—a tour designed to be an education for the entire family.[1] The lessee of Brightwood was the newly arrived British minister to Washington, Sir Edward Thornton.[2] Having heard much about the oppressive torridity of the Potomac Valley, and quite as much about the delightful coolness of the Berkshire region, Sir Edward was determined to find a summer home in the latter. An hour's stroll about the house and grounds of Brightwood convinced him that that was just the place he wanted; and the Englishman's wholesomely refined appearance and stately charm of speech and manner convinced Josiah that here was just the tenant he wanted.[3] So the doctor's worry about leaving his fine country place idle and fallow came to a quick and happy end.

Neither Josiah nor Elizabeth Holland had ever been abroad before, and all three of the children were now old enough to learn much from foreign travel.[3] Theodore, the baby, was in his tenth year; Annie and Kate were young ladies in their middle or later teens.[4] The plans of the tour called for lengthy sojourns in places that the Hollands should find most interesting; for French and German instruction for all of the children; and for music lessons for the two girls. An afterthought was that Mrs. Holland, long a sufferer from eye

1 Plunkett, *op. cit.*, pp. 74–76.

2 W. H. Judson memorial article on Holland, Chicago *Tribune,* Oct. 22, 1881.

3 See above, p. 10, footnote 36.

4 See Bianchi, *op. cit.*, pp. 184, 207.

trouble, should consult Dr. Albrecht von Gräfe, of Berlin, at that time probably the foremost oculist of Europe.[5]

So it was that on Monday, May 25, 1868, the Springfield *Republican* contained the following item:

Dr. Holland and family leave Springfield today for New York, whence they will sail on Wednesday, in the steamer Manhattan, intending to spend two years or more in travel.[6]

Before the *Manhattan* had passed Montauk Point, Josiah, ensconced in a deckchair, was regaling Elizabeth and the children with eloquently enthusiastic comments upon their European itinerary [7] and its real significance—comments not a whit less fascinating because of their frequent repetition at Brightwood since early spring.[8] First of all, they would visit England—"Our Old Home," as Hawthorne had so aptly called it. Of course they would see Oxford and Cambridge and Stratford-on-Avon, as well as the score or more of places that American tourists always visit in London. Probably they would catch more than one glimpse of Britain's noble little widow-queen as she rode out of the grounds of Buckingham Palace to take her daily airing in St. James's Park. Surely, at one time or another, they would catch sight of the distinguished Mr. Gladstone, England's real chief executive, as he emerged from or entered No. 10 Downing Street. Perhaps they could even arrange to meet the big, gruff, shaggy Laureate at Farringford, and the wicked but warm-hearted and dynamic little "Boz" at Gad's Hill; [9] certainly meeting the two most illustrious English authors of the day was an experience much to be craved. There were, however, other prospective delights in England—delights even greater or, at least, more edifying than those mentioned. They must, for instance, run down to Plymouth, in Devon, and view the

[5] Plunkett, *op. cit.,* pp. 74–76.

[6] *Op. cit.*

[7] For list of the European countries visited by the Hollands, see New York *Times,* Oct. 13, 1881.

[8] See above, p. 10, footnote 36.

[9] See above, pp. 76, 80–81.

place whence the *Mayflower* had sailed on her immortal voyage. They must go to Bedford, the shrine of the Nonconformist saint, John Bunyan. Back in London they must betake themselves on the Sabbath—on more than one Sabbath, in fact—to Newington Butts Tabernacle; for here it was that Charles Haddon Spurgeon, most eloquent and consecrated preacher in the realm, held forth.[10] St. Paul's Cathedral and Westminster Abbey were all very well in their way; but, after all, no priest in the Establishment—not even the evangelical and literary Mr. Kingsley—could deliver a message of the devotional, spiritual quality of Brother Spurgeon's.

Up in Scotland they would make the conventional tour of Princes Street, Calton Hill, Abbotsford, the Trossachs, Ayrshire, and Kelvingrove Park. In that Presbyterian land, however, they would experience their deepest thrill when they reached the east end of High Street, Edinburgh; for here they would reverentially enter the well-preserved house of John Knox.

On the Continent they would visit Belgium, with its historic Waterloo; Prussia, with its clean, orderly, new-looking Berlin (which one day, perhaps, would become the great capital of a united Germany); and the Italian peninsula, with its landmarks of the Caesars and the Renaissance. They would visit France, particularly that modern Sodom, Paris (which they would probably disapprove of almost as heartily as Helen Pendennis disapproved of Brussels). In Paris, no doubt, they would glimpse the suavest monarch in Europe, the dapper, black-bearded Louis Napoleon, and his worldly but exquisite consort, Eugénie. For Josiah, however, the richest experience of the Paris sojourn would be the rare privilege of conducting the Sunday-school in the American (Calvinistic) Church.[11] How refreshing was even the thought of that little spiritual oasis in a desert of Romanism and in-

---

[10] For short biographical sketch of Charles Haddon Spurgeon (1834–1892), see *Encyclopaedia Britannica,* XXI, 268.

[11] Plunkett, *op. cit.,* p. 119.

fidelity! [12] They would visit that European sore spot, Austria, —including, of course, its Gomorrah-like capital, with its beautiful blue Danube, its massive Schonbrunn Palace, and its degenerate Hapsburgs.[11] They would visit Switzerland, that scenic land of lands, which once gave refuge to the noblest Frenchman of them all: John Calvin. In Switzerland they would join the Roswell Smiths.[13]

That Josiah Holland received a liberal education from the Old Country it would be absurd to doubt; indeed, his *Every-Day Topics* in *Scribner's* attest repeatedly to that fact.[14] It is equally obvious, however, that in Europe, as in the South twenty years earlier, he carried his village New England aura with him wherever he went. As Mrs. Plunkett has expressed it: "He came back [to the United States] singing louder paeans than ever that God had hidden America till the fulness of time." [15]

Before embarking upon his voyage, Holland had been offered the editorship of *Hours at Home,* a magazine published by Charles Scribner for three years with indifferent success.[16] Naturally the publisher had felt that the wide popular acclaim of J. G. Holland's writings, together with Holland's long and valuable experience on the Springfield *Republican,* made the author of *Bitter-Sweet* and the Titcomb editorials an ideal man to revive a languishing periodical. Holland, not greatly impressed by the future possibilities of *Hours at Home,* had asked time to think the matter over in Europe, and Scribner had gladly consented to leave the offer open.[17] As matters turned out, *Hours at Home* was never to be revived. Another and much more flourishing magazine, however, was soon to be published by Scribner with the assistance of Holland.

11 Plunkett, *op. cit.,* p. 119.
12 For Holland's moral attitude toward Paris and Vienna, see above, p. 114.
13 See above, p. 65, footnote 36.
14 See above, p. 74.
15 Plunkett, *op. cit.,* p. 76.
16 *Ibid.,* p. 77.
17 Plunkett, *op. cit.,* p. 77.

One summer evening in 1869, in Geneva, Switzerland, Holland took a stroll with Roswell Smith—a stroll that led them to a bridge spanning the historic Rhone.[18] Up to this time the paths of these two Americans had not crossed frequently; but as prominently active laymen in their respective churches, the Congregational and the Presbyterian, they had discovered that they possessed many interests in common. Their first meeting, as was observed in a previous chapter, had occurred at Lafayette, Indiana, whither Josiah Holland had gone on one of his earlier lecture tours.[19] Since a considerable number of Holland's lectures were "return engagements," Holland and Smith had had several subsequent meetings in Lafayette. Indeed, the intimacy of the two men had become such that they and their families had arranged to tour part of Europe together.[19] For some eighteen years Smith had practised law at Lafayette. He was, however, a Connecticut Yankee by birth, was a graduate of Brown University, and between the ages of fourteen and seventeen had worked for the New York publishing house of Paine & Burgess.[20] As Holland, years later, recalled the momentous Geneva stroll, he recollected that he and Smith had formed their business partnership while loitering on the bridge.[21] Was it not singularly appropriate that these two earnest disciples of John Calvin should have held their most memorable conference in Geneva of all places, even though they were to talk magazines rather than theology?

In this particular "Geneva Conversation," Smith told Holland of his desires to give up the law, move back East, and form some sort of business connection with a New York publishing firm.[21] Holland, in turn, told Smith of his *Hours at Home* offer, of his growing conviction that *Hours at Home* could never be made a success, and of his strong confidence that there was a distinct field for an entirely new American

18 Plunkett, *op. cit.*, p. 78. See also above, p. 54, footnote 36.
19 See above, p. 54, footnote 36.
20 For short biographical sketch of Roswell Smith (1829–1892), see *Dictionary of American Biography*, XVII, 339–340.
21 Plunkett, *op. cit.*, p. 78.

magazine—a magazine with high literary and artistic standards, yet with a much broader popular appeal than the *North
American,* the *Atlantic,* or *Harper's.*[22]

The upshot was *Scribner's Monthly,* a periodical named in
honor of Charles Scribner, whose generous offer of an editorship had really touched Josiah Holland. The publishing arrangements for the new magazine were unusual; for, strictly
speaking, the magazine was not to be published by the book
house of Scribner at all. The magazine firm was to be known
as Scribner & Company, in contradistinction to the book firm
of Charles Scribner & Company. Holland, the editor-in-chief
of the magazine, was to take three-tenths of the shares of
stock in the new corporation; Smith, the publisher and business manager, was to take three-tenths of the shares; and the
book firm of Charles Scribner & Company was to take the
remaining two-fifths of the shares.[23]

Buoyant with enthusiasm for the new venture, and eager to
get things going, Holland arrived in New York in May
1870.[24] Smith, who had arrived some time ahead of him, had
already completed the necessary business arrangements.[25] Just
six months later, in November 1870, *Scribner's Monthly*
made its first appearance.[26]

The New York to which Josiah Gilbert Holland and his
family moved, and of which he was soon to become a leading
citizen, was as incomparably the greatest American city as is
the New York of today. Counting the four hundred thousand
in Brooklyn, it had a million and a half of inhabitants—
more than twice the population of Philadelphia, its nearest
rival. Chicago, a raw prairie town less than half as large as
the Quaker City, had scarcely begun to assert itself as a
metropolis.[27] And yet the New York of 1870 would have ap-

<hr>

[22] See Robert Underwood Johnson: *Remembered Yesterdays,* Boston, 1923,
pp. 82–84.

[23] R. U. Johnson, *op. cit.,* pp. 82–84.

[24] See above, p. 10, footnote 36.

[25] Plunkett, *op. cit.,* p. 78.

[26] *Op. cit.,* Vol. I, No. 1.

[27] Nevins, *op. cit.,* p. 75.

peared a quaint little town to the Gothamite of to-day. It had no skyscrapers, no subways, no trolley cars. Its elevated railways were just emerging from the blueprint stage, the first "L" being opened that very year from the Battery to Thirtieth Street by way of Ninth Avenue.[28] People who rode about Manhattan were conveyed mainly in horsecars, in hackney cabs, or in lumbering stages. Fourteenth Street was "uptown," and Twenty-third Street was decidedly "uptown." The dismal stretches above Central Park were occupied by rundown farms, squatters' shanties, and herds of goats.[29] The town had three or four subscription libraries, but no great public library.[30] There was no Metropolitan Museum of Art.[31] There was no great symphony orchestra.[32] The only prominent legitimate theatres were Wallack's, the Union Square, Booth's, the Fifth Avenue, the Lyceum, and the Grand Opera House, the first two of which were occupied by stock companies.[33] There was only one apartment house, a new structure on Eighteenth Street.[34] Of the few large hotels the Astor, opposite the post-office, and the Fifth Avenue, at the corner of Twenty-third Street, were most notable.[35] The largest store, at Broadway and Eighth, was kept by A. T. Stewart, predecessor of John Wanamaker.[35] There was no Times Square, no Herald Square, most of the daily newspapers being housed in what a contemporary described as "tall buildings" in Park Row. Perhaps the most fashionable place of worship was Grace Church, at Broadway and Tenth, a large proportion of whose aristocratic communicants still lived within sound of its bells.[36] What a contrast was that

[28] Nevins, *op. cit.*, p. 82.

[29] *Ibid.*, p. 82.

[30] *Ibid.*, p. 243. See also R. U. Johnson, *op. cit.*, pp. 162–163.

[31] Nevins, *op. cit.*, pp. 262–263.

[32] However, a very good orchestra assembled and conducted by Theodore Thomas did give frequent concerts. R. U. Johnson, *op. cit.*, p. 168. See also Nevins, *op. cit.*, p. 91.

[33] R. U. Johnson, *op. cit.*, p. 164.

[34] Nevins, *op. cit.*, p. 208.

[35] R. U. Johnson, *op. cit.*, p. 162.

[36] For general sketch of New York in the seventies, see R. U. Johnson, *op. cit.*, pp. 153–170.

little old New York, with its cozy "downtown," to the thundering, conglomerate world metropolis of these nineteen-thirties! Today, of course, the Manhattan sojourner can do all his shopping, see all of his night life, and take in all of the theatrical hits without even venturing below the garish Forties of the Murray Hill district.

For all its comparative insignificance, however, the New York of the seventies was a most fascinating town. A. Oakley Hall—weak and futile, but suave, scholarly, and colorful—was its mayor.[37] Astors and Lorillards and Vanderbilts rode sleek four-in-hand equipages up and down its Avenue.[38] On fine Sunday afternoons smart top-hatted, frock-coated gentlemen, accompanied by smart crinolined ladies, promenaded Broadway between Union Square and Madison Square. On weekdays flower girls, Spitz-pup vendors, and toy-women hawked their wares along lower Broadway—the more enterprising hawkers equipped with capacious laundry baskets. Along the Rialto and in the shopping district, shabby but picturesque sandwich men advertised the newest plays.[39] On New Year's day, in the fashionable region of brownstone fronts, everybody who was Anybody made or received formal calls amid much convivial popping of corks.[40] A contrast to present-day Gotham! Yes. But an even greater contrast to the staid little Springfield that Josiah Holland had left forever behind!

After several strenuous days of house-hunting, Josiah and Elizabeth found a town house which took the fancy of both of them. The location was far enough uptown to be in a quiet and thoroughly desirable neighborhood, yet not too far from the Scribner office, the best stores, and the Hollands' favorite New York church. The house, which had just been erected, was large and comfortable-looking without being unduly showy. Its feature which probably appealed most

[37] See Harry J. Carman: "Abraham Oakley Hall," VIII, 114–116, *Dictionary of American Biography*. New York, 1932.
[38] R. U. Johnson, *op. cit.*, p. 169.
[39] William H. Rideing: "Life on Broadway." *Harper's*, LVI, 229–239.
[40] R. U. Johnson, *op. cit.*, p. 168.

strongly to Josiah was a large, sunny attic room, which had been designed for billiards, but which Josiah promptly decided would make him an admirable study. The place chosen was 46 Park Avenue, between Thirty-fifth and Thirty-sixth streets.[41] Commenting upon this house, an Illinois friend and admirer of Holland wrote proudly:

The writer of this notice enjoyed Dr. Holland's princely hospitality recently at his family residence . . . in New York City, for which he paid the sum of $76,000, besides the cost of elegant furnishings and appointments.[42]

Before we consider the career of *Scribner's Monthly,* we must reiterate the fact that Josiah Holland and Roswell Smith were wonderfully congenial spirits—much more congenial than Josiah Holland and Sam Bowles had ever been. At the time when the *Scribner's* was started, Smith was forty-one years old—just ten years Holland's junior. Smith, like Holland, was a tall, big-framed, sturdy-looking man; but in other physical particulars the two men did not greatly resemble each other. Smith's long curly hair and luxuriant beard, which were already noticeably graying, and the kindly placidity of his habitual facial expression, caused people to remark that Roswell Smith reminded them of Henry Wadsworth Longfellow.[43] Smith was an admirable man to do business with; for, although he was shrewd, venturesome, and acquisitive, he was scrupulously honest and very generous. Like Holland, he was devoutly religious and strait-lacedly ascetic. An upstanding pillar in the Presbyterian church, Smith also found time to serve as a director of the American Tract Society. In this connection, it should be remarked that when the stockholders of the Scribner magazine company assembled for their first annual meeting, Smith suggested that their deliberations should be preceded by a prayer.[44] Most of the stockholders were astonished at this suggestion; but

41 Plunkett, *op. cit.,* p. 87. See also above, p. 10, footnote 36.
42 See above, p. 165, footnote 2.
43 R. U. Johnson, *op. cit.,* pp. 96–98.
44 Ellsworth, *op. cit.,* p. 10.

Holland, of course, was delighted. Indeed, Josiah's one regret was undoubtedly that he himself had not thought to make the suggestion. Needless to say, the opening of the Holland-Smith stockholders' meeting with prayer became an annual procedure.

Josiah Holland could hardly have found a more congenial, more sympathetic business partner than Roswell Smith. Although the two men often disagreed regarding details of policy, and although Holland often felt called upon to veto Smith schemes that appeared to him unduly rash, their disagreements were always goodnatured; there is not the slightest evidence that the two ever really quarreled. In fact, in all their relations, both business and social, they were the warmest of friends.[45]

The establishment of *Scribner's Monthly* created no real sensation, for in 1870 the American magazine was neither a new nor an unfamiliar phenomenon. As early as 1741, two magazines, the *American Magazine* and the *General Magazine,* had been started in Philadelphia,[46] and by 1850 more than five hundred periodicals (exclusive of newspapers) had made their appearance in this country.[47] In the remaining twenty years before the inception of the old *Scribner's* that amazingly long list had been augmented by eleven "leading periodicals." [48]

Most of these periodicals, to be sure, had been decidedly ephemeral, some of them having continued for only a few months.[49] Several others, however, had had long and successful careers. In this latter category must be listed such periodicals as the *North American Review* (1815–   ), *Godey's Lady's Book* (1830–1898), the *Knickerbocker Magazine*

---

[45] R. U. Johnson, *op. cit.,* pp. 96–98.

[46] Mott, *op. cit.,* p. 787.

[47] See chronological list compiled by Mott, pp. 787–799.

[48] Percy H. Boynton: *A History of American Literature,* Boston, 1919, chart opposite p. 486.

[49] For example, the *American Magazine* (Jan.–Mar., 1741) and the *Western Literary Journal and Monthly Review* (June–Nov., 1836). Mott, *op. cit.,* pp. 787, 803.

(1833–1865), the *Southern Literary Messenger* (1834–1865), the *Democratic Review* (1837–1859), *Graham's Magazine* (1841–1859), *Littell's Living Age* (1844–   ), *Harper's Magazine* (1850–   ), and the *Atlantic Monthly* (1857–   ).[48] Moreover, since we are concerned with magazines in particular rather than with periodicals in general, it should be observed that all of the periodicals in the foregoing list are to be classed definitely as magazines.

In differentiating the magazine from other types of periodicals, we may, I think, accept Professor Mott's statement that the term *magazine* "is . . . understood . . . to refer to a stitched or stapled pamphlet, usually with a cover," [50] and that the magazine is "issued more or less regularly . . . [contains] a variety of reading matter . . . [and] has a strong connotation of entertainment." [50] This definition would obviously exclude newspapers on the one hand and specialized professional journals on the other. It would also exclude the old British "reviews," such as the *Edinburgh Review,* in which—until recent times, at least—the pages have been devoted entirely to criticisms of books.

In an earlier paragraph we remarked that several of the American magazines issued prior to 1870 enjoyed long and successful careers. The longevity of these magazines we have already indicated. Their popularity may be gauged by circulation figures. For example, the circulation of *Graham's* reached 135,000 by 1850; that of *Harper's,* 125,000 by 1854; and that of *Godey's,* 150,000 before 1877.[51] Before 1850, of course, circulations were considerably smaller than any of those listed above. In 1826, for instance, the *North American Review* had only about three thousand subscribers; [52] from 1835 to 1837 the circulation of the *Southern Literary Messenger* grew from some seven hundred to some five thousand; [53] and even as late as 1849 a *Godey's* edition of forty

---

⁴⁸ Percy H. Boynton: *A History of American Literature,* Boston, 1919, chart opposite p. 486.

⁵⁰ Mott, *op. cit.,* p. 7.

⁵¹ Boynton: *Hist. of Amer. Lit.,* pp. 491–492.

⁵² Mott, *op. cit.,* p. 514.

⁵³ Boynton: *Hist. of Amer. Lit.,* p. 499.

thousand was acclaimed as "unprecedented." [52] Still, the average circulation of all American monthly periodicals in 1850 was said to have been in excess of seven thousand,[52] a figure indicative of a relatively large magazine reading public by the middle of the last century.

Reasons for the popularity of magazines, both before and after 1870, are not difficult to find. As Professor Cairns has pointed out: "The magazines offer the writings of the best authors, artistically printed and often admirably illustrated, far cheaper than such work can be purchased elsewhere." [54] Moreover, the magazines, unlike most books, offer an anthological variety of subject matter and keep constantly abreast of the times. In short, as Professor Mott says, the popular magazines of this country have been generally "miscellaneous, entertaining, and mercurial." [55]

In accepting the editorship of a magazine, J. G. Holland was entering no unsurveyed or uncultivated field. Long before 1870 there had been a number of really prominent American magazine editors. There had been, for example, James Russell Lowell, of the *Atlantic Monthly;* Edgar Allan Poe, of the *Gentleman's* and *Graham's* respectively; George P. Morris and N. P. Willis, of the *Home Journal;* Charles Fenno Hoffman and Lewis Gaylord Clark, of the *Knickerbocker;* James Russell Lowell and Charles Eliot Norton, of the *North American Review;* and Paul Hamilton Hayne, of *Russell's.*[56] And most of these men did not owe their fame solely or even primarily to their editorial positions; most of them were at least moderately successful as creative writers. Lowell and Poe, for instance, need no introduction even to the most superficial student of American literature. Willis was a highly versatile and extremely popular writer in his day.[57] Morris and Hoff-

---

[52] Mott, *op. cit.,* p. 514.

[54] William B. Cairns: "Later Magazines." *Cambridge History of American Literature,* III, 299.

[55] Mott, *op. cit.,* p. 7.

[56] Boynton: *Hist. of Amer. Lit.,* pp. 488–498.

[57] See above, pp. 71–72.

man were gifted song-writers.[58] Hayne was one of the most prolific lyrical poets of the South.[59]

Holland must have realized, however, that the field of magazine-editing was not all a garden of roses or an orchard of luscious fruit. Circulation figures were deceptive. Advertising, as we shall see,[60] was as yet undeveloped. Editors, on the whole, commanded but paltry salaries. The checks sent to contributors were correspondingly small.

The deceptive thing about the circulation lists was that many of the subscribers did not meet their financial obligations. Some persons were far in arrears. Exasperated editors often threatened to publish lists of delinquents.[61] More patient and conciliatory editors tried to stimulate subscription payments by publishing honor-rolls of prompt remitters.[61]

And [says Professor Mott] how wearisomely reiterated are the dunning notices to delinquent subscribers! Some publishers try to break the monotony of such pleas by variety and wit in their expression. Godey writes: "We are frequently asked for an autograph. There is one certain way of procuring it: Remit us three dollars, and we will send it, affixed to a receipt, in a most flourishing style. . . ." And many a magazine in its swan-song laid the responsibility for its death upon its own well-wishing but non-paying subscribers.[62]

These being the circumstances, it is evident that in the middle years of the nineteenth century the publishers of our American magazines could hardly have afforded to pay their editors munificent salaries. As a matter of fact, one thousand dollars a year appears to have been a notably large stipend. This was the sum received by R. W. Griswold and Bayard Taylor as successive editors of *Graham's,* and it was likewise the figure at which William Gilmore Simms accepted the editorship of

[58] *Cambridge History of American Literature,* 1, 279–280.
[59] Boynton: *Literature and American Life,* p. 576.
[60] See below, pp. 183–184.
[61] Mott, *op. cit.,* p. 515.
[62] *Ibid.,* pp. 514–515.

the *Southern Quarterly*.[63]. Appreciably smaller was the fifteen dollars a week received by Poe as editor-in-chief of the *Southern Literary Messenger*.[63] On a comparative basis, of course, these figures did not look nearly so bad in 1850 as they would look today. As Professor Mott points out, "All of these payments are to be regarded in the light of living costs of the period."[64] Salaries for other occupations were correspondingly low. College professors, for instance, averaged about six hundred dollars a year; schoolteachers were extraordinarily lucky if they got ten dollars a month and board; and even the governor of a wealthy and populous state such as Connecticut was willing to serve at a stipend equal to the editorial salary paid by *Graham's*.[65] Nevertheless, at a time when John Jacob Astor had accumulated between twenty and thirty million dollars,[66] and when Jenny Lind commanded a thousand dollars a night,[67] a salary of a thousand a year could hardly have been regarded as princely.

Low pay, however, was only one of the financial difficulties encountered by the American magazine editor at the middle of the last century. The other big difficulty was that the publishers could not offer very attractive rates to the most desirable contributors. So far as the general run of contributors were concerned, it was said in 1848 that they were "mostly unpaid."[68] More prominent writers fared better than that; but, on the whole, not particularly well. Poe, for instance, received only four or five dollars a page for prose in *Graham's* (one of the best-paying magazines of its day); and Lowell and Longfellow received respectively thirty and fifty dollars a poem in the same periodical.[69] The two thousand a year offered to Irving by *Knickerbocker* for the *Wolfert's Roost* papers sounds truly munificent—until we note that Irving had

---

[63] Mott, *op. cit.*, p. 512.
[64] *Ibid.*, p. 513.
[65] *Ibid.*, p. 513.
[66] Arthur D. H. Smith: *John Jacob Astor, Landlord of New York*, New York, 1929, p. 289.
[67] *Encyclopaedia Britannica*, III, 125.
[68] Mott, *op. cit.*, p. 512.
[69] *Ibid.*, p. 507.

great difficulty in collecting what he had been promised.[70] The kernel of the difficulty is revealed in these words, written from an editorial point of view by N. P. Willis:

> As to the original American production, we shall, as the [book] publishers do, take what we can get for nothing (that is good), holding, as the [book] publishers do, that while we can get Boz and Bulwer for a thank-ye or less, it is not pocket-wise to pay much for Halleck and Irving.[71]

Before accepting the editorship of the old *Scribner's,* the prudent Josiah Holland must have considered carefully the drawbacks as well as the advantages of magazine journalism. Ultimately he must have decided that the latter outweighed the former. Perhaps the astute Roswell Smith could solve the problem of delinquent subscribers and ill-paid contributors. And, so far as the scale of editorial salaries was concerned, Holland had no personal worries; for he himself was to be a member of the firm.

The first issues of *Scribner's Monthly* made a widely favorable impression—so widely favorable, we may be sure, as to bring *Harper's* to a speedy realization of the fact that at last it had a real rival in the illustrated magazine field.[72] And it soon became apparent that as rapidly as possible the new monthly intended to introduce attractive innovations.

As a starter, *Scribner's Monthly* was inheriting two small subscription lists: that of the already-mentioned *Hours at Home,* and that of *Putnam's Monthly Magazine,* which, for not quite three years, had struggled along in a none-too-successful effort to revive an earlier *Putnam's.*[73] In this connection, a perusal of Holland's opening editorial makes it clear that Holland and Smith expected to build their subscription list largely upon the wide personal following that Holland had gained as author and as lyceum lecturer. Said the editorial in part:

[70] Mott, *op. cit.,* pp. 510–511.
[71] Henry A. Beers: *Nathaniel Parker Willis,* Boston, 1885, p. 240.
[72] Of course, however, *Harper's* did not publicly admit this realization.
[73] Boynton: *Hist. of Amer. Lit.,* p. 499.

It is an exceedingly pleasant reflection to the editor that he and those for whom he prepares this magazine are not strangers. In books, newspapers, periodicals, and public addresses, he and they have met many times during the last twenty years. In that period he has experienced much of their kindness, and they have had abundant opportunity to become acquainted with him. To their generous confidence he appeals in presenting to them this new enterprise. He asks them to believe that it is his purpose to obtain for them the best reading that money will buy, to furnish the finest illustrations procurable at home and abroad, and to make a magazine that they will all desire to possess, and will all feel the richer for possessing. . . .

We shall try to make a magazine that is intelligent on all living questions of morals and society, and to present something in every number that will interest and instruct every member of every family into which it shall have the good fortune to find its way.[74]

The first volume of *Scribner's Monthly* contained parts of lengthy illustrated serials by Hans Christian Andersen and George Macdonald respectively; a three-installment novelette by Rebecca Harding Davis; half a dozen short stories, including "Huldah the Help," by Edward Eggleston; and more than a score of poems. Its illustrated articles included "Life in the Cannibal Islands," a richly informative essay on New Zealand, by J. C. Bates; "Fairmount Park," an interesting account of Philadelphia's huge playground, by Newton Crane; "Strasburg after the Surrender," a timely Franco-Prussian war article, by M. B. Riddle; and "King Gambrinus and his Subjects," a diatribe against Bavarian beer-drinking, by William Wells.[75] This last-named article, which bears all the earmarks of having been solicited if not directly inspired by Editor Holland, comes much nearer to being downright propaganda than any other contribution to the volume. In this article, both the text and the grotesque illustrations undertake to show that beer is inherently and necessarily a most demoralizing beverage. The writer concludes his remarks with the in-

---

[74] *Op. cit.*, I, 106. Nov., 1870.
[75] *Ibid.*, I. Nov., 1870–Apr., 1871.

genuous assertion that "statistics prove" [76] that the Bavarians, who are the heaviest beer-drinkers in the world, are likewise the most ignorant, the most superstitious, the most unprogressive, the most cowardly, and the most unhealthy of Germans.[76] That this article was hailed with delighted approval by all Good Templars and Rechabites goes without saying. In this connection, we may suspect that the average American temperance zealot of sixty or seventy years ago was much more likely to be a reader of a first-class magazine than is his counterpart of these nineteen-thirties. At any rate, abstinence-from-beer propaganda would look odd in the *Harper's* or the *Atlantic* of today; it would look still odder in the *American Mercury*.

At the very beginning, *Scribner's Monthly* followed the old American magazine custom of withholding the names of individual contributors. In the earliest issues, for example, the only *Scribner's* authors whose names were attached to their work were such foreign celebrities as Andersen and Macdonald. Not until the appearance of the first table of contents for the entire first volume, in April 1871, were the names of most of the contributors revealed.[77] Apropos of this fact, it should be remarked that the practice of withholding magazine authors' names was one of long standing. In 1859 James Russell Lowell, then editor of the *Atlantic Monthly*, had expressed definite opposition to the publishing of names.[78] And, as one literary historian has truly remarked, up to the seventies the majority of magazine articles were as strictly anonymous as were the majority of newspaper articles.[79] Both Holland and Smith, however, felt that magazine authors were as fully entitled to public recognition as were book authors. They felt, moreover, that the publication of prominent names would be of distinct commercial value to the magazine. Consequently, it was not long until the names of leading *Scribner's* contributors, particularly the writers of

[76] *Op. cit.,* I, 497. March, 1871.
[77] *Op. cit.*
[78] Ellsworth, *op. cit.,* p. 49.
[79] *Ibid.,* p. 49.

serials, were attached regularly to their contributions.[80] That other magazines soon recognized the wisdom of this new policy may be seen from an examination of old *Atlantic* files.[81] *Harper's* was somewhat slower in coming round, but in due time it also followed suit.[81]

Another attractive new feature inaugurated by *Scribner's Monthly* was the improved process of engraving. Illustrations in the old *Harper's,* the old *Putnam's,* and other ante-bellum magazines look rather crude to us, and this crudeness is largely due to clumsy, primitive methods of transferring artists' drawings to engravers' blocks. Prior to the seventies the only known way to make woodcuts was the very slow, laborious backhand copying of the original pictures upon the wooden surfaces.[82] But Alexander Wilson Drake, art editor of the new *Scribner's Monthly,* was mainly instrumental in changing all this. Drake, an enterprising and talented young New Yorker with valuable experience both as a painter and as a wood engraver, quickly recognized the success of experiments in transferring pictures from paper to wood by the photographic process. He saw, as other engravers came to see a little later, that both in speed and in accuracy the photographic process was immeasurably superior to the awkward backhand method of drawing line for line.[83] The result was that *Scribner's Monthly* immediately surpassed all of its competitors in the matter of attractive illustrations. The further result was that British authorities were soon admitting that the best contemporary illustrations were being printed in America, not Europe.[84] Beginning in 1875, Drake had a most able assistant in the person of Timothy Cole, who

[80] R. U. Johnson, *op. cit.,* p. 88.

[81] The practices of the three magazines in 1881 may be seen from the following instances: *Scribner's* published Cable's *Delphine* with the author's name at the beginning of each installment (*op. cit.,* XXII, 22 *et seq.*); the *Atlantic* published Howells' *Dr. Breen's Practice* with the author's name at the end of each installment (*op. cit.,* XLVIII, 145 *et seq.*); *Harper's* published Mrs. Woolson's *Anne* without the author's name. In all three magazines the verse and the short articles were still, for the most part, unsigned.

[82] R. U. Johnson, *op. cit.,* pp. 99–100.

[83] *Ibid.,* pp. 99–100.

[84] Ellsworth, *op. cit.,* pp. 70–71.

ultimately surpassed Drake himself as a wood engraver. Cole's beautiful reproductions of famous paintings, which accompanied the late W. C. Brownell's articles on art, made *Scribner's Monthly* easily the most artistic general magazine of its day.[84] Incidentally, another very important contributor to the esthetic excellence of the old *Scribner's* was Theodore Low De Vinne, internationally famous exponent of artistic printing, from whose press issued all but the first few volumes of the Holland-Smith magazine.[85]

Another *Scribner's* innovation, probably instituted by Smith, but certainly approved by Holland, was the acceptance of advertising upon a large scale. William W. Ellsworth is not quite accurate in his statement that "up to the beginning of that periodical [*Scribner's Monthly*] magazines did not print advertising at all";[86] for, as a matter of fact, *Harper's* printed miscellaneous advertising as early as 1864,[87] and the *Atlantic* as early as 1860.[87] Mr. Ellsworth is, however, quite correct in his implication that *Scribner's Monthly* was the first high-grade magazine to solicit advertising—the first high-grade magazine to consider extensive advertising entirely compatible with the tone and dignity of a superior periodical.[87] From the very start, *Harper's* had advertised Harper books; but its miscellaneous advertisements had never exceeded fifteen or twenty to the issue, and all of these advertisements had been small and inconspicuous. In fact, at about the time *Scribner's Monthly* was founded, *Harper's* had actually rejected a proposition to advertise the Howe Sewing Machine on its back cover for one year for $18,000.[87] Moreover, as Roswell Smith recognized, *Harper's* advertising rates were so steep as to discourage rather than invite advertisers. *Harper's* charged $500 a page for an ordinary page of each issue; $1,000 a page for space next to reading matter; and $1,000 a page for space on the cover. *Scribner's Monthly* decided to charge $100 a page for an ordinary page; $200 a

<hr>

84 Ellsworth, *op. cit.*, pp. 70–71.
85 R. U. Johnson, *op. cit.*, pp. 108–112.
86 Ellsworth, *op. cit.*, p. 121.
87 Frank Presbrey: *The History and Development of Advertising*, p. 466.

page for space next to reading matter; and $150 a page for space on the cover.[88] It is, therefore, not to be wondered that the Holland-Smith firm were soon getting all of the advertisements that they could find space to print. Today, as we all know, the price of a good magazine is invariably much lower than the cost of publication; and the only commercial value of a large circulation lies in increased value of advertising space.[89] *Scribner's Monthly,* however, was the first magazine really to appreciate this obvious fact.

Closely related to the problem of magazine advertising is the problem of magazine distribution. Up to the time when *Scribner's Monthly* was established, the method of paying magazine postage was one that we should consider indeed peculiar. All postage was paid quarterly at the post-office by the subscriber.[90] Roswell Smith concluded that this was a ridiculous system—a system that tended to drive people away from taking magazines. Why, he asked, should not the publishers pay the postage? The postage bill would be relatively small; and, anyhow, the prepayment of postage would probably result in a noticeably larger subscription list. True, no subscriber ever paid more than fifteen or twenty cents postage a quarter, but these payments were manifestly a nuisance. Holland and Scribner were interested in Smith's suggestion, but they wondered about the feasibility of attaching stamps to thousands of magazines each month. Well, why bother with stamps at all? Why not arrange with the postal authorities to make wholesale payments of magazine postage? To us of today, these questions of Smith's are all so very simple that we wonder how it could ever have been necessary for anyone to ask them. Thanks to Roswell Smith, American magazines were soon being distributed in a new manner—a manner that won the good will of subscribers everywhere.[90]

It takes more, however, than generous advertising and

<hr>

88 Presbrey, *op. cit.,* p. 469.
89 *Ibid.,* p. 471.
90 Ellsworth, *op. cit.,* p. 11.

postal prepayment to make a magazine popular. It takes more, even, than attractive illustrations and beautiful printing. And here we come to the big part played by Editor J. G. Holland in the success of *Scribner's Monthly*. *Scribner's*, from the day of its first appearance, bore the subtitle *An Illustrated Magazine for the People*. It was just that—in the best sense of the word. Of course it made no particular appeal to "the people" in the Jacksonian sense; that is, to the illiterate or the vulgar. It did, however, win a much wider clientele than any first-class magazine had ever won before. *Harper's* and the *Atlantic* and the *North American* had gone regularly into the homes of the leading professional men in communities large and small throughout the country. *Scribner's Monthly* reached the families of the more substantial business men as well.[91]

A particularly good reason for the old *Scribner's* winning of this wider clientele lay in the fact that the Holland-Smith magazine was not afraid to tackle controversial subjects, especially those pertaining to politics and religion. Up to 1870, American magazines of general appeal had cautiously avoided such subjects on the ground that whatever interest they might arouse, they would likewise kindle such resentment as to alienate more readers than they could hope to gain. Editor Holland, however, stoutly insisted upon bringing these debatable topics out into the open; he was firm in the conviction that since "the two subjects in which the people of this country are most interested are politics and religion,"[92] those subjects ought to be discussed most freely, not tabooed. As a result, *Scribner's Monthly* "took a conspicuous stand in the advocacy not merely of civil-service reform and religious liberalism, but of international copyright, kindergarten instruction, tenement-house improvement, and other causes."[93] And thereby, thanks to Josiah Holland's courage and sagacity, this forward-looking magazine "not only lived

[91] Presbrey, *op. cit.*, p. 469.
[92] R. U. Johnson, *op. cit.*, p. 87.
[93] Nevins, *op. cit.*, p. 245.

and prospered . . . but gained enduring distinction." [94]

Turning to more purely literary materials, we find that under J. G. Holland's astute editorship *Scribner's Monthly* published such interesting and memorable fiction as Henry James's *Adina*,[95] William Dean Howells' *A Fearful Responsibility*,[96] Bret Harte's *Gabriel Conroy*,[97] Rebecca Harding Davis' *Natasqua*,[98] George Macdonald's *Wilfrid Cumbermede*,[99] Frances Hodgson Burnett's *Louisiana*,[100] George W. Cable's *The Grandissimes*,[97] and Mrs. Oliphant's *At His Gates*,[101] as well as the Holland novels that we considered in our last chapter. Most of the authors' names just mentioned are almost as familiar today—at least, to the student of literature—as they were threescore years ago. George Macdonald is, perhaps, nearly forgotten; but up to the time of his death at an advanced age in 1905 he remained one of the conspicuously popular British novelists. Macdonald was a Scotch Calvinistic minister, and, as might be supposed, he wrote novels that were as ethical and evangelical in tone as the novels of Holland himself.[102] Cable and "Fanny" Burnett were real *Scribner's* discoveries. In the seventies both of them were youngsters,[103] and it was through the columns of *Scribner's Monthly* that both of them first attracted nation-wide attention. Among the notable poets whose work appeared in the old *Scribner's* were Richard Watson Gilder, Edmund Clarence Stedman, and Richard Henry Stoddard.[104] It will thus be observed that Josiah Gilbert Holland had rather good editorial taste.

Further light on this matter of Holland's editorial taste is shed by two unpublished Holland letters, both of them writ-

---

[94] Nevins, *op. cit.*, p. 245.
[95] *Op. cit.*, VIII, 33 *et seq.*
[96] *Ibid.*, XXII, 276 *et seq.*
[97] See above, p. 164, footnote 61.
[98] *Op. cit.*, I, 1 *et seq.*
[99] *Ibid.*, p. 90 *et seq.*
[100] *Ibid.*, XIX, 512 *et seq.*
[101] *Ibid.*, III, 355 *et seq.*
[102] See above, p. 77.
[103] Born 1844 and 1849 respectively.
[104] Ellsworth, *op. cit.*, p. 45.

ten in 1878. Speaking of Stedman's "Meridian," a poem read at the twenty-fifth anniversary of the Yale class of 1853, on June 28, 1878, Holland wrote these appreciative words:

> Bonnie-Castle
> Alexandria Bay, N.Y.
> July 16, 1878

My dear Stedman:

I have just finished reading [in proof] your long poem [which will appear] in the August "Scribner," and I hope you will let me tell you of the strong, pure satisfaction it gives me. To me it speaks of a broader, deeper, mellower man than anything of yours I have ever read.

I have no college memoirs that would give to a production of this sort a fictitious or factitious value; so it seemed to me that you would be glad to know just how it impressed "an outsider." It is pure, elevated, temperate, strong, and it must have been received with great favor by your friends to whom it was delivered. After all, is there anything better than the "old fashioned" poem for a public occasion? I doubt it.

Hoping you are passing a pleasant summer, I am

> Yours always truly,
> J. G. Holland [105]

Equally appreciative is a letter that Holland wrote a few months later to the German poet Ferdinand Freiligrath, upon receipt of seven metrical translations which the latter had made from German into English. Holland wrote as follows:

> Scribner's Monthly,
> 654 Broadway, N.Y.
> Oct. 1, 1878

Dear Mr. Freiligrath:

Several months ago I received a number of poems from your daughter by your hand—translations from the German. I immediately wrote you that the poems ought to have a fitting introduction to the English reading public, and that I should be delighted to get such an introduction from yourself. For this, of

---

[105] For the use of this letter I am indebted to Miss Mary A. Benjamin, 501 Madison Avenue, New York City.

course, I should expect to pay our best prices. If you should choose
to write it in German I would get it translated though I have no
fault to find with your English. Did you get the letter? [106] Please
tell me what your conclusion is and very greatly oblige,

Yours always truly,
J. G. Holland [107]

Yes, Josiah Gilbert Holland was an appreciative as well as an
astute editor.

It should, however, be pointed out that Holland had a
most able assistant in the person of Richard Watson Gilder.
Gilder, although a much younger and less experienced man
than Holland, was possessed of a finer discrimination and a
decidedly more catholic and cosmopolitan outlook.[108] Undoubtedly it was Gilder rather than Holland who first appreciated the talents of that promising young Southerner,
George W. Cable. Undoubtedly, too, Gilder's monthly department *The Old Cabinet* is of far more enduring literary
value than Holland's *Topics of the Time*.

But Holland's editorial influence must not be minimized.
It was Holland more than anyone else who made *Scribner's
Monthly* a distinct public educational force. It was at Holland's suggestion that the Southern people were ingratiated
and the Northern people enlightened by a series of illustrated
articles on the New South—articles from the pen of Edward
King.[109] The King articles, by the way, were published in
book form in 1875, under the title *The Great South,* and
enjoyed a wide sale.[110] The timeliness of these articles may be
seen from the fact that not until the inauguration of President Hayes in 1877 did a post-bellum chief executive adopt a
sane and at the same time conciliatory attitude toward the

---

[106] The reason for Freiligrath's failure to answer Holland's previous letter
is more obvious to us than it was to Holland. The sad fact is that Freiligrath
had died more than two years earlier (March 18, 1876), a circumstance which
had evidently escaped Holland's notice or eluded his memory.

[107] For the use of this letter I am indebted to Miss Mary A. Benjamin, 501
Madison Avenue, New York City.

[108] R. U. Johnson, *op. cit.,* p. 89. See also Ellsworth, *op. cit.,* pp. 43–44.

[109] Ellsworth, *op. cit.,* pp. 50–51.

[110] *Universal Cyclopaedia,* VI, 637.

South.[111] It was, moreover, Holland who, partly through his own *Topics of the Time* and partly through articles by the Reverend William Cleaver Wilkinson and the Reverend Augustus Blauvelt, first popularized the merits of biblical higher criticism.[112] And this, in the United States of the seventies, was a courageous thing to undertake.

To Editor Holland, I think, even more than to Publisher Smith, we must credit the phenomenal success of *Scribner's Monthly* during the eleven years of its existence. In that period of a trifle over a decade, the old *Scribner's* more than tripled its original circulation of forty thousand; [113] and in the United States of the seventies, with its relatively small, relatively unenlightened population, that was indeed a wonderful feat for a high-toned magazine.

[111] Frederic L. Paxson: *The New Nation*, Boston, New York, Chicago, 1915, p. 85.
[112] R. U. Johnson, *op. cit.*, pp. 86–87.
[113] Boynton: *Hist. of Amer. Lit.*, p. 499.

IX

In Conclusion

During his eleven years' residence in New York, Josiah Gilbert Holland became, as we have already pointed out, a leading citizen of the metropolis. From his third-story sanctum, two flights above the Scribner store at 743 Broadway,[1] he wielded an influence comparable to that of a daily newspaper editor. And those were the days of the great personal journalists: William Cullen Bryant, of the *Evening Post;*[2] Charles Anderson Dana, of the *Sun;*[2] and Horace Greeley, of the *Tribune!*[2] In his monthly *Topics of the Time* (his *Every-Day Topics* as they appeared in *Scribner's*) Holland labored unceasingly and, on the whole, effectively, to improve public morals, public manners, and public taste.[3] And for a man of his humble origin and his stubbornly provincial morality, Josiah Gilbert Holland acquired astonishingly good taste. With just a little more urbanity, just a little more open-mindedness, just a little more of a cosmopolitan outlook, just a little more of a sense of humor, Holland might have become a nineteenth-century American Joseph Addison.

Let us draw the curtain, for the moment, upon Josiah Holland's naïve faith in the supremacy of the New England Calvinistic rural ethical code,[4] upon his enthusiasm for Anthony Comstock,[5] upon his antipathy for Walt Whitman.[6] Let us draw the curtain upon Whitman's cruel but by no means

[1] This was the address at the end of Holland's career. (Ellsworth, *op. cit.,* p. 24). An earlier address had been 654 Broadway. (See above, p. 187.)

[2] Willard Grosvenor Bleyer: *Main Currents in the History of American Journalism,* Boston, New York, Chicago, 1927, pp. 143, 236, 305.

[3] See above, V, 68 *et seq*.

[4] See above, p. 66.

[5] See Holland's "Topics." *Scribner's Monthly,* XXII, 456–457.

[6] See above, pp. 74–75.

utterly false words: "He [Holland] was a man of his time, not possessed of the slightest forereach; . . . the style of man . . . who can tell the difference between a dime and a fifty-cent piece—but is useless for occasions of more serious moment." [7] Let us draw the curtain upon Holland's distress at George Eliot's unconventional relations with George Henry Lewes,[8] upon his disapproval of Dickens' paganism,[9] upon his reprehension of Thackeray's unspirituality.[9]

Let us focus our eyes, for the moment, upon a pleasanter side of the picture. And here we shall see Josiah Gilbert Holland as the envoy of literature and art to thousands of American homes in an age when few of our people had contact with good bookstores and good libraries, and still fewer had contact with metropolitan galleries.[10] We shall see Holland as—quantitatively, at least—the greatest American dispenser of sweetness and light in his day.[11]

Yes, J. G. Holland was a leading citizen in the eighth decade of the last century, an apostle of culture, a patron of arts and of artists. The intellectuals and the esthetes of the seventies might be captious of the good Dr. Holland's provincial naïveté, but most of them took genuine pleasure in dropping in at the evening receptions in the Holland town house on Park Avenue; for here one might meet such interesting personages as Kate Field, "Fanny" Hodgson (Burnett), Helen Hunt (Jackson), Bret Harte, John Hay, Robert Underwood Johnson, Charles Dudley Warner, and Richard Henry Stoddard. And though Stoddard might exclaim wistfully, "Good heavens, boys, where's the whisky?"—though coffee and tea would invariably be the most potent beverages served—everyone present would have a really delightful time.[12]

Outside of the literary and the editorial fields, Holland's

[7] Horace Traubel: *With Walt Whitman in Camden*, Boston, 1906, p. 184.
[8] "Topics." *Scribner's Monthly*, XXI, 791.
[9] See above, pp. 80–81.
[10] Nevins, *op. cit.*, pp. 242, 260.
[11] See above, pp. 2, 120, 164.
[12] For an account of the Holland receptions, see R. U. Johnson, *op. cit.*, p. 90.

importance as a citizen may be seen in the public and quasi-public positions that he held. Probably the most conspicuous of these positions was the presidency of the New York City Board of Public Instruction, to which he was elected for the term beginning January 1, 1873.[13] That a man who had been a resident of the metropolis for less than three years should be thus honored was indeed a tribute to the high esteem in which Holland was held by hosts of his fellow New Yorkers; and Josiah, we may be sure, fully appreciated the honor. In this office, however, he was not to find much happiness. Back in his Springfield *Republican* days, as we have observed, he was not very political-minded.[14] And now both the politics and the routine of the Board of Public Instruction soon proved a vexation to him. What with the wire-pulling of selfish interests and the nagging of the daily and the weekly press, Holland found his school-board job to be anything but a sinecure. Should the Board of Public Instruction retain as its clerk a man who was an avowed Roman Catholic? Regardless of personal merits and qualifications, should Roman Catholics be employed as teachers in the public schools? Did not Roman Catholic parents, whenever and wherever it was at all possible, send their children to the parochial schools in preference to the public schools? Was it not high time that the Board of Public Instruction inaugurated a program of retrenchment? Had not the expenditures for schools become scandalously large? Were not the Republican office-holders in New York too prone to emulate the inefficiency, the laxity, and the extravagance of the disgraceful Grant administration in Washington? These were some of the questions that rose to plague Josiah Holland and to distract his mind from the much more congenial matters of writing, editing, and lecturing. Three months of this turmoil was quite enough. It was, undoubtedly, with a sigh of relief that he reached the end of his brief term of office on April 5, 1873. On that date,

<hr>

[13] For this information I am indebted to Mr. Joseph Miller, Jr. (1934), Secretary of the New York Board of Education.

[14] See above, p. 39.

through the provisions of a new municipal charter, the old
Board of Public Instruction gave way to a Board of Education—a board that was different in personnel as well as in
name.[15] But Holland never lost interest in educational affairs; his *Topics* contain frequent and sometimes thoughtful
references to the function and the administration of schools.[16]

In previous chapters we have had more than one occasion to
speak of Josiah Holland's religious activities. In New York, of
course, he continued to be an ardent church worker. But here
he was faced with a problem such as he had not confronted
since his days in the South more than a score of years earlier.
The problem was this. Relatively few communities outside of
the New England states have ever been strongholds of Congregationalism; [17] and Manhattan Island has not been an exception to this general rule. Even today Manhattan boasts
only half a dozen Congregational churches as compared with
more than twoscore Presbyterian, and three or four thousand
Congregational communicants as compared with thirty or
forty thousand Presbyterian.[18] When the Hollands moved to
New York the prominent Congregational church in the met-
tropolitan area was Henry Ward Beecher's church, the Plymouth, in Brooklyn.[19] And when it is considered that the
Brooklyn of the early seventies was separated from Park
Avenue by miles of tedious horse-car and ferry-boat routes, it
may be readily seen that it was a real task for the Hollands
to get to a New York church of their own faith and polity.
For a few strenuous Sundays they tried it. But soon they gave
it up as a bad job; for, as Josiah sadly and truly remarked:
"This is much harder than a trip to Bridgeport." [20]

Only a few short blocks from the Holland residence on

[15] For dates and other objective facts, see above, p. 192, footnote 13. For
reference to charges of extravagance and Catholic influence, see "Topics."
Scribner's Monthly, VI, 622–623. Sept., 1873.

[16] See especially *Every-Day Topics*, II, 156–189.

[17] Fish, *op. cit.*, p. 184. See also *Encyclopaedia Britannica*, VI, 253.

[18] *World Almanac* (1937), pp. 433, 505.

[19] *Encyclopaedia Britannica*, III, 305.

[20] See above, p. 10, footnote 36. This was several years before the Tilton
scandal damaged Beecher's reputation. (Nevins, *op. cit.*, p. 313.)

Park Avenue stood the Brick Church, at Fifth Avenue and Thirty-seventh Street, one of the two leading Presbyterian churches of the metropolis. Thither the Hollands began to drift. The services there were simple and in the best of evangelical taste. The sermons, generally free from discussions of peculiarly Presbyterian doctrine and polity, were of just the proper degree of liberalism to please Josiah. The Brick Church soon became a Holland habit.[20]

But still the family hesitated about uniting with a Presbyterian church. It was not that either Josiah or Elizabeth was hidebound in any strictly sectarian sense. As early as 1861 Josiah had written:

Every denomination or form of religion has its excellencies, its necessities for certain natures, and its legitimate and honored field; but none of them hold [*sic*] exclusively the keys of happiness or heaven.[21]

And there is not the slightest reason to suppose that Elizabeth was more sectarian than Josiah. By the eighteen-seventies, undoubtedly, almost any evangelical communion would have been fairly acceptable to either of the Hollands; in other words, almost any orthodox Protestant body except the Lutheran and the Episcopal. Certainly among Calvinistic denominations there was little difference except as to church organization. Traditions, however, are precious. Had not both the Hollands and the Chapins been Congregationalists for more than two hundred years? To them a change of denomination, even though the change should be little more than nominal, was not a step to be taken lightly. Hence, for many months the Hollands continued as regular attendants of the Brick Church without becoming communicants.[22]

This state of affairs worried Josiah a great deal. One day, over two years after the family had settled in New York, he exclaimed: "Mother, it isn't right that we should go on be-

<hr>

20 See above, p. 10, footnote 36.
21 *Books, Authors and Art.* Springfield (Weekly) *Republican,* Feb. 16, 1861.
22 See above, p. 10, footnote 36.

ing 'Sunday bummers.'[23] Visiting a church, Sabbath after Sabbath, without accepting its full fellowship and its full responsibilities, isn't doing the work of the Lord. It isn't setting the kind of example that I want to set to my great audience of young people." Elizabeth agreed.[22] On the following Sunday morning—a Sunday in December 1872—the Hollands filed up to the front pew of the Brick Church and received the right hand of fellowship.[24]

So it came about that Josiah Holland, during his last earthly years, labored in the Presbyterian row of the Lord's vineyard. The Reverend Llewelyn D. Bevan, pastor of the Brick Church during the greater part of these years, has testified both as to the regularity of Josiah Holland's church attendance and as to Josiah's zeal for engaging prominently in every church and Sunday-school activity open to the layman.[25] The Holland pew was near the front of the church, and seldom during services was it unoccupied. The Sunday morning that did not find Josiah Holland in his accustomed place just beneath the pulpit was indeed a rarity. And he did not hide his ecclesiastical talents under a bushel. Whether singing a hymn in his earnest tenor, or joining heartily in a responsive reading, or passing the collection plate, he let his light so shine before men that they might see his good works.[25] Of the official positions that he held in the Brick Church the most responsible was that of trustee, which he graced from 1878 until his death.[26]

Here and elsewhere, perhaps, we have dwelt a little overmuch upon Holland's religiosity—or, rather, we have dwelt insufficiently upon his humanity. Walt Whitman peevishly complained of Holland's "strut,"[27] but that particular com-

<hr>

[22] See above, p. 10, footnote 36.

[23] By "Sunday bummers," Holland meant persons who visit church after church without uniting with any of them. (*Every-Day Topics*, II, 52–55.)

[24] Shepherd Knapp: *Records of the Brick Presbyterian Church of New York*, New York, 1909, p. 109.

[25] Plunkett, *op. cit.*, pp. 172–174. See also above, p. 10, footnote 36.

[26] For this information I am indebted to Miss Adair Black, Secretary of the Brick Church.

[27] Traubel, *op. cit.*, p. 184.

plaint appears to have been as groundless as it was biased. As a matter of fact, neither in "Titcomb's" own writings nor in the testimony of contemporaries, do we find evidence that Josiah Gilbert Holland was an obnoxiously conceited man. That Holland—like every provincial who fails, more or less, to outgrow a circumscribed early environment—was unduly opinionated touching matters of ethics, religion, temperance, and woman suffrage is all too patent; in fact, we have already had occasion to remark about it several times. But this is not to say that Josiah Holland was arrogantly egotistical. As a matter of record, one finds not a few evidences of Holland's modesty, even in his most prosperous and influential years. In this connection, it is interesting to read a sentence from a letter written by Holland to E. C. Stedman in 1877: "I have had," he confesses here, "none of Longfellow's rest and 'wherewithal,' nor until I was thirty did I ever know people who lived in 'sweetness and light.' " [28] And this not the bragging of a complacent self-made man, but rather the humble admission of one who was painfully conscious of his handicaps.

An especially pleasant anecdote exemplifying Holland's humanity, his kindly consideration for colleagues and subordinates, is related by Robert Underwood Johnson, who, as a youth of twenty, became a member of the *Scribner's* editorial staff in 1873.

My novitiate on the magazine [writes Mr. Johnson] did not occupy the designated three months, for after three weeks Doctor Holland came to me one day as I sat at my desk and, putting his hand in a fatherly way on my shoulder, said very gently, "Johnson, if you like us as well as we like you, you may hang up your hat and call it a bargain." [29]

On a later page, speaking of the fact that Dr. Holland was much beloved by his associates, Mr. Johnson recalls that for thirty-two years the members of the *Century* staff reverently

<hr>

[28] Laura Stedman, and George M. Gould: *Life and Letters of Edmund Clarence Stedman*, New York, 1910, II, 574.

[29] R. U. Johnson, *op. cit.*, p. 84.

celebrated the anniversary of Holland's death by draping his portrait with the vine and berries of the bittersweet.[30]

And Josiah Holland was as generously sympathetic toward struggling young writers as he was toward his associates. Recalling his own early privations and discouragements, he felt a real kinship for obscure, impecunious youths and maidens who, battling against formidable odds for a place in the literary sun, brought or mailed more or less promising manuscripts to 743 Broadway. Gilder, much more critical in literary and artistic matters, took a more objective, more impersonal attitude toward these would-be geniuses—an attitude that the warm-hearted Doctor considered a bit harsh. "I do believe, Gilder," said Holland impatiently one day, "that you have an antipathy to any one who wants to write for this magazine." [31]

Incidentally, Josiah's heart was big enough to offer hostel for obscure old writers as well as for obscure young ones. Contemplating some author who had reached ripe years with but scant recognition, he must often have paraphrased the words of John Newton, "There but for the grace of God goes Josiah Holland." In this connection, the late Professor Brander Matthews recalled that when Charles Kingsley, English writer-clergyman, visited New York in the winter of 1874, the *Scribner's* staff invited all of its contributors to a reception held in Kingsley's honor. Among the guests was a timid spinster who had made the trip from her New England village home to New York especially for this great occasion. The kindly Holland, noticing that the poor lady was much less fluent with her tongue than with her pen, joined with Roswell Smith in devoting much of the evening to her in order to save her from being a forlorn wallflower.[32]

We have spoken of J. G. Holland's prominence as a citizen of New York. We should add that he acquired a genuine affection for the metropolis. Like many another person of

<hr>

30 R. U. Johnson, *op. cit.,* p. 88.
31 *Ibid.,* p. 90.
32 Brander Matthews: *These Many Years,* p. 222. New York, 1917.

small-town birth and rearing, he found the varied and intensive human activity of the great city a stimulus. Despite the
fact that he often sang of the joys of country life in the conventional romantic manner,[33] he really delighted in the clang
and clatter, the rattle and roar, of Manhattan. He delighted,
more than he ever quite wished to admit, in strolling through
the thick of the crowds on Broadway. Metropolitan libraries,
metropolitan concerts, metropolitan churches, metropolitan
manners were an ever growing charm and thrill to him.[34] In
an amateurish and Puritanic way, also, he cultivated no little
appreciation of art galleries.[35]

Even the theatre came to cast its spell over him. Early precept, lifelong habit, and an inflexible conscience forbade him
to become an inveterate theatre-goer; but on more than a
few winter evenings he fared forth with childlike joy to see
Edwin Booth or Joe Jefferson, Charlotte Cushman or Maggie
Mitchell.[34] He who had once condemned all plays and players
and playhouses as works of the devil could now bring himself to say:

As a people, we have no such superfluity of amusements and
recreations that we can afford to hold one under ban that is in
itself harmless and legitimate. We work under great pressure, and
need much more recreation than we get. If a man thus pressed
feels that a pure dramatic representation refreshes him, he ought
to be at liberty to avail himself of it, and the time is certainly
coming when he will do so. The histrionic art is as legitimate as
any art, and any man or woman who practises it worthily . . .
well deserves our honor—ay, our honor and our sympathy, for the
art-life is a hard life to live under any circumstances. To be obliged
to rely for a livelihood upon the plaudits of the multitude, and
to be subject to the caprices of the press and the public, and the
jealousies that are inseparable from all art-life, is a hardship from
which the bravest man and woman may well shrink. If, among
those who have so many temptations to strike a low key that may

---

[33] As we have seen, *Bitter-Sweet, Kathrina,* and *The Mistress of the Manse*
are rural or small town in their settings.
[34] See above, p. 10, footnote 36.
[35] See above, pp. 86–88.

at least please "the groundlings," there is a considerable number who appeal to the nobilities of human nature, let us give them our hands and help them to build up a pure taste in the public mind. We have only to remember that the theatre is with us, that it will stay, and that the Church has a great responsibility concerning the stage of the future. If it supposes that condemning it at a street's length, and indiscriminately, will discharge its duty, it will find itself sadly mistaken.[36]

There were, of course, times when the metropolis palled upon Josiah Holland. Seldom, however, was this true in the winter. Recalling the hardships and the tedium of rural and small-town New England during the months of cold weather and short daylight, he found New York, with its cheery gas lights, its colorful shop-windows, and its never ending stream of diversions a happy contrast to his earlier environment.[37] But when Manhattan pavements began to bake in late May or early June, he had a different feeling; he thought wistfully of cooler, quieter, more open spaces.

We have no doubt [he said] that people in the country wonder why New Yorkers are willing to leave their splendid and commodious houses, and submit to the numberless inconveniences and inferior fare of way-side places. They would have but to spend one active winter in the city to understand it all. They would then know how precious the privilege would be to flee from hot sidewalks and burning walls, and the ceaseless din of wheels, and lie down, care-free, in the country silence, beneath an appletree, or a maple, with the fresh green earth around and the wide blue heaven above them.[38]

During the first two or three years after their removal to New York the Hollands made Brightwood their summer home.[37] Both Josiah and Elizabeth, however, felt that Brightwood was quite too expensive a place to retain for the few short months in which they could now occupy it. Consequently, when George C. Fisk, an old Springfield friend,

---

[36] *Every-Day Topics,* I, 244–245.
[37] See above, p. 10, footnote 36.
[38] *Every-Day Topics,* I, 250.

offered to buy the place in 1873, they sold it without much hesitation.[39]

During the next few summers they visited such resorts as Long Branch and Saratoga;[40] but Josiah, at least, did not find these places to his liking.

There is [he declared] no objection to the filling up of the fashionable watering-places by fashionable people who have nothing to do the whole year round but to play. There are enough of these to populate Newport and Saratoga and Long Branch, and there will be enough of those who are amused for a little time by looking at them to keep the hotels full; but the well-to-do working men and women can do infinitely better for themselves and their children than to seek dwellings in such places for the summer. What they want is liberty, away from the centres of observation, where they can dress as they choose and do what they like. The very soul of play is liberty, and there is no true recreation without it.[41]

"What we need," he insisted, "is a quiet summer home of our own—a place where we can rest as we please, and play as we please." The possibility of obtaining a summer cottage in Springfield occurred to the family; but the children protested that Springfield without Brightwood would not quite be Springfield, and Josiah and Elizabeth were inclined to agree with them.[40]

A trip to Alexandria Bay, Jefferson County, New York, in the Thousand Islands region, finally solved the problem of a Holland summer home. In 1877 Josiah purchased one of the smaller islands near the village.[42] Upon this island, on a bluff just above the shore, he erected a three-story cottage, to which he gave a favorite name—Bonnie Castle.[43]

Regarding Josiah's life at Bonnie Castle, Mrs. Plunkett has piously, if superfluously, remarked that "when Dr. Holland betook himself thither for his summer rest he did not

---

[39] For this information I am indebted to Mrs. Isabel R. Dickinson, of Springfield, Mass.

[40] See above, p. 10, footnote 36.

[41] *Every-Day Topics,* I, 250.

[42] New York *Times,* Oct. 13, 1881.

[43] Plunkett, *op. cit.,* p. 122 and picture opposite.

leave his religion behind." [44] The village of Alexandria Bay boasted neither a Congregational nor a Presbyterian church, but it did have a Calvinistic church, a small Dutch Reformed. As a matter of course, Josiah Holland hastened to become a regular worshipper at this little church, as well as a generous financial contributor to it.[44]

A better instance of Holland's humanity—an instance that affords a refreshing and pleasantly surprising sidelight upon the Doctor's hobbies—was related by a writer in *Harper's* a few weeks after the Doctor's death. On the shore immediately below Bonnie Castle stood a boathouse,[45] in which was kept one of Josiah's most treasured playthings, a steam launch. As the *Harper's* writer relates:

His especial recreation [during summer vacations on the St. Lawrence] was yachting upon the river in his steam-launch, and it was his pride that it should outsail all other craft upon those waters. His hearty hospitality welcomed his guests to a sail, and when he directed the full power of the steam to be applied, the quivering vessel darted . . . with appalling swiftness . . . through a devious channel where one sudden touch of the shore would have instantly sunk her.[46]

There was, then, something of the sportsman, something even of the daredevil, about Josiah Holland.

Speaking of Holland's fondness for his launch, the late Robert Underwood Johnson recalled only a few years ago:

My wife and I visited him there [at Alexandria Bay] with great enjoyment. To see him in the stern of the boat was almost like recalling the days of the Indians. He was so tall, straight, dark, and well poised.[47]

One Alexandria Bay episode revelatory of the extent to which J. G. Holland had become a national celebrity is set forth by Mrs. Plunkett in these words:

[44] Plunkett, *op. cit.*, p. 122.
[45] *Ibid.*, and picture opposite.
[46] *Op. cit.*, LXIV, 147. Dec., 1881.
[47] Letter from R. U. Johnson to the author, March 22, 1934.

People visited his summer home as though making a pilgrimage to a shrine, and carried away relics of every kind, begging sometimes even for a handful of pebbles out of the roadway.[48]

Relatively few authors, we may infer, have been so canonized by their lay contemporaries. To find a parallel we must recall, perhaps, the pilgrimages to Tennyson's retreat on the Isle of Wight. Here, by the way, is fresh evidence that Holland was revered by the prosperous as well as by the humble. People of scant means and restricted opportunities do not tour the Thousand Islands region in great numbers.

By a peculiarly fitting coincidence, *Scribner's Monthly* ended its career within a few weeks of its editor-founder's death. The suspension of the old *Scribner's* resulted in a serious disagreement between the Scribner magazine firm and the Scribner book firm—in other words, between J. G. Holland and Roswell Smith on the one hand, and Charles Scribner the younger on the other. A Presbyterian divine by the name of Charles S. Robinson, friend and pastor of Smith, was the unwitting cause of the difficulty. The Reverend Mr. Robinson had submitted a manuscript to the Scribner book firm, and the book firm had rejected that manuscript.[49] Thereupon Smith assured Robinson that the magazine firm would be glad to publish the manuscript—publish it in book form. This assurance evoked the immediate protest of Scribner, who insisted that the contract between the book firm and the magazine firm did not authorize the latter to publish any books whatsoever. To Scribner's protest Smith and Holland replied that by oral agreement with Scribner's father they had reserved the right to publish books—a right, however, which they had not had occasion to exercise until the Robinson incident had arisen. Unfortunately, the third party to this oral agreement could not corroborate the statement, for the elder Scribner had died soon after the founding of the

<hr>

48 Plunkett, *op. cit.,* p. 190.
49 R. U. Johnson, *op. cit.,* pp. 82–83.

Monthly. The younger Scribner, although not doubting the word of Smith and Holland, felt that the publication of books by the magazine firm would be contrary to the spirit, if not to the letter, of the contract.[50]

The upshot of the matter was that Scribner sold all of his magazine holdings to Smith, giving the latter a free hand to publish both magazines and books, but stipulating that the Smith firm should not use the name *Scribner.* Scribner, in turn, agreed that he would publish no Scribner magazine for at least five years. Holland likewise sold his holdings to Smith and to other members of the magazine firm, and agreed to edit a new Smith magazine in which he would be a salaried employee rather than a stockholder. In this manner the Scribner magazine firm changed to the Century Company, book and magazine publishers, and brought out the first issue of the *Century Magazine* in November 1881,[51] precisely eleven years after the inception of the old *Scribner's.* The *Scribner's* subscription list was, of course, transferred bodily to the *Century,* and in appearance, make-up, and business arrangements, the new magazine was identical with the old. An entirely separate and distinct periodical, *Scribner's Magazine,* published by the Scribner book firm (now Charles Scribner's Sons), appeared in January 1887, as a rival of the *Century* and *Harper's.*[52]

A short time before the climactic events recorded in the last two paragraphs, the health of J. G. Holland had reached an alarming state. Although still as active and alert as ever, he had become increasingly subject to heart attacks. In particular he had noticed that in climbing the two flights of stairs leading to his Broadway sanctum, he had begun to suffer spells of dizziness and heartburn. His physician diagnosed his ailment as angina pectoris and warned him that he might die very suddenly.[53] This warning, doubtless, was what prompted

[50] R. U. Johnson, *op. cit.,* pp. 82–83.
[51] *Op. cit.,* I, No. 1.
[52] R. U. Johnson, *op. cit.,* pp. 82–83.
[53] Plunkett, *op. cit.,* p. 150. See also Ellsworth, *op. cit.,* p. 24.

him to sell his stock holdings to other members of the magazine firm.

Josiah Holland lived to edit only one number of the *Century*, and he did not live to see that number upon the newsstands. On the afternoon of October 11, 1881, he sat at his desk in the new *Century* office facing Union Square. For some weeks he had been feeling extraordinarily well, and on that particular afternoon he remained late at the office to finish an editorial tribute to the martyred President Garfield, who had died only three weeks earlier. The tribute completed, he closed his desk, refused the offer of a ride, and walked energetically homeward.[54] At dinner that evening he talked enthusiastically about the new magazine and about his own editorial and authorial plans. He repeated a statement made in one of his most recent *Topics:* that he hoped to continue addressing his large public for many years to come.[55]

At six o'clock the next morning Mrs. Holland was awakened by a terrifying moan. Before any other member of the household could reach the bedchamber, Josiah Gilbert Holland was dead.[56] The late editions of the morning papers announced that Editor Titcomb, discoverer of one of America's greatest reading publics, had written "thirty." [57]

The Holland funeral, a very private and simple affair without pallbearers, was held at the Park Avenue residence, the services being conducted by Holland's pastor, Dr. Bevan.[58] The body was taken to Springfield for interment.[58] Memorial services were held at the Brick Church in New York, at the Memorial Church in Springfield, at the Dutch Reformed Church at Alexandria Bay, and at the Congregational Church at Holland's native Massachusetts village of Belchertown.[59]

The death of J. G. Holland created a very considerable stir—probably as great a stir as that of any American writer

---

[54] Plunkett, *op. cit.,* pp. 151–152.
[55] See above, p. 10, footnote 36.
[56] Plunkett, *op. cit.,* p. 152.
[57] *Ibid.,* p. 153.
[58] *Ohio State Journal,* Oct. 19, 1881.
[59] Plunkett, *op. cit.,* pp. 159, 168, 171, 179–180.

up to that time. Mrs. Plunkett cannot be far wrong when she says:

Of course every leading newspaper had an article, more or less carefully written, containing an estimate, more or less just, of the elements and value of his literary work.[60]

For Josiah Gilbert Holland was easily one of the most outstanding public figures of his day. Naturally such religious journals as the *Christian Union* and such bucolic journals as the *Rural Home* lauded the good Doctor to the skies.[61] But the great metropolitan dailies added their tributes too—the *Evening Post,*[62] the *Times,*[63] the *Tribune,*[62] the *World,*[62] the *Sun,*[62] the Chicago *Tribune,*[64] the St. Louis *Globe-Democrat,*[62] and the Cleveland *Leader*[63]—and these included journals that had often spoken scornfully of Josiah Holland's literary mediocrity, his triteness, and his intellectual parochialism.[65] All of them now recognized Holland as having been a phenomenal influence. So, likewise, did a few of the foreign journals, notably the London *Academy* and the *Canadian Monthly.*[66]

Verse tributes included three quatrains by Edmund Clarence Stedman,[67] two sonnets by Helen Hunt Jackson,[67] and a seven-stanza elegy by the Reverend Washington Gladden.[67] Of the numerous personal expressions one of the most noteworthy was that of John Greenleaf Whittier, who, in a letter to Richard Watson Gilder, on October 24, 1881, spoke of Holland as "poet, novelist, historian, and last, not least, the most successful of editors."[68] Another noteworthy expression came from John Burroughs, who, as a genuine admirer of Walt Whitman,[69] had not been upon cordial terms with

60 Plunkett, *op. cit.,* p. 192.
61 *Ibid.,* pp. 198, 201–203.
62 *Ibid.,* pp. 192–195.
63 See below, p. 206.
64 *Op. cit.,* Oct. 22, 1881.
65 R. U. Johnson, *op. cit.,* p. 85.
66 Plunkett, *op. cit.,* pp. 196–197.
67 *Ibid.,* pp. 153–157.
68 *Century Magazine,* I, 471. Jan., 1882.
69 R. U. Johnson, *op. cit.,* pp. 332–333.

J. G. Holland. Said Burroughs in a letter to Robert Underwood Johnson:

I am more shocked and grieved at Holland's death than I expected I should be. He was little to me personally, and yet I find that he helped uphold and warm and render inhabitable the world in which I lived. The loss of every such man leaves a void to the heart and the imagination. . . .[70]

The New York *Times,* which for many years had been one of Holland's severest critics,[71] now graciously referred to him as "one of the most celebrated writers which [*sic*] this country has produced." [72]

The Cleveland *Leader,* at that time a Republican morning paper of great sectional influence and truly national reputation,[73] declared editorially:

By the death of Dr. J. G. Holland, which occurred yesterday at his New York residence, the literary world lost one of its brightest lights. . . . Of Dr. Holland's literary efforts, or of his prominence as a lecturer, little need be said. He was a man of our day, and his works are found on every bookshelf the delight of all. . . . In their sorrow the bereaved ones may be assured of the sympathy of the entire reading world.[74]

Representative of small-town editorial opinion is the following excerpt from the Alton (Illinois) *Weekly Democrat:*

The death of Dr. J. G. Holland, editor of Scribner's Magazine [*sic*], makes a great void in the world of letters. In American magazine literature his loss will be deeply felt.[75]

Equally representative is the Champaign (Illinois) *County Gazette's* reference to Holland as "an author of world-wide reputation." [76]

Along with these newspaper tributes should be mentioned

<hr>

70 *Ibid.,* p. 342.
71 See R. U. Johnson, p. 85.
72 *Op. cit.,* Oct. 13, 1881.
73 George Henry Payne: *History of Journalism in the United States,* New York and London, 1920, p. 334.
74 *Op. cit.,* Oct. 13, 1881.
75 *Op. cit.,* Oct. 21, 1881.
76 *Op. cit.,* Oct. 19, 1881.

meetings held in commemoration of the deceased author. For instance, at a teachers' institute at St. Joseph, Illinois, on Saturday, November 5, 1881, special memorial papers were read on "the two great Americans who have recently passed away—President James A. Garfield and Dr. J. G. Holland." [77] And in this same connection the following notice in the Mansfield (Ohio) *Herald* is as revelatory as it is pertinent:

A tribute to the memory of Dr. J. G. Holland will be paid by the Mansfield Lyceum and Reading Union on Friday evening next at the Methodist Church. The exercises will consist of essays biographical and in relation to his literary work, select readings, etc., with appropriate music.[78]

On the Holland monument, in the Springfield Cemetery, just below a profile bronze medallion, appear these characteristic words:

FOR THE GREAT HEREAFTER I TRUST IN THE INFINITE LOVE AS IT IS EXPRESSED TO ME IN THE LIFE AND DEATH OF MY LORD AND SAVIOUR JESUS CHRIST.[79]

The editorship of the *Century* fell to Holland's chief lieutenant, Richard Watson Gilder, a charming and able poet-gentleman who truly graced his chair until his death in 1909.[80] To say that Gilder, with his rich creative gifts, his ripe culture, and his urbane outlook, improved the magazine is not to disparage the sturdy pioneering of his less talented, less cultivated, less sophisticated predecessor. Gilder accomplished many admirable things that were beyond Holland's powers, but neither Gilder nor any other man of his type could have built the foundation that the old *Scribner's* laid for the *Century*. Holland, with his brisk energy, his shrewd but generous business sense, his startling fusion of the esthetic dilettante and the Puritan zealot, and his extraordinary popular following, was the one man to perform that great task.

[77] Champaign (Ill.) *County Gazette,* Oct. 26, 1881.
[78] *Op. cit.,* Nov. 3, 1881.
[79] Plunkett, *op. cit.,* p. 208 and picture opposite.
[80] R. U. Johnson, *op. cit.,* pp. 132–133.

Bibliography

BOOKS AND ARTICLES QUOTED OR CITED IN THIS VOLUME

Adams, James Truslow: *New England in the Republic*. Boston, 1926.

Allen, Hervey: *Israfel*. New York, 1934.

Barton, William E.: *The Life of Abraham Lincoln*. Indianapolis, 1925.

Beecher, Lyman: *Autobiography and Correspondence*. New York, 1863, 1865.

Beers, Henry A.: *Nathaniel Parker Willis*. Boston, 1885.

Bernbaum, Ernest: *The Drama of Sensibility*. Boston, New York, Chicago, 1915.

Bianchi, Martha Dickinson: *Life and Letters of Emily Dickinson*. Boston and New York, 1924.

Blackmar, Frank W.: *Charles Robinson*. Topeka, Kansas, 1900.

Bleyer, Willard Grosvenor: *Main Currents in the History of American Journalism*. Boston, New York, Chicago, 1927.

Bloom, Margaret: "Emily Dickinson and Dr. Holland" (Article in the *University of California Chronicle*, XXXV, *q.v.*) Jan., 1933.

Boynton, Percy H.: *A History of American Literature*. Boston, 1919.

Boynton, Percy H.: *Literature and American Life*. Boston, New York, Chicago, 1936.

Brooks, Van Wyck: *The Flowering of New England*. New York, 1936.

Buchan, John (editor): *A History of English Literature*. New York, 1927.

Cairns, William B.: "Josiah Gilbert Holland" (Article in the *Dictionary of American Biography*, *q.v.*).

Cairns, William B.: "Later Magazines" (Chapter XIX of the *Cambridge History of American Literature*, *q.v.*).

Cambridge History of American Literature. Cheap edition. 3 vols. New York, 1933.

Cambridge History of English Literature. Cheap edition. New York, 1933.

Carman, Harry J.: "Abraham Oakley Hall" (Article in the *Dictionary of American Biography, q.v.*).

Casner, Mabel B., and Gabriel, Ralph Henry: *Exploring American History.* New York, 1931.

Chapin, Charles Wells: *Sketches of the Old Inhabitants of Springfield.* Springfield, Mass., 1893.

Clark, Solomon: *Antiquities of Northampton, Massachusetts.* Northampton, 1882.

Coffman, George Raleigh (editor): *Five Significant English Plays.* New York, 1930.

Cubberley, Ellwood P.: "Education, United States" (Article in the *Encyclopaedia Britannica, q.v.*).

Davis, William T.: *Bench and Bar of the Commonwealth of Massachusetts.* Boston, 1900.

De Bow, J. D. B.: *Compendium of the Seventh Census.* Washington, 1854.

Dickey, Marcus: *The Youth of James Whitcomb Riley.* Indianapolis, 1919.

Dictionary of American Biography. 20 vols. New York, 1928–1936.

Eggleston, Edward: "Josiah Gilbert Holland" (Article in the *Century Magazine,* I, Dec., 1881, *q.v.*).

Ellsworth, William W.: *A Golden Age of Authors.* New York and Boston, 1919.

Encyclopaedia Britannica. 14th edition. 24 vols. London and New York, 1929.

Fish, Carl Russell: *The Rise of the Common Man.* New York, 1927.

Garnett, Edward, and Gosse, Edmund: *An Illustrated History of English Literature.* 4 vols. New York, 1903, 1935.

Gay, Richard L.: *Gazetter of Hampshire County, Massachusetts.* Springfield, n.d.

Grant, Ulysses S.: *Personal Memoirs.* 2 vols. New York, 1885–1886.

Greenslet, Ferris: *Life of Thomas Bailey Aldrich.* Boston and New York, 1908.

Halleck, Reuben Post: *History of American Literature.* New York, Cincinnati, Chicago, 1911.

Harte, Geoffrey Bret (editor): *Letters of Bret Harte*. Boston and
    New York, 1926.
Haworth, Paul L.: *The United States in Our Own Times*. New
    York, 1920.
Herndon, William H., and Weik, Jesse W.: *Abraham Lincoln*.
    New York, 1888, 1906.
Hibben, Paxton: *Henry Ward Beecher, An American Portrait*.
    New York, 1927.
Higginson, Thomas Wentworth: *Carlyle's Laugh, and Other Sur-
    prises*. Boston and New York, 1909.
History of the Connecticut Valley. 2 vols. Philadelphia, 1879.
Holland, Josiah Gilbert: (For complete chronological list of Hol-
    land's books, see below, p. 213).
Hooker, Richard: *The Story of an Independent Newspaper*. New
    York, 1924.
Howe, Will D.: "Whittier" (Chapter X of Macy's *American
    Writers on American Literature*, q.v.).
Howells, Mildred: *Life in Letters of William Dean Howells*.
    Garden City, N.Y., 1928.
Hudson, William Henry: *An Introduction to the Study of Liter-
    ature*. Boston, New York, Chicago, 1913.
Johnson, Clifton: *Historic Hampshire in the Connecticut Valley*.
    Springfield, Mass., 1932.
Johnson, Oliver: *William Lloyd Garrison and His Times*. Lon-
    don, 1882.
Johnson, Robert Underwood: *Remembered Yesterdays*. Boston,
    1923.
Jones, Howard Mumford: "Longfellow" (Chapter IX of Macy's
    American Writers on American Literature, q.v.).
Knapp, Shepherd: *Records of the Brick Presbyterian Church of
    New York*. New York, 1909.
Lewis, Lloyd: *Sherman, Fighting Prophet*. New York, 1932.
Lodge, Henry Cabot: *Daniel Webster*. Boston, 1883.
Longfellow, Samuel: *Life of Henry Wadsworth Longfellow*. Bos-
    ton and New York, 1886, 1891.
Lyman, P. W.: "J. G. Holland Memorial Address." Belchertown,
    Mass., 1881 (unpublished).
Macy, John (editor): *American Writers on American Literature*.
    New York, 1931, 1934.

Matthews, Brander: *These Many Years*. New York, 1917.

Maurice, Arthur Bartlett: "Literary Magazines" (Chapter XXXIV of Macy's *American Writers on American Literature, q.v.*).

The Meadow City's Quarter-Millennial Book. Northampton, Mass., 1904.

Merriam, George S.: *The Life and Times of Samuel Bowles*. 2 vols. New York, 1885.

Monroe, Paul: "Education" (Chapter XXIII of the *Cambridge History of American Literature, q.v.*).

Morison, S. E.: *Oxford History of the United States*. 2 vols. London, 1927.

Mott, Frank Luther: *A History of American Magazines, 1741–1850*. New York and London, 1930.

National Cyclopedia of American Biography. 15 vols. New York,1891–1916.

Nevins, Allan: *The Emergence of Modern America*. New York, 1927.

Onderdonk, James L.: *History of American Verse,* Chicago, 1899–1901.

Orians, G. H., "Censure of Fiction in American Romances and Magazines, 1789–1810" (Article in *Publications of the Modern Language Association of America*, LII, March, 1937, *q.v.*).

Parrington, Vernon L.: *Main Currents in American Thought* (Vol. II, *The Romantic Revolution in America*). New York, 1927.

Pattee, Fred Lewis: *Century Readings for a Course in American Literature*. Third edition. New York, 1926.

Paxson, Frederic L.: *The New Nation*. Boston, New York, Chicago, 1915.

Payne, George Henry: *History of Journalism in the United States*. New York and London, 1920.

Phillips, Ulrich B.: *Life and Labor in the Old South*. Boston, 1929.

Plunkett, Mrs. H. M.: *Josiah Gilbert Holland*. New York, 1894.

Poe, Edgar Allan: "The Poetic Principle" (Essay first published in the *Home Journal,* Aug. 31, 1850. Reproduced by Robert Shafer, *q.v.*).

Pollitt, Josephine: *Emily Dickinson*. New York and London, 1930.

Presbrey, Frank: *The History and Development of Advertising*. Garden City, N.Y., 1929.

Quinn, Arthur Hobson: *American Fiction*. Students' edition. New York, 1936.

Rideing, William H.: "Life on Broadway" (Article in *Harper's Monthly Magazine,* LVI, Jan., 1878, *q.v.*).

Roe, Frederick William (editor): (See under Ruskin).

Rowe, Henry Kalloch: *The History of Religion in the United States*. New York, 1924.

Rowland, Dunbar: *History of Mississippi*. 2 vols. Jackson, Miss., and Chicago, 1925.

Rowland, Dunbar: "Mississippi" (Article in *Encyclopaedia Britannica, q.v.*).

Ruskin, John: *Selections and Essays*. Edited, with introduction, by Frederick William Roe. Modern Student's Library. New York, 1918.

Saintsbury, George: *A Short History of English Literature*. New York, 1898.

Shafer, Robert: *American Literature*. (An anthology). Garden City, N. Y., 1926.

Smith, Arthur D. H.: *John Jacob Astor, Landlord of New York*. New York, 1929.

Stedman, Edmund Clarence: *An American Anthology, 1787–1900*. Boston and New York, 1900.

Stedman, Laura, and Gould, George M.: *Life and Letters of Edmund Clarence Stedman*. New York, 1910.

Sweet, William Warren: *The Story of Religions in America*. New York and London, 1930.

Tate, Allen: *Jefferson Davis: His Rise and Fall*. New York, 1929.

Traill, H. D., and Mann, J. S.: *Social England*. 6 vols. New York, 1909.

Traubel, Horace: *With Walt Whitman in Camden*. Boston, 1906.

Universal Cyclopaedia and Atlas (Charles Kendall Adams, editor-in-chief). 12 vols. New York, 1901, 1903, 1905.

Van Doren, Carl: *The American Novel*. New York, 1921.

Whipple, Edwin Percy: *American Literature, and Other Papers*. Boston, 1887.

Winston, Robert W.: *High Stakes and Hair Trigger*. New York, 1930.

World Almanac and Book of Facts. Issued annually. New York, 1937.

BOOKS BY JOSIAH GILBERT HOLLAND

History of Western Massachusetts. Springfield, 1855.
The Bay-Path. New York, 1857.
Bitter-Sweet. New York, 1858.
Timothy Titcomb's Letters to Young People. New York, 1858.
Gold Foil Hammered from Popular Proverbs. New York, 1859.
Miss Gilbert's Career. New York, 1860.
Lessons in Life. New York, 1861.
Letters to the Joneses. New York, 1863.
Plain Talks on Familiar Subjects. New York, 1865.
Life of Abraham Lincoln. Springfield, 1865.
Kathrina. New York, 1867.
The Marble Prophecy. New York, 1872.
Arthur Bonnicastle. New York, 1873.
Garnered Sheaves. New York, 1873.
The Mistress of the Manse. New York, 1874.
The Story of Sevenoaks. New York, 1875.
Every-Day Topics. First Series. New York, 1876.
Nicholas Minturn. New York, 1877.
The Puritan's Guest, and Other Poems. New York, 1877.
Garnered Sheaves (enlarged edition). New York, 1879.
Every-Day Topics. Second Series. New York, 1882.
Complete Works (uniform edition). New York, 1882.

MAGAZINES CONSULTED

Atlantic Monthly, Vols. III (1859), IV (1859), VII (1861), XV (1865), XX (1867), XXXVII (1876).
Century Magazine, Vol. I (1881–1882).
Democratic Review, Vol. XX (1847).
Education, Vol. XII (1892).
Forum, The, Vol. XV (1893).
Harper's Monthly Magazine, Vols. XXXVI (1867–1868), XXXVIII (1868–1869), XLVI (1872–1873), XLVII (1873), L (1874–1875), LII (1875–1876), LVI (1877–1878), LX (1879–1880), LXIV (1881–1882), LXXIV (1886–1887).
Independent, The, Vol. XLVI (1894).
Methodist Quarterly Review, Vol. XXXIII (1851).
Nation, The, Vols. XVII (1873), XXI (1875), XXXIII (1881).

North American Review, Vols. LXXXV (1857), CI (1865), CXXV
    (1877).
Publications of the Modern Language Association of America.
    LII (1937).
Scribner's Monthly, Vols. I (1870–1871), VI (1873), XXI (1880–
    1881), XXII (1881).
Union Magazine, Vol. II (1847).
University of California Chronicle, Vol. XXXV (1933).

NEWSPAPERS CONSULTED

Alton (Illinois) *Weekly Democrat,* Oct. 21, 1881.
Champaign (Illinois) *County Gazette,* Oct. 19 and 26, 1881.
Chicago *Tribune,* Oct. 22, 1881.
Cleveland *Leader,* Oct. 13, 1881.
Columbus *Ohio State Journal,* Jan. 6, 11, and 12, 1872; Oct. 14,
    1874; Oct. 19 and 20, 1881.
Mansfield (Ohio) *Herald,* Nov. 3, 1881.
New York *Times,* Oct. 13, 1881.
Oberlin (Ohio) *Lorain County News,* Oct. 24, 1860; Nov. 7, 1860;
    Jan. 28, 1863; Feb. 11, 1863; Nov. 25, 1863; Dec. 9 and 16,
    1863; Oct. 23, 1873; Nov. 13, 20, and 27, 1873.
Oberlin (Ohio) *Weekly News,* Nov. 18, 1875.
Springfield (Massachusetts) *Republican,* Jan. 1, 1861; Feb. 16,
    1861; Mar. 2 and 9, 1861; Nov. 23, 1861; May 17, 1862;
    July 19, 1862; May 25, 1868.
Vicksburg (Mississippi) *Sentinel,* Oct. ?, 1881.

Index